P9-EKD-466

LIGHT *from the* CHRISTIAN EAST

An Introduction to the Orthodox Tradition

JAMES R. PAYTON JR.

An imprint of InterVarsity Press
Downers Grove, Illinois

InterVarsity Press
P.O. Box 1400, Downers Grove, IL 60515-1426
World Wide Web: www.ivpress.com
E-mail: email@ivpress.com

InterVarsity Press® is the book-publishing division of InterVarsity Christian Fellowship/USA®, a student movement active on campus at hundreds of universities, colleges and schools of nursing in the United States of America, and a member movement of the International Fellowship of Evangelical Students. For information about local and regional activities, write Public Relations Dept., InterVarsity Christian Fellowship/USA, 6400 Schroeder Rd., P.O. Box 7895, Madison, WI 53707-7895, or visit the IVCF website at <www.intervarsity.org>.

Design: Cindy Kiple
Images: transfiguration icon: Museum of Art, Novgorod, Russia/The Bridgeman Art Library
candles: Jivko Kazakov/iStockphoto

ISBN 978-0-8308-2594-3

Printed in the United States of America ∞

Library of Congress Cataloging-in-Publication Data

Payton, James R., 1947-
Light from the Christian East: an introduction to the Orthodox tradition / James R. Payton, Jr.
p. cm.
Includes bibliographical references and index.
ISBN-13: 978-0-8308-2594-3 (pbk.: alk. paper)
1. Orthodox Eastern Church. I. Title.
BX320.3.P39 2007
281.9—dc22

2007016688

P 21 20 19 18 17 16 15 14 13 12 11 10 9 8 7 6 5 4 3 2 1
Y 25 24 23 22 21 20 19 18 17 16 15 14 13 12 11 10 09 08 07

To Sharon

who has brought light into my life

in so many ways

Contents

ACKNOWLEDGMENTS

I AM INDEBTED TO MANY PEOPLE WHO HAVE contributed to this book in various ways. My first debt, in order, is to Clair Davis, professor of church history at Westminster Theological Seminary in Philadelphia, under whom I first studied Eastern Orthodoxy. Through his course I was introduced to a field of study which has continued to intrigue me for more than thirty years. Several Orthodox scholars have further stimulated my interest in and understanding of the faith they embrace: the works of John Meyendorff, Kallistos (Timothy) Ware, Alexander Schmemann and Vladimir Lossky have been sources of continual enrichment. From Western Christian authors, I am especially indebted to volumes written by Jaroslav Pelikan (who in 1998 converted to Orthodoxy).

Over the last twenty years, the priests and congregations of several Orthodox parishes in Hamilton, Ontario—St. Demetrios Greek Orthodox Church, Holy Resurrection Romanian Orthodox Church, St. Nicholas Serbian Orthodox Cathedral, Panagia Greek Orthodox Church and St. Vladimir Ukrainian Orthodox Cathedral—have accorded me and my students (fellow Western Christians, all) gracious reception and unstinting hospitality at many Orthodox services and events; I am grateful to them all. I am especially indebted to Fr. Stevo Stojsavljevich of St. Nicholas Serbian Orthodox Cathedral and to Fr. Bohdan Hladio of St. Vladimir Ukrainian Orthodox Cathedral (since 2005 serving as Chancellor of the Ukrainian Orthodox Church of Canada), for frequent conversation, encouragement and patience as I plied them with questions and sought to benefit from their understanding and experience. This book could not have been written without them.

I am grateful for the sabbatical granted me in 1999 by Redeemer University College, which allowed me to focus entirely on the early stages of this project. I am also indebted to several colleagues at Redeemer: I have enjoyed and benefited from discussions about Eastern Orthodoxy with David Koyzis, Wayne Norman,

Jacob Ellens, Al Wolters and David Benner (now Distinguished Professor of Psychology at the Psychological Studies Institute, Atlanta, Georgia); two others, Jitse van der Meer and Tom McCormick, offered helpful comment on earlier drafts of some chapters of the book. Over the years, many students have taken the course on Eastern Orthodoxy which I have taught for several years at Redeemer; I have been enriched by their interest in learning and fascination with an approach to the Christian faith so different from their own. Their frequent assurances that they found the study intellectually, spiritually and personally enriching encouraged me to put into book form what we had considered together.

I am deeply indebted to my editor, Joel Scandrett, and his colleagues at InterVarsity Press. They have been unfailingly encouraging, supportive and helpful throughout the process that has led to the publication of this book. I am also grateful to Bradley Nassif and James Stamoolis, as well as an unnamed Orthodox scholar from Romania, who painstaking read through an earlier draft of this book and offered valuable suggestions for its improvement. Their work has made this a much better volume. I also express my gratitude to Judy Reveal, who prepared the author and subject indexes. For any errors or faults that remain, I am solely responsible.

I am also grateful for the privilege of teaching a course on Eastern Orthodoxy and the annual two-term church history sequence offered at Redeemer University College. This has afforded me the opportunity to devote special attention over the last two decades both to Orthodoxy and to the church fathers, whose writings are so important within Orthodoxy. I have frequently cited patristic writings in the material which follows; unless otherwise noted, all patristic translations are my own.

Last, but certainly not least, I express my deep gratitude to my wife, Sharon, and to our children, Chris (and Liza), Trevor (and Erin), Jessica and Chris. Family life ablaze with the mysteries of joy, trust and love is a wonderful preparation for exploring Eastern Orthodoxy.

PROLOGUE

THIS BOOK IS FOR WESTERN CHRISTIANS WHO WOULD LIKE to learn more about Eastern Orthodoxy. For those who have learned to appreciate the insights of other Christian traditions than their own, this book offers the opportunity to be enriched by one with which few of us in the West are well acquainted. Eastern Christianity has its own distinctive approaches to the faith, and studying these Orthodox distinctives can be stimulating and edifying.

In this ecumenical age, we have found that faithful Christians can listen to and profit from others without forsaking either their own tradition or the Christian faith, and can do so without falling into a boundary-less relativism. Western Christians and Eastern Orthodox can and should speak with and listen to each other in ways that enable us to enrich each other and together draw nearer to that fullness of development to which we are all called in Christ (Eph 4:13). This book is offered as a contribution to such dialogue.

In what follows, I will clarify some terms used in this volume. After that, I will briefly indicate why we in the Christian West have usually known little about the Christian East. Then I will point out the particular focus of the treatment that follows, so readers will know what to expect.

TERMINOLOGY

As to the terminology adopted in this book, first of all, "Western Christianity" is a general term encompassing both Roman Catholics and Protestants, with all the subsets of the latter—including mainline churches, evangelicals, the "free" churches, charismatics of various stripes and fundamentalists. We Western Christians have usually been more aware of the differences between us than the similarities which mark us, so the term may at first be surprising, even in our ecumenically open age. Suffice it to note here that Eastern Christians, for all the differences they acknowledge among Western Christians, nevertheless discern overarching similarities among us. They have observed that, while Western Christians often have opposing views, those views are all responses to the same basic questions; those questions have shaped Western Christianity. However, Eastern Christianity has been shaped by significantly different questions.[1] Thus, the Orthodox discern a similarity in basic approach throughout Western Christianity, an approach different from the one Eastern Christianity has taken.

Second, we will often use the designation "Orthodox" or "Orthodoxy" without the adjective, "Eastern." While it has become common for Western Christians to refer to "*Eastern* Orthodoxy," this is not the usual Orthodox practice: they rarely use the adjective, unless they are consciously relating to Western Christianity. This book will follow this Orthodox pattern: when a contrast is being pointed out with Western Christianity (or if clarity otherwise recommends it for Western Christian readers), "*Eastern* Orthodoxy" will be used. When we are dealing with the teachings and practice of Eastern Christianity itself, we will use the designation "Orthodox."

Third, "Eastern Orthodoxy" and "Eastern Christianity" will be used interchangeably. I acknowledge that "Eastern Christianity" is actually somewhat broader than "Eastern Orthodoxy," since Eastern *Christianity* includes, in addition to the Orthodox, a few churches which split from the main body of Orthodoxy along the historical way. However, these churches—collectively called *Oriental* Orthodox—are few in number by comparison with the Eastern Orthodox, and we in the West are less likely to encounter them. Beyond this argument from size and presence, though, I note that even the distinctions between the Oriental Orthodox and the Orthodox mainstream are variations on a shared approach, one different in striking regards from Western Christian perspectives. Using Eastern Orthodoxy (or Orthodoxy) and Eastern Christianity as synonyms will allow for variation in terminology and still honor the basic Eastern Christian perspective.

Finally, when I use the designation "the West," I intend the geographical and cultural area where Western Christianity has developed over the last several centuries—specifically, Western Europe and North America. Orthodoxy's historical pathway has wound through Eastern Europe and Russia, as well as the Middle East. References to "the Christian West" intend no claim to specifically Christian foundations of any Western nations or any comment as to the actual practice of

---

[1]For a pointed presentation of this assessment, see the excerpts from the third letter of the nineteenth-century Russian lay theologian Alexei Khomiakov to William Parker (November 28, 1846), as cited in chap. 1, n. 2 (www.geocities.com/trvalentine/orthodox/khomiakov_palmer03.html).

Christianity in the West; the same qualification applies to my usage of "the Christian East." What I am referring to with either designation is the geographic area within which Western Christianity or Eastern Christianity developed and flourished.

Why Has Orthodoxy Remained Unknown to Us?

Why, though, have we in the Christian West usually known so little about Eastern Orthodoxy? In large part, that situation can be accounted for by historical factors—what we have focused on in Western historical study and also what has happened to the Orthodox in the last few centuries. In the West, our historical awareness has rarely ventured east of the German-speaking lands of Europe; our familiarity with the history of Eastern Europe and of Russia, the areas in which Eastern Orthodoxy has flourished, has been limited, at best. Even Western Christian treatments of church history have concentrated virtually exclusively on the Western Christian heritage; few such volumes accord more than a passing glance at Eastern Christianity. Perhaps unintentionally, but nevertheless surely, we have long ignored—and, consequently, been ignorant of—that vast segment of Christendom which has continued from the Greek church fathers of antiquity to the present and is known as Orthodoxy. What occasioned this?

During the last six centuries, the West rose to world dominance, and our historical interests have focused on our culture, its background, and its accomplishments. By contrast to our Western experience, as of 1453, all but one of the Orthodox churches had fallen under the domination of the Ottoman Turkish Empire; for more than half a millennium they languished in this oppressive atmosphere, but they survived. Only the Russian Orthodox Church knew freedom during that time, but it was usually dominated by the tsars; beyond that, Russia was so exotic and unquestionably foreign to Western experience that understanding of its experience in any regard—including its religious commitment—was minimal. Beyond all this, for most of the last half of the twentieth century, with the Communist domination of Russia and Eastern Europe, the vast majority of worldwide Orthodoxy was captured behind the Iron Curtain. Given Soviet Communism's atheistic basis, the Orthodox churches faced intense hostility; given the Russian Communist control of information dissemination, that half-century proffered little opportunity to become acquainted with Orthodoxy. Thus, for several centuries, obstacles have cluttered the path toward familiarity with Orthodoxy. That, along with Western culture's longstanding and undeniable self-preoccupation, has conspired against Western Christians learning much about Eastern Christianity.

In the last few generations, though, the obstacles have been getting cleared away. The substantial emigration from various Eastern European countries and from Russia since the late 1800s offered a small window on the faith to which so many of these people were committed. This opening has been dramatically increased in the last few years: with the collapse of the Communist Bloc in 1989 and the Soviet Union in 1991, Orthodoxy entered upon a freedom unknown for several centuries. Since then, Western Christians have had more opportunity to become acquainted with this Eastern Christianity which has stood faithful to its ancient roots through centuries of dreary oppression and, more recently, fiendish persecution.

As some acquaintance has developed, Western Christians have often been struck by approaches and emphases in Eastern Orthodoxy which distinguish it from Western Christianity. The desire to understand these distinctives has spawned further interest in Eastern Christianity. This book has been written to respond to that interest in things Orthodox.

FOCUS: ORTHODOXY'S "DISTINCTIVES"

Even so, we Western Christians should recognize that in asking about the distinctiveness of Eastern Christianity, we are assuming and reflecting our Western Christian perspective. From the vantage point of an Eastern Christian, those "distinctives" are, simply, what Christianity is all about. Correlatively, that Eastern Christian could speak of distinctives of Western Christianity, and do so by pointing to items which we probably take for granted as essential to Christian faith and practice. Learning from each other requires openness and humility.

For us Western Christians, becoming acquainted with Eastern Orthodox distinctives can be enriching: it can stimulate a renewed appreciation of the depths and riches of the Christian faith, the Scriptures, doctrine and the joyful privilege of worshiping and serving God. As a Western Christian myself, I have experienced this. Over the last few years, I have also had the privilege of helping numerous Western Christians explore Eastern Orthodoxy; they too have found the experience rewarding. In this book, I seek to present some of those Orthodox distinctives in a way that we in the Christian West can understand and appreciate.

I hope that Orthodox readers will find this book helpful too. It may serve to remind them of the richness of their tradition by letting them see it anew through the eyes of a Western Christian who deeply appreciates their heritage. I trust that the presentation of Orthodox distinctives, against the backdrop of Western Christian patterns, will help Orthodox readers see how to relate their faith to that of their Western Christian acquaintances (and thus how to communicate better with them), in addition to serving as a review of significant elements of their heritage of faith and practice.

Teaching at a small undergraduate university has helped prepare me for this venture: curricular necessities and budget constraints force professors at such institutions to teach more than just in the areas of expertise developed during their graduate training. Specifically, I have taught courses in the histories and cultures of ancient Greece and ancient Rome, the Middle Ages and the Reformation era in Western Europe, Byzantium, Eastern Europe, Eastern Orthodoxy and church history. Together, these have given me the opportunity to examine and compare cultures and perspectives as they developed in the West and in the lands where Eastern Orthodoxy has taken root, have enabled me to discern commonalities and differences in historical and doctrinal patterns, and have acquainted me with the scholarly divergences of interpretation which require caution.

In what follows, I have tried to survey the terrain fairly without running roughshod over either historical or doctrinal qualifications upon which someone might insist. Comparing the different cultural settings in the Greek-speaking and the Latin-speaking halves of the ancient Roman Empire has necessitated a broad sweep, as has comment on either "the Christian East" or "the Christian West" in subsequent historical periods. It has also been necessary to sketch out common patterns in Western Christianity's approaches to the faith, so as to set forth the different approaches found in Orthodoxy. Consequently, I have had to paint the picture, at times, with rather broad strokes, historically and doctrinally; the need for both brevity and general comparisons prohibited too much qualification. If we were examining Western Christian perspectives themselves, these presentations would require greater nuance, but my purpose has been to show basic patterns or similarities among Western Christian perspectives, for all their admitted diversity, as they have been discerned by the Orthodox or by Western Christian scholarship.

This book will not attempt to recount the long history of Eastern Orthodoxy, to present a complete exposition of Orthodox doctrine or to present a collection of significant utterances by Orthodox authors; all these can be found in other volumes currently available. The purpose of this volume is to introduce Western Christian readers to some of the distinctive perspectives and emphases of Eastern Orthodoxy in a way that facilitates understanding and appreciation. To achieve this, I have sometimes found it preferable to shape the treatment by categories familiar to Western Christian thought (as, e.g., with "The Accomplishment of Salvation" [chapter seven] and "The Application of Salvation" [chapter eight]); usually, though, the treatment follows categories common to Orthodox thought.

This book is intended to serve as a stimulus to Christian growth and development—but obviously in an ecumenical sense. I hope that reading this volume and reflecting on what it presents will be enriching to the piety and insight of Western Christians. With that, they should be drawn to a greater appreciation for brothers and sisters in the Eastern Christian tradition. If some of those Orthodox brothers and sisters also find this book helpful, I will count the labor expended in producing this work doubly blessed.

At the beginning of the third millennium, it may seem odd to devote attention to a segment of Christendom which traces its roots back to the earliest history of the Christian church and emphasizes its fidelity to that antiquity: after all, with the constant advertising brouhaha in the West about new and improved products, Christians too can become impatient with that which is longstanding. But we must remember that Christianity is, undeniably, a historical religion; the Christian faith is rooted in the soil of history. Into history God sent his Son to accomplish salvation—in this world, and in time as we mark it on calendars. He also promised to be with us throughout history, to its end (Mt 28:20), and to guide his church by the Holy Spirit (Jn 16:13). The path Orthodoxy has traversed over the centuries shows Christ's faithfulness to his promises and to our Eastern Christian brothers and sisters; considering what they have learned is a way to appreciate his work among them—and might even stimulate us to become more familiar with the history of Western Christianity than we often are. If this can help wean us from our cultural obsession with the allegedly "new and improved," it would also enable us better to live up to the apostolic summons not to be conformed to this present world (Rom 12:2); if we have ears to hear what the Spirit has said (Rev 3:13) to the Orthodox churches through their long history, we may ourselves find ways to live more faithfully in our own day. Recent history has shown the resilience and strength of Orthodoxy, which survived the worst that its atheistic Communist foes could do. Indeed, the survival of Eastern Orthodoxy through the past half-millennium shows that this portion of Christendom possesses considerable spiritual resources—resources from which Western Christians might well learn.

My approach in this book does not imply that I think all things Eastern Orthodox are as well as they might be. Respected and often outspoken Orthodox leaders recognize foibles, problems and areas that need to be vigorously addressed in their communions, whether in the émigré Orthodox churches in Western Europe and North America or those in Eastern Europe and the former Soviet Union. It would be arrogance on the part of an Orthodox Christian to assume that nothing could be improved within Orthodoxy. Equally, it would be hubris for Western Christians to act as if they had so well mastered the Christian faith and its practice that they could not sit at the feet of Eastern Christians and learn from them. On either side, that kind of arrogance is spawned by ignorance, cradled in pride and nurtured in a triumphalism that cannot rightly claim the name Christian.

This book should also not be taken to imply that the Christian East is only to be teacher. Indeed, there is much in Western Christianity that might be of benefit to Eastern Christianity. However, this book is intended to set forth some of the riches of Eastern Orthodoxy for Western Christians—specifically, for those who have already learned to appreciate insights of other Christians in the West and who are willing to open themselves to enrichment from the Eastern Orthodox tradition. I hope that through this book some light from the Christian East will fall on our pathway and help us see even better how to journey through this life toward the ultimate hope set before us.

1

Historical Perspectives

THE DISTINCTIVE EMPHASES FOUND WITHIN CHRISTIANITY, both Eastern and Western, have developed over the course of several centuries. They are rooted in the different ways the gospel was appropriated in the Latin and the Greek cultures of the Roman Empire during the period of the ancient church. Subsequently, the particular distinctives of Eastern Orthodoxy were elaborated during the Byzantine era. In the trying circumstances faced by Eastern Christianity since the fall of Constantinople, these distinctives have not only been preserved and practiced, they have also received further elaboration. By tracing the history traversed by Orthodoxy in the following overview, with special focus on what has shaped its distinctive approaches and emphases, we will be in a better position to understand and appreciate those distinctives.

The Ancient Church: Unity and Diversity

The fifth book of the New Testament presents the story of the apostolic witness spreading outward from Jerusalem, into Judea, through Samaria, unto the ends of the earth (Acts 1:8). The book culminates with St. Paul preaching the gospel in Rome (Acts 28:23-31). Within a little more than three decades after the death and resurrection of Christ, the Christian message could be heard throughout the Roman Empire and in the capital itself. Even within the confines of Caesar's household (Phil 4:22), there were people who had responded with faith in Christ. "The ends of the earth" had been reached, with the proclamation of the gospel in the capital of the Roman Empire. Rather than marking the end of history, both of the church and of the present age—as some early Christians thought it would—this humble triumph of the spread of the gospel opened up a wide new history of the church within this age.

The path of the church would involve many tortuous turns and difficult struggles in the following 250 years, but remarkable—and, indeed, quite unexpected—

developments lay in store for it. By the early fourth century, the emperor himself, Constantine the Great, had embraced Christianity; before the end of the fourth century, under Theodosius the Great, Christianity became the official religion of the empire. It is scarcely surprising that enthused leaders of the church saw in all this the realization of the eschatological declaration "the kingdom of the world has become the kingdom of our Lord and of his Christ" (Rev 11:15 RSV). Their determination to transform that earthly empire from within, so that it would become in reality what it was in promise, was a faithful response to the glorious opportunity afforded them.

Pursuing such a transformation would require the discerning application of all that Christ had commanded (Mt 28:20) to the manifold situations confronting the church throughout the empire. It would entail not only a careful listening to the deepest questions of the respective cultures that the Roman Empire had absorbed but also offering relevant responses that could be understood by the members of those cultures. Such an endeavor would not be a new venture for the church: it would be a broadening of what had been its practice since the church first began to spread.

When the Christian message originally moved out of the confines of Palestine, it entered regions of the ancient world that had not been molded by the experience of the Jewish people. As it did so, that Christian message encountered established cultures, which the early Christian church needed to understand if it was to bring the gospel with clarity into those cultures. More than that was needed, however; the church also had to find ways to communicate the gospel to the people whose thought patterns, attitudes and approaches to life had been shaped by those cultures.

Sometimes, communicating the gospel faithfully might require direct challenge to prevailing thought patterns and the endeavor to replace them with Christian alternatives. At other times, it might involve an appreciation of attitudes that could be transformed from within to serve the glory of Christ. St. Paul indicates that the goal of his ministry was to "take every thought captive to obey Christ" (2 Cor 10:5). There is nothing in that passage to suggest that this was a determination unique to him; indeed, it seems evident that he saw no other option, whether for other apostles and leaders of the church or for any of its members.

Working thus within various cultural settings did not, however, lead to doctrinal division within the church. To the contrary, the early church gloried in the unity which marked its faith and practice in whatever tongue, tribe, people or nation (Rev 7:9) it was found: there was "one Lord, one faith, one baptism" (Eph 4:5). This was true not only during the lifetime of the apostles but in the ensuing centuries as well. To the apostolic fathers of the late first and the second centuries, the church's continuity in the apostolic message indicated both the Lord's faithfulness to his promises to be with it to the end of the age (Mt 28:20) and to guide it into all truth (Jn 16:13), and also the church's faithfulness in preserving and proclaiming what he had imparted to it.[1] According to the church fathers of the late second and the third centuries, the continuing unity in teaching and practice to be found throughout the church, in whatever region of the world it had taken root, testified to the presence and leading of the Holy Spirit within it. That unity in the apostolic message was, in their understanding, both gift and task, and they sought strenuously to remain within the apostolic teaching and practice.[2]

However, this unity did not issue into a bland sameness or preclude divergences of approach on various matters. The very use of different languages—Greek in the eastern half of the Roman Empire and Latin in the West—inevitably involved certain differences. Moreover, the Latin and the Hellenistic worlds were themselves different in several regards. In relating with relevance to the respective cultures in which the church took root, attitudes and approaches which became commonplace in ecclesiastical life in one culture would not necessarily be found in churches in the other. Just as absorption of people groups into the Roman Empire had not meant the eradication of the various subject peoples' cultures, likewise as the church subsequently spread into those cultures, the Christian message did not eradicate them as intrinsically evil. In this way, the Christian church took on various shades of emphasis, depending on where it was found within the ancient world; however, it did not thereby lose its unity in faith and practice. This assured the leaders of the church that, for all the differences in particulars which might be noted, they were nonetheless still one.

We need to keep this ecclesiastical pattern of acculturation in mind in order to appreciate what took place in the early church in general, and the roots of Eastern Christianity's distinctiveness in particular. To understand this, it may be helpful to remind readers of what they have probably been taught about the roots of Western civilization.

---

[1]These emphases appear in St. Clement of Rome's *Letter of the Romans to the Corinthians* 42:1-2 and 44:2; in St. Polycarp's *Letter to the Philippians* 3:2 and 7:2; and in St. Ignatius of Antioch's *Letter to the Ephesians* 3:2, as well as in his *Letter to the Smyrneans* 1:2 and 8:2.

[2]This perspective is pervasive among the leaders of the church during this period. It is especially prominent in the works of three of the most significant of them: see the arguments in St. Irenaeus of Lyons *Against Heresies* 1.10.2; 3.3.1-2; 3.4.1-2; 4.20.1; 5.20.2; Tertullian *Prescriptions Against Heretics,* chaps. 6, 9, 12 and 13 (with special stress in chaps. 20, 28, 32); and St. Cyprian *On the Unity of the Catholic Church,* chaps. 5 and 23.

Textbook treatments of the ancient period of Western civilization commonly emphasize the foundational contributions of Greece and of Rome, the two great civilizations that shaped the world into which the Christian message was first proclaimed. The great gifts of ancient Greece to Western civilization were democracy, on the one hand, and the stress on human reason, on the other. Rome's chief bequests lay in other fields. For one, its emphasis on law has profoundly molded Western attitudes toward law, nation and justice. For another, Rome was wise enough to adopt the insights and practices of those nations it conquered, rather than to eradicate them or reject and then reinvent analogues to them; however, it first adapted them to mesh with its own distinctive Roman approaches. This Roman orientation implanted deeply within the Western psyche a concern to understand how something holds together, how it works and how it affects (or would affect) the system already in place. These Greek and Roman emphases had already molded the cultures into which Christianity first spread. To appreciate that influence, however, we need to consider how the ancient Greek contribution itself had been reshaped by the time the Christian message began to be heard.

The culture of ancient Greece, which spawned democracy and the emphasis on reason, flourished from the sixth through the fourth centuries B.C. As that culture was subsequently spread throughout the world in the wake of the conquests of Alexander the Great, that *Hellenic* culture was transformed into *Hellenistic* culture. Thus modified, Greek influence permeated the leading strata of the entire ancient Near Eastern world well before Rome swallowed up the region into its empire.

Alexander saw himself as benefactor to the known world in imparting the benefits of Hellenic culture to it. As that culture permeated the ancient Near East, it was assimilated and adapted to the quite different cultural milieus into which it entered: it became *Hellenistic* culture which, though rooted in ancient Greece, was nonetheless something distinct from it. Hellenic culture had flourished in the close confines of the Greek *polis* ("city-state"); Hellenistic culture reigned within the much more impersonal structures of the large kingdoms that developed out of Alexander's empire.

Not surprisingly, Hellenic experimentation with democracy passed from the scene in the Hellenistic age. However, the emphasis on reason survived, even though it was transformed. In the Hellenistic period, philosophers continued to engage in searching theoretical speculation, but they manifested considerably less confidence than their Hellenic predecessors that human reason could lead to the embrace of ultimate truth. With their forebears in the glory days of ancient Athens, the Hellenistic thinkers still used their reasoning capacities to discourse on beauty, goodness, justice and their noumenal kin; even more, those philosophers reflected on fate, tragedy and the host of related phenomenal experiences which had been so graphically portrayed by the playwrights of the Hellenic era and were always relevant to the human condition. In seeking to relate such dissimilar concerns in a largely impersonal cosmopolis, these Hellenistic philosophers placed limitations on what bare reason might hope to attain; they made room for a "Beyond" which even reason could not reach. This was the intellectual culture in the eastern half of the Roman Empire into which the Christian message entered and to which it sought to speak.

In the western half of that empire, the situation was quite different. The Roman world had not been profoundly affected by Hellenistic attitudes. It had long since developed its own approach to life, culture, government and mutual responsibility before encountering the cultural results of Alexander's conquests. Where the Hellenistic emphasis on reason had remained primarily the province of the cultural elite in the ancient Near East, the Roman emphasis on practicality and adaptability could be assimilated by virtually anyone in society; consequently, it could and did seep much more deeply into the habits of thought of the common people. Furthermore, the emphasis on law, for all the need it undeniably had of specialist practitioners, could and did touch on the lives of the average Roman. The more ethereal and intellectually reflective stance of the leading cadres of Hellenistic culture was not particularly attractive to Roman society.

The stark difference in the respective cultures is obvious in the following contrast. Hellenistic culture had produced many brilliant philosophers who explored profoundly what reason could (and could not) offer; even so, during its more than millennial existence, Rome produced no great philosophers. There was, of course, no lack of great minds among the Romans; however, the best and brightest of Rome's gifted pursued law rather than philosophy. Even those who, like Cicero and Seneca, appear to have been philosophically attuned were really interested in questions of ethics—that is, of the *practical application* of thought to life; this was a distinctively Roman approach to and adaptation of the life of the intellect.

As the Christian message spread into these divergent cultures, it came to people whose attitudes and concerns had been shaped by those cultures. These people had the same longings, needs and ultimate concerns as any human would, but the particular ways in which they thought, acted and lived, and the questions with which they wrestled, were inevitably shaped by and inextricably bound up with the cultures in which they had grown up.

Thus, contextualization was not a merely theoretical issue but the need of the hour for the fledgling church. Without departing from the teaching of Christ and the apostles, the church nevertheless, in bringing the gospel relevantly to each of these great cultures, spoke it into those cultures in ways that their people could understand. Those who heard the gospel and responded in faith also incorporated it in terms of the concerns they already knew and the questions with which they traditionally wrestled. Because of this, from early in the church's existence, different emphases and stresses in teaching and preaching emerged in the two halves of the Roman Empire. These distinguishable emphases did not contradict each other, but they were nevertheless different. Each was a relevant response to the distinct culture into which the gospel had come. A consideration of two historic contrasts in Christian emphasis, as these arose within the two cultures, may elucidate the general pattern of these differences.

In the first place, during the early third century a significant difference arose between Christian leaders in the two halves of the empire as to how best to present the claims of Christianity. In the eastern part, in the intellectual center of Alexandria, Clement of Alexandria and his student Origen sought to demonstrate that Christianity was the culmination of the best that Hellenic and Hellenistic thought had produced. They sought points of similarity and contact between the Christian faith and the leading philosophical systems produced by their day[3]—especially Platonism.[4]

By contrast, in the Latin West, Tertullian responded with the trenchant challenge, "What has Athens to do with Jerusalem?" He rejected the Alexandrian attitude, one consonant with the Hellenistic intellectual culture to which Clement and Origen sought to bear witness. In Tertullian's estimation, Greek patterns of

[3]The results of their attempts would be challenged by subsequent Greek church fathers who, while they did not repudiate the project of Clement and Origen, sought to achieve it in a manner that precluded the assimilation of the Christian faith to the pagan influences of Greek and Hellenistic intellectual culture—the pattern which these later Greek church fathers discerned in the approach of Clement and Origen; cf. the treatment below, chap. 2, pp. 52-55.

[4]"Platonism" had become the catchall designation for philosophical thought in the Greek-speaking world long before Origen's time. The package of thought was not a straightforward continuation of Plato's teaching, however; it included many other elements that had commended themselves to philosophers since Plato's time. It has become common to refer to the "Platonism" that Origen and subsequent Christian leaders interacted with as "Neo-Platonism." This is anachronistic, however, for Origen. The philosopher who developed the coherent philosophical position subsequently known as Neo-Platonism was Plotinus, a contemporary of Origen. Plotinus's presentation of philosophy (which he called "Platonism") so quickly commended itself to philosophers of his time and subsequently that one can use the designation as the description for philosophical thought in ancient civilization in the generation immediately after Origen (d. 254). Consequently, most of the time when ancient philosophical thought is mentioned in our presentation from this point onward, it will be appropriate to denominate it "Neo-Platonism."

thought could not be appropriately adapted and adopted by Christians.

However, Tertullian's response was no less shaped by his culture than was that of the Alexandrian thinkers. For all his denunciation of the Hellenistic orientations of the Alexandrians, Tertullian's response was typically Roman: he was focused on the question of how to adapt and adopt what had gone before and now had been conquered by ultimate truth, the Christian faith. Further, in the rest of Tertullian's writings, his apologetic stance toward the surrounding world was one of the lawyer arguing his case for Christianity against all claims of its challengers; his own theological and personal ascetical practices were also focused on matters of law, ethics and practical usefulness. The Alexandrians might well have parried Tertullian's thrust with the challenge, "But what has Rome to do with Jerusalem?"

In both cases, the Hellenistic and Roman cultures into which Christianity had been introduced had shaped the way in which Christian claims were presented and which claims were emphasized by those who called others to faith in Christ. Yet for all their differences in strategy and particular emphases, Tertullian from the Latin West, and Clement and Origen from the Hellenistic East, all embraced the one Christian faith and stressed the unity of faith among the churches throughout the world.

Second, the difference between the cultures of the two halves of the empire led to differences in the focus and emphasis of the church in each half as it appropriated Christian teaching. As heir to the emphasis of Roman civilization, Christianity in the Latin West was much concerned with law. In that Roman legal tradition for which the Roman Empire was justly famous, concerns with status before the law, with guilt and justice, with debt and credit, and with other similar matters were foundational, ultimate considerations. Consequently, it is hardly surprising that Western Christian theology, ecclesiastical practice and piety all came to reflect concerns with matters that properly belong in a court of law—specifically, in God's court. This was true already in the period of antiquity; it remained so throughout the Middle Ages in the West; it is unmistakable in the concerns of the Protestant Reformation as well. Questions of merit and debt, of satisfaction and payment, of justification and condemnation, are all appropriate and natural questions within this approach. To this day, Western Christianity has been shaped by this ancient Roman heritage which has been transmitted down through the centuries.

In contrast, the eastern half of the Roman Empire was not preoccupied with questions of law and legal standing. The prior concerns of Hellenistic intellectual culture shaped both the questions asked and the answers given by the church in that culture. In the East, those questions, rooted in careful philosophical thought, converged especially on the contrast between light and darkness, life and death, spirit and matter, and on the limitations of human reason. Christians in the East sought to address the underlying questions of their society by emphasizing those elements of the apostolic message that spoke to such issues. Questions of guilt and legality, for example, or of satisfaction and payment were not the main issues for Eastern Christianity; instead, Eastern Christians focused on the struggle between good and evil, between light and darkness, on the process of salvation, on the gift of eternal life and on communion with God. Even so, Christianity in the East was reserved about the capacities of human reason to express adequately the mysteries of the faith. These emphases were already present in Eastern Christianity during the period of antiquity; they remained central in subsequent centuries; and they have continued to be the issues on which Eastern Orthodoxy has focused to the present day.

These differing emphases between Western and Eastern Christianity need not be viewed as mutually exclusive, but can be seen as complementary. Neither has been, of course, exclusively the prerogative of one group or absolutely foreign to the other, since both find emphasis in the apostolic witness in the New Testament. Nevertheless, the differences are there, and they have been there since Christian antiquity.

However, the distinctions between Western and Eastern Christian approaches did not split the ancient church; the two segments of the one church worked together. A remarkable unity of teaching and confession marked the church throughout the empire. Whatever differences Tertullian and his heirs might discern from Clement and Origen and their successors (or vice versa), the ancient church fought together for the faith of the gospel (Phil 1:27). Challenged at the end of the first and throughout the second centuries by Gnosticism; in the second and third by Marcionism, Montanism and Modalism; and in the fourth and fifth by Arianism, Apollinarianism, Nestorianism and Eutychianism, the ancient church, West and East, stood together to defend apostolic teaching during the trinitarian and christological controversies.

In these controversies, the theologians of the Christian East played the predominant role. To be sure, the controversies themselves had arisen in the eastern half of the empire, so response from within the Christian East was to be expected. Of course, Western Christian leaders involved themselves in the controversies; however, both in number and influence, the church fathers of the Christian East dominated the response to the heretical challenges during the period of Christian antiquity. Moreover, when the ecumenical councils were called that dealt with the trinitarian and christological heresies, they all met in the eastern half of the empire: Nicea (325), Constantinople (381), Ephesus (431) and Chalcedon (451). At each of those councils, while Western Christian representatives took part in the deliberations, the major role was played by the leaders of the Christian East. In view of the intellectual leadership of the Greek-speaking East within the empire, this is hardly surprising.

The Byzantine Period

While the different tendencies within Western and Eastern Christianity considered above were already present in the period of antiquity, the continued unity and coordination of the Roman Empire kept them from developing into significantly different directions within the church. However, by the end of the fifth century, a serious change had befallen the known world.

When people of Western European or North American extraction think of the fall of the Roman Empire, they usually date it to sometime in the fifth century. Since Rome was overrun in 410 and again in 455 by Germanic invaders, and the last Roman emperor in the West was removed in 476, it seems warranted to assert that the Roman Empire came to an end in that century. According to Western historiography, that fall ushered in the beginning of the "Middle" Ages—that period lying between the collapse of Rome and the coming of the European renewal movements of the Renaissance and Reformation. This approach makes sense of Western European history, indeed, but it runs aground on the reef of the continued existence and importance of the Roman Empire in the East.

However significant the city of Rome had been for the Roman Empire, by the fifth century it had long since ceased to be much more than a matter of nostalgia. The first Christian emperor, Constantine the Great, had moved the capital of the empire to Byzantium in 330. It remained the seat of all effective Roman government thereafter. The residents of Constantinople and the empire in the East thought of themselves as Romans and saw their empire as the continuation of the Roman Empire.[5] Consequently, however painful the fifth-century loss of Rome and the western provinces was to Byzantium, that city continued to rule over a considerable empire—the eastern half of the Roman Empire.

The loss of the West did not go uncontested: in the sixth century, under Justinian the Great, Byzantium won back a considerable portion of the former impe-

---

[5]The Byzantines referred to themselves, throughout the whole imperial era, as *romaioi*, the Greek term for "Romans" (George Ostrogorsky, *History of the Byzantine State*, trans. Joan Hussey, rev. ed. [New Brunswick, N.J.: Rutgers University Press, 1969], p. 28).

rial holdings in Italy, North Africa and southeastern Spain. However, those western territories were too far from Byzantium for effective control and administration. Over the next few centuries, the West had to make its way, largely, without effective government from the city on the Bosphorus.

Not long after Justinian's time, the Eastern Roman Empire took a significant step. During the first half of the seventh century, the official language of government became Greek rather than Latin. With the West in ruins, few people there were in a position to consult with the imperial court; in the East, fewer and fewer members of that court saw the importance of fluency in a language which, however well it had previously served the empire, was now an anachronism.

With that change in imperial language came a concomitant decline in interest in learning Latin. Byzantine scholarship still had access to all the riches of Hellenic and Hellenistic writings and of the Greek church fathers, so scholars were not greatly disadvantaged by this development. However, the decline in the study of Latin led to a significant decrease in familiarity with the works of either ancient Roman or Western Christian scholarship. For Christians in the West, the desperate situation in the wake of the Germanic invasions meant the loss of effective Christian government, subjection to barbarian rule, and the destruction of most vestiges of civilization and culture. Among these losses was education. The Germanic invasions resulted in the destruction of schools, and both schooling and learning retreated behind the walls of the monasteries, which became the protectors of learning in the West. In such straits, it is scarcely surprising that knowledge of the Greek language became an exotic possession of the few. Given this, not many people in the West could understand the language in which their reputed imperial protectors sought to address them.

This extended comment on the collapse of the western half of the Roman Empire and its results has been necessary in order to appreciate why the differing attitudes of Eastern and of Western Christianity, already recognizable in the period of antiquity, would become so much more pronounced in ensuing centuries. With little communication between the two geographic areas, and what little there was suffering the vagaries of well-meant but often inept translation, it is hardly surprising that misunderstandings arose in the centuries after the fall of Rome, or that the two spheres developed in considerable independence from each other. For our purposes, the significance of this development lies in the context it created for those distinctive approaches which had already begun to manifest themselves in the Christian West and the Christian East to come to fuller growth in ensuing centuries.

The collapse of the West did not immediately issue in any obvious change in the relationship between the church there and in the continuing empire in the East. Indeed, the christological controversies which had agitated the church in the preceding centuries continued: Monophysitism challenged the church in the sixth century, Monotheletism in the seventh, and Iconoclasm—specifically, the question whether the incarnate Christ could be pictorially represented, a distinctly christological question[6]—in the eighth and ninth centuries. As before, these were questions that arose within Eastern Christendom, and they were resolved by ecumenical councils held within its geographic bounds: Constantinople II (553), Constantinople III (680-681) and Nicea II (787). Given the desperate straits faced by Western Christianity during this period, the infrequency of participation in the controversies by Western Christian leaders and the paucity of Western ecclesiastical representatives at the councils are hardly surprising. While the ecclesiastical culture which could spawn and deal with such controversies continued in the Byzantine Empire, the Western Church's situation demanded concern for other issues.

The intellectual leadership of the fifth through the eighth centuries was unquestionably to be found not in the Christian West but in the Christian East. Indeed, throughout the Middle Ages (as they are reckoned by Western historiography), Byzantium was the intellectual and cultural center of the Christian world. In due course, the West would see a new civilization arise during the Middle Ages, built on the remains of Roman achievements and with the admixture of Christian and Germanic contributions. This momentous accomplishment, however important it eventually proved to be for the subsequent development of Western European civilization, was dwarfed by the transformation in the Byzantine Empire. There the Christian church, participating fully in the cultural and intellectual leadership of the time, was able to achieve a Christianization of both state and culture. The emperors were all Christians, some of them gifted lay theologians in their own right. Christian perspectives shaped the schooling and the curriculum. Self-consciously Christian approaches to the heritage of the ancient Greeks, and to how and to what degree it could be used by Christian thinkers, were not only developed but commonly embraced. Much more could be noted about the considerable achievements of the Christian state of Byzantium, but that would take us off the track of our particular concerns. It takes little imagination or preliminary familiarity with the data to appreciate that such accomplishments, especially given

[6]See the treatment below, chap. 11, pp. 188-89.

the lack of input from the Christian West, led to a considerable further development of those distinctively Eastern Christian approaches to faith and practice which were already evident in the period of Christian antiquity.

A cautious attitude regarding the possibilities of merely human reason, including Christian reason, had undergirded and shaped the contributions of the Eastern Christian participants in the trinitarian and christological controversies of antiquity. This same attitude pervaded the subsequent christological controversies of the fifth through the ninth centuries. In each case, the ecumenical councils followed the Eastern Christian attitude in their responses to heresies: the conciliar pronouncements always said as much as was necessary to protect the Christian message of salvation as imparted by the apostles, but they never claimed to explain the truth confessed. The distrust in the capacities of mere human reason to understand the most profound truth, an attitude that had developed during the Hellenistic period, found a welcome home in the attitudes of Eastern Christianity: if even unbelievers could recognize such limitations, who would be foolish enough to countermand that attitude when speaking of the triune God and the one who was both God and man?

This reverence for the mystery of God and of the incarnate Christ also promoted a wonder before the biblical story of creation, fall and redemption. The conflict of light and darkness, the coming of life in conquest of death, the triumph over the demonic powers, and the wonder of relationship with God received constant emphasis in the teaching and preaching of Eastern Christianity. Awe before God's grace and praise for the indescribable benefits he bestows served further to check any presumptuous inclinations to claim to explain the ways of God with humanity. Among Byzantine Christians, it was commonly affirmed that the part of the theologian was to pray, not to explain; put another way, he should remain silent in contemplation of God and his ways rather than open his lips and speak error.

This highlights a notable difference between what was to develop in the Christian West and what was to be found in the Christian East. Along with the later medieval Western European renewal of government, the Christianization of its inhabitants and the call to erect a God-glorifying civilization, there arose a determination to develop an educational system that would serve God's glory and that civilization. The monastic variety of education, which had continued in the centuries since the fall of Rome, could not well serve the needs of the new civilization. About the time that the needs for education were becoming evident—during the eleventh century—the works of Aristotle became much more widely known in the Christian West. (Only a few of his works had survived the Germanic invasions, been copied and become known in Western Europe in the preceding centuries.) The initial hesitation among Western Christian scholars about relying on the works of a pagan for instruction was answered by respected Christian theologians, and the resultant enthusiasm for Aristotle's works knew few limits over the next four centuries. His penchant for categorization, clarity and explanation offered the Christian West new and exciting possibilities for the understanding and mastery of all branches of learning—including theology. Consequently, Western confidence in the ability of the Christian mind to explain truth and account for the ways of God with humanity came to recognize almost no bounds.[7] The difference in perspective and expectation between the Western Christian attitude toward human reason and that which marked Eastern Christianity can hardly be overstated.

However, the Eastern Christian attitude toward reason did not preclude the development of considerable doctrinal sophistication; during the Byzantine period, Eastern Christianity benefited from the insightful teaching of many gifted theologians. However, in Byzantium, speaking of God—what "theology" means—could only arise out of intimate communion with him, a communion nurtured in meditation rather than intellection. Given this orientation, it is not surprising that many of those who became trusted as theologians were monks. To be a theologian was the culmination of a life spent in communion with God, speaking out of the richness of his experienced grace and mercy; it was not the end result of a process of academic instruction. For Eastern Christians, "theology" was not the product of intellectual mastery of appropriate revelatory data. Their viewpoint was well expressed by Evagrius Ponticus when he urged, "If you are a theologian, you will pray truly; and if you pray truly, you are a theologian."

This Byzantine Christian concern for practitioners of Christian meditation who had learned to know God in humility and silence rather than through definitions and schooling alone shaped more than their attitude toward theologians. Eastern Christianity came to require that anyone who would serve as a bishop—the highest-ranking member of the clergy in a city, the one responsible for the direction of all the churches in his diocese—must have been a monk. Ecclesiastical government could only be entrusted to those who had first learned humility before God and love for their fellow human beings; it was not something that was immediately transferable from administrative experience in civil government into the ecclesiastical sphere of rule. This concern for humility and the commitment to wonder before God, rather than confident speech about him, marked Eastern

[7]See the treatment in G. R. Evans, *Old Arts and New Theology: The Beginnings of Theology as an Academic Discipline* (New York: Oxford University Press, 1980).

Christianity throughout the glory days of the Byzantine Empire. They do so unto this day as well.

Another important emphasis in Byzantine Christianity was its appropriation of the dramatic story of God's dynamic dealings with humanity and creation as the mold for theological method. Eastern Christian theologians were familiar, on the one hand, with the flow of the history of redemption in the Scriptures, yet aware, on the other hand, that the pagan thought of Hellenic and Hellenistic culture usually built on static categories; consequently they stressed the dynamic character of all of creation and of God's dealings with it. Simply put, Eastern Christianity refused to follow pagan Greek thought in its fixation on definitions and static categories of analysis. Instead, Eastern Orthodoxy stressed that everything was created by God for development and could not be understood or spoken of correctly apart from that dynamic process. The contrast to classic Greek and to Hellenistic philosophies could hardly be more sharply drawn.

The great period of Byzantine *doctrinal* elaboration came to an end with the conclusion of the Iconoclastic controversies in the ninth century. Thereafter, further refinement came in the area of *spirituality.* In the subsequent five centuries, Byzantine Christianity focused its attention on what can and does take place in intimate communion with God. The lyrical intimacies of the hymns of St. Symeon the New Theologian (949-1022) express a profoundly passionate awareness of divine grace to the unworthy who is nevertheless privileged to commune with God. His approach received further elucidation by St. Gregory Palamas (1296-1359), who defended the claim that one could so commune with God in the depths of one's being as not only to experience the indescribable light which had emanated from Christ on the Mount of Transfiguration but even to reflect it before others. This depth of intimacy with God could not be an abiding experience in this life; even so, anyone who devoted himself or herself to constant prayer—whether a monk or a layperson—might well be blessed with this divine gift. Palamas, himself a monk and later archbishop of Thessaloniki, was the theologian of intimate communion with God; he was the last great theologian of Eastern Christianity before the fall of Constantinople to the Turks in 1453, the event with which the Byzantine period of Orthodoxy's history came to an end.

Before taking our leave of that Byzantine period, we must consider two further matters: the rift which took place between Eastern and Western Christianity and the missionary labors of the Byzantine Church. Without the first, much of subsequent church and world history would have been dramatically different. Without the second, the study of Byzantine Christianity might well be nothing more than a piece of antiquarianism; after all, Byzantium ceased to exist as an empire. However, because of Byzantium's evangelistic endeavors among the various Slavic peoples, there were nations and churches which could and did carry on the practice and teaching of Orthodoxy even after Constantinople's fall.

It is hardly surprising that, in view of the tremendous differences between the situations of Western and Eastern Christianity after the end of antiquity, tensions periodically developed between the two. There were occasional rifts during the ensuing centuries, and ecclesiastical communion was periodically broken. Each of these, however, was eventually healed. Consequently, the mutual denunciations and excommunications in 1054 occasioned no particular anxiety at the time:[8] people expected that, as before, there would be an eventual restoration of that communion. Nevertheless, the division lingered; indeed, it has never been officially healed to the present day.

However, it was not the 1054 schism that drove Western and Eastern Christianity permanently into two rival camps. The event that assured the continuance of this division was the sack of Byzantium and the dismantling of its empire by Western Christians in 1204 during the Fourth Crusade. Although a little-known episode in Western Christianity, it has left lasting scars within Eastern Christianity.

The crusade ideal urged by various medieval popes seemed to the Byzantines a peculiarly quixotic adventurism.[9] Western Christian leaders, with virtually no experience in actually confronting the Muslim military forces, saw the idea of liberating the holy land from control by the infidels as a godly calling, sure of success. For the Byzantines, who had had long experience with the formidable Muslim armies, relationships with the Muslims were concerns of diplomacy and, as occasion demanded, warfare. They were not, however, the stuff of holy war. In Western Christian eyes, the Byzantine attitude constituted cowardly compromise; to Byzantines, the Western Christian attitude seemed foolhardy fanaticism.

During the first three crusades, the Western crusaders expected and, usually,

---

[8]While books by Western authors have often made much of the 1054 division, evidence from the period indicates no particular or unusual anxiety about the most recent split; what made the 1054 schism more significant than its predecessors was that it has never been healed—a datum that the contemporaries, of course, could not have known at the time. For a careful consideration of the question, see Steven Runciman, *The Eastern Schism: A Study of the Papacy and the Eastern Churches During the Eleventh and Twelfth Centuries* (1955; reprint, New York: Oxford University Press, 1997).

[9]The Byzantine emperor Alexius I appealed to Pope Urban II for help in resisting the Seljuk Turks' incursions into Byzantine territory. The pope proclaimed a crusade to liberate the holy land from Muslim control. This was not at all what the emperor requested: Byzantine territory had not included the holy land for more than four centuries by the time of the emperor's appeal.

received unfailing support from the Byzantines in the provision of guides, foodstuffs and other such necessities. However, the Byzantines did not supply armed forces to join the crusading expeditions. When those expeditions encountered insuperable frustrations, Western Christian leaders suspected that the Eastern Christian imperial leadership had undermined the endeavors. In any event, the first three crusades did little to draw the two camps of Christians together.

They had, however, served to acquaint Western Europeans with the riches of Constantinople. Among those considerably impressed were the Venetians, a significant maritime and naval power. When the call for a fourth crusade was issued in the early thirteenth century, the Venetians built ships to transport the Western crusading armies to their destination. Payment for the ships fell seriously short of what had been promised, however, and the Venetians demanded that the crusaders somehow make up the deficit. To do so, the crusaders had to capture certain towns which Venice desired for its trade empire. The ultimate target in this regard became Constantinople itself.

Internal strife in the imperial city afforded the crusaders, who had planned to stop there for provisions in any event, the opportunity to take Constantinople. In 1204, through intrigues within the city, the gates of the impregnable fortress that had been Constantinople were thrown open to the crusaders. What followed was a three-day rampage of destruction, slaughter, rape and pillage. Virtually all the transportable riches of Byzantium were taken; much of the rest was simply destroyed. Eventually, the loot found its way to Western Europe, where much of it can be found today in museums and private collections.

The devastation to Constantinople was horrific, but more than buildings and riches were affected: Eastern Christians suffered the atrocities of rape, murder, mutilation and the other horrors of warfare at the hands not of infidel armies but of supposedly fellow Christians involved, ostensibly, in holy warfare. It was this, and not the 1054 schism—even with the important questions it confronted—that led to the deep chasm between Western and Eastern Christianity that continues to the present.

The Byzantines were eventually able to restore their kingdom. By 1261 the empire erected by the crusaders had fallen to resurgent Byzantine forces, and the Byzantine Empire was reestablished. However, the shock and horror of Western Christian perfidy, so little known to Western Christians in the present, has colored Eastern Christian attitudes and responses to Western Christianity to this day. Given what they experienced, it is hardly surprising that Eastern Christians have continued to be suspicious of Western Christianity—which did not repudiate the travesty of 1204 for nearly eight centuries, until 2001.[10] The Fourth Crusade has soured relations between Eastern and Western Christianity in ways that Western Christians hardly sense but Eastern Christians still taste. Their steadfast determination to remain faithful to their distinctive perspectives can, at least in part, be accounted for by what they experienced at the hands of Western Christians in 1204.

In turning to the missionary labors of Byzantium, we consider endeavors which spread Christianity over a considerable portion of the continent of Europe. In so doing, these evangelistic efforts contributed to the rivalry that was developing between Western and Eastern Christianity, since the area being evangelized lay between the two centers of Rome and Byzantium. That rivalry would lead, among other things, to the Fourth Crusade just considered.

In the mid-ninth century, the pagan Slavic peoples who had spread throughout Eastern Europe became the focus of intense evangelistic activities on the part of both Western and Eastern Christianity. However, Western Christianity required that services be conducted in Latin, the ecclesiastical language of the West. Consequently, mission endeavors were hampered by the inability of those who were being evangelized to understand what was being presented to them. The prince of the earliest Slavic state in Central Europe sought another way.

Rastislav of Moravia contacted Byzantium, seeking missionaries to labor among his people. His desire was to convert to Christianity, but he was aware that there were by that time two rival approaches to it. Since his nation was geographically located between the ecclesiastical spheres of influence of Rome and Byzantium, he figured that he could receive missionaries from either. Fearful of the aggrandizing desires of the powerful German state to his west, which was within the Roman orbit, he sought protection by possible affiliation with the Byzantine sphere of ecclesiastical influence—which would almost certainly bring with it military defense from the powerful Byzantine Empire. In 862 he requested missionaries from Byzantium, but his request included a special requirement: he wanted the evangelistic work and the services of worship conducted in the language of his people.

The Byzantines acquiesced to this request, and two highly respected figures were sent to Moravia. Previously entrusted with delicate diplomatic negotiations by the Byzantine leadership, the scholar Cyril and the monk Methodius were

---

[10]In May 2001, in Athens, Pope John Paul II startled the Orthodox by unexpectedly expressing remorse and asking forgiveness for the sins committed by Western crusaders in 1204. It remains to be seen how the Orthodox will respond to this acknowledgment of the evils committed in the Fourth Crusade. For 797 years, bitter memories of the tragedy have poisoned relationships with Western Christianity.

brothers who had grown up in Thessaloniki. In the region surrounding the city, numerous Slavs had resided for several centuries; like many of their fellow citizens, Cyril and Methodius had become fluent in the Slavic language. Cyril created an alphabet which he used to reduce that language—known then as "Slavonic"—to writing. The alphabet he devised, with some subsequent simplifications, is called "Cyrillic"[11]; it is the alphabet still used by many of the Slavic peoples.

In short order, Cyril and Methodius translated various parts of the Scriptures, the regular services of worship and much other Christian literature into Slavonic. Their work among the Moravians was successful: Rastislav and his people converted to Christianity. However, intrigues within his court, abetted by promises from the German leaders to the west of Moravia, resulted in a palace coup. Rastislav was deposed by a nephew who, cooperating with the Germans, expelled the Byzantine missionaries and brought in Western Christian clergy to take over the fledgling church in Moravia.

In both regards, what took place in the 860s in Moravia was charged with significance for the future of Christianity among the Slavic peoples. In the first place, although initially drawn to Eastern Christianity, the nation of Moravia—composed of the Moravian and large portions of the Slovak and Bohemian tribes of the Slavs—was absorbed within the Roman orbit. They, together with the rest of the Slovak and Bohemian tribes and (in the following century) the Poles—thus, all the West Slavs[12]—were drawn into the sphere of Western Christianity. Second, the success of the endeavors of Sts. Cyril and Methodius showed the way for further evangelization among the rest of the Slavic peoples. Byzantium readily sent the missionaries who had worked in Moravia to Bulgaria, at the request of Khan Boris, who also wanted to embrace Christianity. This evangelistic program, begun in the late 860s, resulted shortly in the conversion of Boris and his nation. From Bulgaria, the Christian faith was brought to the western Balkans, where the Serbs also embraced Eastern Christianity, hearing the message in their own language. Thus, most of the South Slavs were drawn into the orbit of Eastern Orthodoxy. In the following century, Prince Vladimir of Kiev embraced Byzantine Christianity. Converted in 988, he and his people learned the Christian faith in their own

---

[11]The alphabet Cyril devised is known as Glagolitic. Some of his younger collaborators in the mission to the Slavs later simplified the alphabet; it is commonly thought that the leader in this effort was St. Clement of Ohrid, who established a school to prepare students to become translators and priests. The simplified alphabet came to be called Cyrillic, in honor of St. Cyril.

[12]The various Slavic peoples are denominated "West," "South" or "East" Slavs, according to the direction in which they migrated during the sixth through the eighth centuries from their original homeland (in contemporary eastern Poland and western Ukraine).

language. Vladimir's state[13] was then the dominant one among the East Slavs, all of whom embraced Eastern Orthodoxy.

During the Byzantine period of Orthodoxy's history, the distinctive perspectives of Eastern Christianity came to full expression. They were communicated faithfully to the South and East Slavs, who were readily able to understand what was brought to them in their own language. Because of the results of missionary labors among the Slavs, Orthodoxy would continue to live on, even after Byzantium fell to the Ottoman Turks in 1453. Due in part to the Fourth Crusade, the Orthodoxy of those Slavs would remain suspicious of Western Christianity and adamant in its adherence to Eastern Christian perspectives. Even so, while the Slavs imparted their own tones to the distinctives of Eastern Orthodoxy in the period since 1453, those colors have only been further combinations of hues from the Byzantine palette.

1453 TO THE PRESENT

The glorious days of Byzantine Christianity's growth, development and cultural leadership ended with the fall of Constantinople in 1453 to the Ottoman Turks. By that time, much of southeastern Europe had already fallen: Bulgaria, Serbia and what is today Romania were already under Ottoman control by the time Byzantium fell to them. Thus, all the churches of Eastern Christianity—with a single important exception—became subject to the oppressive rule of the Muslim Turks.

As has been the practice with most empires throughout history, so also the Ottoman Turks sought to repress any movement that seemed a possible danger to the continuance of their rule. Thus, the various peoples who had embraced Eastern Christianity found themselves unable to set up their own schools, teach about their heritage, develop their own governments, or even set up clubs to study and cherish their own culture and identity. The Turks forbade any organization that might serve these causes.

Nevertheless, the Muslims had a reputation for religious tolerance. They were respectful of other "peoples of the Book"—that is, the other two religions that (with Islam) built on the ancient Hebrew Scriptures—namely, Judaism and Christianity. To be sure, the leading clergyman within Orthodoxy, the Patriarch of Constantinople, was appointed by the Turkish court. This could and did lead to a certain degree of Turkish influence within the upper echelons of the church's structure. Apart from that, however, the Turks largely allowed the various

[13]The state was known as Kievan Rus'; from it the three nations of Ukraine, Belarus and (European) Russia have descended.

churches to meet without oversight or control by the imperial rulers. In at least two regards, this proved to be significant for Orthodoxy's further development.

In the first place, the church within the various subject nations became the sole place where that people's nostalgia for earlier days of independence could be expressed and hopes for future freedom encouraged. The church in each nation thus ended up serving not only as the place where worship was conducted but also as the sole venue where hopes for national freedom could express themselves. Within the walls of the church, aspirations and longings for rebirth of the nation were nurtured in addition to the spiritual growth of the people. As a result, during the extensive period of Turkish dominance, church became inextricably intertwined with nation: to be Serb meant to be Serbian Orthodox; to be Bulgar meant to be Bulgarian Orthodox; to be Romanian meant to be Romanian Orthodox. This entanglement was so tight that many people in the Balkans had then—and still have—a hard time distinguishing between being a member of a particular national group and being a member of the dominant church within that group.

In the second place, the Turkish practice ensured that neither the leadership nor the membership of the churches would be particularly well schooled in the Eastern Christian faith. Since there could be no schools for these subject nations, there was no way for aspiring clergy to receive any structured training. As a consequence, even with the best of intentions on the part of many clergy, they themselves were not all that well versed in the teachings and insights of Eastern Orthodoxy. As a result, it is scarcely surprising that some of the riches of Orthodoxy remained unexplored by the members of the churches languishing under Turkish rule.

The period of subjection under the Ottoman Turk Empire was a severe time of trial for the peoples and churches of Eastern Christianity. For some, it began by the late fourteenth century; for the rest, it became reality during the fifteenth. For all, it lasted at least four centuries: Serbia, Greece, Romania and Bulgaria did not attain independence from the Ottoman Turks until the nineteenth century.

The significance of this lengthy period of domination can hardly be overstated—especially when we compare their experience with what transpired during that period in Western Europe. Constantinople fell less than four decades before Christopher Columbus discovered the Americas. Since then, the significance of the West for the rest of the world has expanded exponentially: among many other things, the establishment of trade empires, the coming of the Industrial Revolution, the development of democratic institutions, and the whole experience of the nations of North America all occurred since Byzantium fell. During that period, Western civilization saw Western Christianity move from being the dominant cultural force, through the division of the Protestant Reformation and into the period of disdain for Christianity, which became explicit during the Age of Reason and has marked so much of Western history subsequently.

During this whole period of Western Europe's and North America's worldwide economic hegemony, Eastern Christianity—again, with one important exception, to be noted below—enjoyed no freedom, endured much oppression and was allowed no means to insure that its perspectives would be preserved. That it was weakened to the degree that its earlier leadership in theology and practice could not be maintained is hardly surprising; that it survived at all is a testimony to the faithfulness of God to his people.

One of the ways God protected Eastern Orthodoxy was the continued influence of Mount Athos. This monastic center in northeastern Greece was already a respected center of spirituality in the last centuries of the Byzantine Empire. Given the centrality of monastic practice and insight for theology and church life in Byzantine Christianity, the fact that the Turks left Mount Athos alone and that they allowed numerous Orthodox Christians to journey to and establish monastic centers there was enough to assure that a continuing source of spiritual and theological leadership would be available to the Orthodox churches. Thus, the very strength and approach of Eastern Christianity, as it had developed during the Byzantine period, was providentially used to assure the continuation of Eastern Orthodox emphases.

The sole exception to the general observation that Orthodox churches fell under Turkish domination was the Russian Orthodox church. The Kievan state had been destroyed by the Mongol invasions in the mid-thirteenth century, and its people had languished under the Mongols' harsh rule until the early fifteenth century. By the closing decades of the Byzantine Empire's existence, however, a Russian state under the leadership of Moscow rather than Kiev had emerged. Given the importance played by that state and by Russian Orthodoxy in the subsequent history of Eastern Christianity, it is worthwhile to consider what that church was like.

The Russian state collectively understood its survival through the period of Mongol subjugation as God's blessing for remaining faithful to him. During the whole period, they had continued to practice the Eastern Christianity they had earlier embraced. Suspicious of the desperate attempts by Byzantine emperors to secure Western Christian aid against the Turks—attempts which, at the Council of Florence in 1439, had gone as far as to deny certain Eastern Orthodox distinctives in favor of Western Christian ones—the Russian leaders of both church and state were not surprised when Byzantium fell to the Turks in 1453. In the Russian assessment, that collapse was a divine judgment on apostasy.

As the sole Orthodox nation remaining after the fall of the Byzantine Empire, the Russians soon came to see themselves with a special calling in the world: to them had fallen the mantle of imperial leadership for the Christian Empire founded long ago on the Bosphorus by Constantine the Great. The Russian ruler took on the title "Tsar"—the Russian word for "Caesar"; Moscow came to be seen as the "Third Rome."[14] The Russian nation saw itself as "Holy Mother Russia," the privileged heir to the dignity of visibly embodying Christ's rule on earth and, for that reason, becoming the object of hatred to all those nations opposed to Christ and his rule. This, of course, bred a suspicion of the designs of other nations against Russia; with the coming of the Age of Reason in the West, Orthodox Russia was only further convinced of its reading of history, of its divine calling and of its danger from the West.

As a consequence, some Russian Orthodox leaders stressed the distinctiveness of Orthodox perspectives over against Western Christianity, both Roman Catholic and Protestant. Suspicious of Western Christian approaches, during the nineteenth century the Russian Orthodox articulated and maintained an acute and accentuated awareness of Orthodox distinctives in contrast to Western Christianity. When the Bolshevik revolution burst upon Russia in 1917, many Russians fled to the West. There they sought to maintain faithfulness to Orthodox perspectives, while also publishing works that would allow Western Christian readers to become familiar with Eastern Orthodoxy in all its riches and its distinctiveness. Two institutions which have especially served in this regard are St. Sergius Theological Institute in Paris and St. Vladimir's Theological Seminary in New York. Through the works authored by professors at these institutions, Western Christian readers have, in recent generations, had an unusual and hitherto unprecedented opportunity to learn about Orthodoxy.

Even so, the work of these institutions did not attract much attention in the broader ecclesiastical world. To many, it appeared little more than a desperate at-

---

[14]This designation builds on the ancient Christian understanding that God had providentially prepared the world for the coming of Christ with the establishment of a universal empire centered in Rome. When Constantine the Great transferred the capital from Rome to Byzantium, he styled the new capital "New Rome." This "Second Rome" was the center of the Christian empire which, according to ancient Christian understanding, by divine right ought to rule over the entire world for the sake of Jesus Christ. The Russians appropriated this understanding of God's providential guidance of history and applied it to their situation; the classic formulation of this conviction is found in a letter of 1510 from the Russian monk Filofey of Pskov to Tsar Basil III (English translation available in Basil Dmytryshyn, *Medieval Russia: A Source Book, 850-1700,* 3rd ed. [Philadelphia: Holt, Rinehart and Winston, 1991], pp. 259-61).

tempt to preserve the vestiges of a world long gone: not only Byzantium, but now Holy Mother Russia had ceased to exist, since it was officially an atheist state. With nearly all the remaining Orthodox churches having also been swallowed up into the post-World War II Soviet orbit, it seemed to many Christians in the West that Orthodoxy was doomed to extinction.

However, the events of the last two decades—with the collapse of the Communist empire in Eastern Europe in 1989 and of the Soviet Union in 1991—have confronted the Western world with the continued strength of Eastern Orthodoxy. Until the collapse of the Iron Curtain, some 80 percent of the approximately 250 million Orthodox Christians worldwide lived within the Soviet empire. Along with the other Christian churches there, Orthodoxy suffered vigorous, virulent opposition from the atheistic regimes of the Soviet Union and its satellites. As the largest and most historically and culturally influential of the branches of Christendom in that geographical area, Orthodoxy attracted the special attention of its Communist overlords. Unquestionably, the Russian Orthodox Church suffered; not only was it assaulted by persecution and martyrdom but clerical collaboration with official policy and secret police undercut confidence among many that it could always be trusted. Few people in the increasingly secular West, even committed Christians, offered much hope that Eastern Christianity would survive.

Consequently, as the Soviet empire crumbled many people in the West were unprepared to appreciate or understand the continuing presence and strength of the Orthodox churches in the Communist lands of Eastern Europe and the U.S.S.R. When the Iron Curtain came down, what the world saw was a church that still stood: the gates of hell had not prevailed against it (Mt 16:18). In a secularized Western world where the separation of church and state has developed from a constitutional perspective into an intellectual presupposition, it is not surprising that Western journalists hardly knew what to make of this phenomenon—and consequently said little about it. However, even committed Christians from the West seemed surprised to discover that Orthodoxy was alive and mostly well after the devastations of Communist oppression.

However, for those who make a study of Eastern Orthodoxy, the surprise will disappear. In its place will arise an appreciation of the riches of biblical and apostolic insight within Eastern Christianity, and especially of its distinctive emphases and approaches. As we can see from this historical overview, those distinctives have unfolded and been elaborated over the course of centuries. Their study is both challenging and stimulating.

Prior to embarking on that study, another preliminary step is required: we need to consider and evaluate certain Western Christian attitudes which have developed toward Eastern Orthodoxy, attitudes that have either inhibited understanding of Eastern Orthodoxy or misrepresented it.

2

WESTERN REACTIONS

BEFORE WE CAN PROCEED WITH AN EXAMINATION of distinctive Eastern Christian perspectives, it would be helpful to point out and respond to some erroneous perceptions about Eastern Orthodoxy that have developed among some Western Christians. The historical treatment in the previous chapter offers enough background to understand both the allegations and the responses appropriate to them. These Western Christian responses fall into three types. Some readers may have encountered one or more of them. The first two arise from different kinds of Western Christian commitment; the third reflects concerns raised by some Western Christian scholars.

"BASICALLY THE SAME AS ROMAN CATHOLICISM"

The first reaction would most likely be heard from evangelicals—whether laypersons, clergy or scholars—who have looked at little more than the externals of Eastern Christianity. This reaction assesses Eastern Orthodoxy as "basically the same as Roman Catholicism" or as "a Greek version of Roman Catholicism." From this perspective, since Roman Catholicism needs to be viewed with suspicion,[1] Orthodoxy deserves the same treatment.

It is not hard to understand where such a reaction comes from. When one considers the ornate ritual of the services of worship, with prescribed liturgies, the use of incense and the liturgical vestments—all of which are found in both Roman Catholicism and Orthodoxy—and compares that with most varieties of evangeli-

[1]Much has happened since Vatican Council II (1962-1965) to enable Protestants and Roman Catholics to draw nearer to each other, and the mid-1990s "Evangelicals and Catholics Together" documents have shown greater mutual respect. However, from many quarters of evangelicalism, significant opposition still arises against Roman Catholicism. The presentation of this first reaction does not take into account the recent rapprochements between Roman Catholicism and Protestantism; rather, it reflects attitudes which have been common among evangelicals in the past (and remain common in many circles in the present) vis-à-vis Roman Catholicism—and, by extension, Eastern Orthodoxy.

cal worship services, one can appreciate why evangelicals would find Eastern Orthodox worship practices foreign. Since their most common referent for such worship would be Roman Catholic church services which they have seen on television or might have attended, it makes sense that they might lump an Orthodox service into the same category.

Moreover, positive references in Orthodox worship to the Virgin Mary, to saints and to tradition might confirm such an assessment to evangelicals. Since they have probably rarely if ever heard these mentioned in a positive sense but know that Roman Catholicism refers appreciatively to them, it might seem warranted to cast Roman Catholicism and Orthodoxy into the same pot. Any further comments they might hear with regard to sacraments, monks or ecclesiastical hierarchy might well confirm the assessment.

In response, three points can be made. In the first place, the axiom that a person's reaction tells more about the person than it does about what stimulated it applies here. For all its strengths in other regards, evangelicalism generally manifests little awareness or appreciation of the history of the church's worship. Apart from the evangelical wings of the Anglican and the Lutheran traditions, evangelicalism is generally nonliturgical in its sensibilities. The usages noted above, against which many evangelicals would probably react as foreign, have marked the liturgies of the church and its teaching through the ages. During Christian antiquity and the Middle Ages, the above practices were found throughout the church. To be sure, some of them were scrapped and others were modified in the Protestant Reformation. But what has developed up to the present day in much of North American evangelicalism is a service so austere in its elimination of the historic liturgies and prayers of the church, so bereft of appeal to anything other than the mind (and sometimes not even that) and so focused on the present, that awareness of other Christians from bygone eras in anything more than a passing illustration within a sermon would be exotic. Without a doubt, many evangelicals would find a number of the accepted worship practices in Roman Catholicism and in Orthodoxy strange. However, a study of Christian worship through the ages would raise questions about the grounds for this evangelical reaction; indeed, from that vantage point, the sort of worship services one typically finds in most evangelical churches (apart from the Lutheran and Anglican ones, that is) would be indicted as deficient.

Second, it is undoubtedly true that, on the above-noted matters as well as others which could be added, Roman Catholicism and Eastern Orthodoxy speak about ideas and doctrines some evangelicals would probably find strange. Nevertheless, the historical treatment in the previous chapter should suggest to us that they do so in significantly different ways, or from divergent perspectives. It is true that on the surface marked similarities appear to the evangelical critic. However, when examined more carefully to see what is actually being affirmed and practiced, one finds that Roman Catholicism and Orthodoxy regularly deal with topics and practices that appear similar from quite dissimilar perspectives and with significantly different understandings. What we have considered in our historical overview has special relevance here: the difference between the cultural backgrounds in the Latin West and the Greek East all the way back to antiquity, and as assimilated and elaborated further by Western and Eastern Christianity, have led to quite different, even opposing, attitudes toward a variety of doctrines and liturgical practices. As a result, the various evangelical criticisms of Roman Catholic practices and teachings are not usually to the point for their Eastern Christian counterparts. Dissimilar patterns of doctrine and practice that developed in the Christian East and the Christian West gave rise to real differences behind these superficial similarities. Since Protestant responses were shaped in reaction to Roman Catholic understanding, they usually do not relevantly address the Eastern Christian perspective.

The third response to this evangelical reaction may well be startling to evangelicals—or to any Protestant, for that matter. This response is to present how Orthodox spokespersons analyze Western Christianity, in contrast to that of the East. This analysis is so frequently found among the Orthodox that we in the Christian West need to hear and appreciate it.

From an Orthodox standpoint, Roman Catholicism and Protestantism (of whatever sort, evangelical or otherwise) are merely two sides of the same coin. A classic formulation of this assessment comes from the nineteenth-century Russian lay theologian Alexei Khomiakov:

> All Protestants are Crypto-Papists; and, indeed, it would be a very easy task to show that in their Theology (as well as philosophy) all the definitions of all the objects of creed or understanding are merely taken out of the old Latin system, though often made negative in the application. In short, if it was to be expressed in the concise language of algebra, all the West knows but one datum, *a;* whether it be preceded by the positive sign +, as with the Latins, or with the negative −, as with the Protestants, the *a* remains the same. Now, a passage to Orthodoxy . . . is rushing into a new and unknown world.[2]

[2]Excerpted from the third letter of Alexei Khomiakov to William Palmer (November 28, 1846); cited from www.geocities.com/trvalentine/orthodox/khomiakov_palmer03.html.

As Khomiakov recognizes, Eastern Christianity comes at almost everything from a different stance and with a different attitude than does Western Christianity. Again, this relates to and reflects the differences in development and perspective that can be traced all the way back to antiquity. What is probably surprising to Western Christians is that, from an Eastern Christian's viewpoint, Western Christians—for all their admitted differences from each other, especially the divide between Roman Catholicism and Protestantism—nevertheless approach issues with the same mindset, asking the same kinds of questions and coming up with the same kinds of answers.

While this invites much more extensive treatment, we will restrict our consideration to two main points. In the first place, for all the differences between Roman Catholics and Protestants about how a person can be acceptable to God, both approach the question as basically a legal matter—that of a person standing before God in the divine law court. Both Roman Catholicism and Protestantism look on this issue as the ultimate question with regard to a person's relationship to God. However, while Eastern Christians recognize that all humans do and must stand before God as Judge, the basic question for Orthodoxy is not one of legal standing.[3] Second, from an Eastern Christian perspective, all Western Christians manifest the same attitude toward doctrinal statements and the claims of theology: that these statements explain the truth and that theologians are called and the church is expected to be concerned with such doctrinal "orthodoxy." While the Orthodox are definitely not incautious about doctrine, the Eastern Christian approach to the truth claims of doctrine and to doctrine's place within the church is substantially different from the approaches of Western Christians, of whatever stripe.[4]

The purpose of considering this Orthodox reaction is not simply to allow Eastern Christians to get their chance to return the favor by throwing the evangelical into the Roman Catholic pot. Rather, it has been, on the one hand, to invite evangelicals humbly to question whether they may themselves be far closer to Roman Catholicism on some important matters than they have recognized to this point. On the other hand, it has also been to challenge evangelicals to consider whether the Western Christian approach to theology, doctrinal statements and the relationship of these to the church indeed reflects the only proper way to view these matters. With the profusion of argument found so frequently and constantly in Western Christianity (and especially in evangelical circles) about ever

---

[3]On this, see below, chap. 6; see also the treatment in chap. 8.
[4]See the treatment below in chap. 3.

more arcane points of doctrinal distinction, it might be liberating to ask whether this stance is a culturally conditioned one, rather than necessarily the best one possible. If evangelicals can at least entertain that question, they will be in a better position to consider, appreciate and possibly learn from an Orthodox approach to these matters.

"An Ossified Relic of the Christian Past"

A second frequent reaction to Eastern Orthodoxy is one more likely to be uttered by those who consider themselves "progressive" in doctrine, worship or church practice (whether in mainline Protestant churches or in evangelical ones). This reaction would dismiss Eastern Orthodoxy as "an ossified relic of the Christian past." Implicit in this reaction is the laudable desire for the church to engage its contemporary culture in a relevant fashion; equally implicit is the questionable attitude that whatever has long been practiced must be stale and stultifying. In either event, this reaction dismisses Orthodoxy in the present day.

According to this assessment, while the early church developed and grew, at some point in the past this ceased to be true of Orthodoxy. What one now finds in the respective Orthodox churches and in their doctrine is precisely and only what could be found centuries ago. According to this characterization, Eastern Orthodoxy has become a stuffy museum rather than a living church.

It is unquestionably true that Orthodoxy has sought to remain true to ancient Christianity. Through the centuries, Eastern Christianity has emphasized the importance of not departing from the apostolic heritage. Because of this, Orthodoxy has shown itself inimical to change. What one can encounter in Orthodox worship today would be hardly different from what one might have encountered in virtually any century in the Christian East over most of the last two millennia. From the perspective of Eastern Christianity, such constancy is not something to be regretted, but a mark of being "the one, holy, catholic and apostolic Church" (as confessed in the Nicene-Constantinopolitan Creed). Orthodoxy glories in its faithfulness to the church of antiquity and in its steadfast adherence to this pattern through the ages, down to the present day.

It may seem, therefore, that the criticism is valid. However, one must not too readily assume the common Western Christian attitude that change or development is always positive; the way cancer progresses gives the lie to that. Furthermore, an awareness of the history of the development of doctrine, church practice, church government or worship patterns in Western Christianity should be enough to give the critic pause: many of these changes have not been healthy for the church, and not all can legitimately claim to have been rooted in the apostolic message. Change in itself no more assures genuine vitality than a lack of change prohibits it. To use a relevant analogy, many people vibrantly involved in questions of culture, society and worship collect and use antiques.

To bring this point to bear on the question of Orthodoxy, one should recognize that there is certainly a difference between a museum, on the one hand, and a house built long ago in which a contemporary family lives, on the other. The latter is what Orthodoxy claims to be. For those who have eyes to see, it is clear that Orthodoxy continues to have a remarkable vitality and an unexpected strength.

If nothing else, the events of the last few years in the former Soviet bloc have indicated that Eastern Orthodoxy has managed to retain a supple strength that is anything but "ossified" and a vitality that has continued to attract adherents even under the burden of persecution and oppression. While it is undoubtedly true that some who flocked to Orthodox churches during the waning days of the former Soviet empire did so out of political or rebellious reasons rather than from genuine devotion, it must be acknowledged that much spiritual commitment was evident as well. The Orthodox (and, indeed, other) churches stood through the worst onslaughts of a heinous foe and prevailed.

Those who bemoan the increasingly secular and amoral nature of Western culture should perhaps question whether our Western churches' rush for contemporaneity and relevance may itself be in some significant way a contributing factor in that cultural decline. It might well be that the kind of strength and vigor that a supposedly ossified ecclesiastical body manifested in an unfriendly culture is just what ours needs. At the least, we ought to admit that, whether a Western Christian wants to embrace the Eastern Christian attitude toward change or not, the common Western Christian criticism that Orthodoxy is an ossified relic of the Christian past has been belied by events of the immediate past.

Another reason that some Western Christians might look on Eastern Christianity as ossified is the remarkable agreement in doctrine which marks the entire Orthodox communion. To a Western Christian, enamored of variety and independence in so many areas of life and thought, and used to the multiplicity of denominations which affords so many options for theological preference, the thought of a worldwide communion in which there is so little doctrinal variation as there is in Eastern Orthodoxy might seem a proof of doctrinal ossification—as well as being frighteningly repressive. A Western Christian might well ask whether such widespread agreement would be possible if faith were still living and careful thought were taking place.

Indeed, from the experience of Western Christianity, it seems virtually unimaginable that even a small denomination would know such unanimity as is manifest throughout the whole of Orthodoxy. Within Western Christianity, we have become used to—if not necessarily comfortable with—a situation in which many church leaders and theologians feel free to reject even tenets of the faith that have been enshrined from antiquity in the creeds of the universal church: to name only a few such points, the genuine deity of Jesus Christ, his incarnation, his virgin birth and his bodily resurrection have all been either treated as dispensable or reinterpreted in such a way as to be virtually unrecognizable as what the church has held through the ages. Given this experience in so much of Western Christianity, it is startling to learn that none of these teachings is rejected by any clergyman or theologian within the whole worldwide communion of Orthodoxy. There are, to be sure, some differences of position on doctrinal tenets beyond those affirmed in the ancient creeds, but these differences have not led to divisions within the Orthodox churches and have not undercut the overall doctrinal unanimity within Orthodoxy.

Within the wide scope of Western Christianity, it has become less and less clear what is essential to genuine Christian faith. In a world that desperately needs to hear the Christian message, it must be frankly admitted that many church leaders and theologians in Western Christianity have rendered that message unclear and its contents ambiguous. By contrast, Eastern Christianity offers a ringing affirmation of what that message is—namely, the apostolic message enshrined in the ancient creeds of the church, celebrated in the liturgy, defended in tradition and proclaimed in preaching.

In all this, the importance of tradition for Eastern Orthodoxy comes to the fore. While we cannot consider that broad and intriguing topic here,[5] a few comments can nevertheless be made. From the perspective of much of Western culture, tradition is something to be feared as stultifying. We crave the new and fresh, not what has been around for a long time, and we often superficially think that tradition must be our enemy.

However, only a little reflection will show that no family, group or culture can exist without some patterns of operation and agreed-upon assumptions. What has been found workable in the past so becomes a part of our approach to life that we take it for granted—roughly, that is what tradition is. *Tradition* must be distinguished from *traditionalism,* which follows past practices without thought or ap-

[5]See the treatment of tradition's relationship to Scripture below, chap. 12.

preciation. As one of the outstanding historians of Christian thought has written, "Tradition is the living faith of the dead, traditionalism is the dead faith of the living."[6] Traditionalism is always stultifying within the church; tradition cannot be. The Eastern Orthodox wholeheartedly embrace tradition.

While a church bound up in traditionalism will almost certainly not be able to speak relevantly to its culture, a church that embraces the tradition of the church, all the way back to the apostles, will inevitably do so. While Eastern Christianity clings to that tradition which stems from Christian antiquity, it has done its best to remain alert to contemporary questions and address them. Works by Orthodox professors from St. Sergius Theological Institute in Paris, Holy Cross Greek Orthodox School of Theology in Massachusetts, and St. Vladimir's Seminary in New York, plus those written by Orthodox monks and ecclesiastical leaders from many cultures, have all sought to interpret Eastern Orthodoxy to the contemporary world. They have not been performing cardio-pulmonary resuscitation on a corpse or trying to keep a comatose Orthodoxy on life-support systems; they have been showing the relevance of the ancient Christian faith as maintained and practiced through the centuries by Eastern Orthodoxy for the contemporary world.[7]

For a variety of reasons, then, the charge of ossification so often leveled against Eastern Christianity must be rejected. Furthermore, as with the first reaction against Orthodoxy, so too with this second one, an Eastern Christian could turn the tables on Western Christianity and charge it with being more inclined toward ossification than Orthodoxy. We need to consider that possibility—again, not simply to allow our reaction to be turned against us, but to consider what the Orthodox find dangerous for Christianity in our attitudes and approaches.

Were one to compare the general approach to doctrine taken by Western Christianity, on the one hand, and by Eastern Orthodoxy, on the other, it could well be argued that Western Christianity's approach would be more likely to lead to ossification. In the West, it has long been common for doctrine to be

[6]Jaroslav Pelikan, *The Vindication of Tradition* (New Haven, Conn.: Yale University Press, 1984), p. 65.
[7]E.g., Peter Bouteneff, *Sweeter Than Honey: Orthodox Thinking on Dogma and Truth* (Crestwood, N.Y.: St. Vladimir's Seminary Press, 2006), offers an appreciative Orthodox assessment of and response to postmodern thought while setting forth Orthodox perspectives on speaking truth. Archbishop Anastasios (Yannoulatos), *Facing the World: Orthodox Christian Essays on Global Concerns* (Crestwood, N.Y.: St. Vladimir's Seminary Press, 2003), addresses the promises and challenges of human rights, globalization, dialogue with Islam and culture from an Orthodox perspective. John Behr, *The Mystery of Christ: Life in Death* (Crestwood, N.Y.: St. Vladimir's Seminary Press, 2006), manifests thorough familiarity with and appreciative responses to recent and contemporary biblical exegesis and theological developments while calling such scholarship to return to patristic approaches to Scripture and doctrine—the path followed in Orthodoxy.

constructed in systems. While the various systems of doctrine presented by Western Christianity may significantly differ among the various denominational traditions—and, indeed, even within them—the same basic pattern usually prevails.

In this pattern, a particular structure is discerned in the way the doctrines of Christianity relate to each other. Teaching about doctrine or books written to present doctrine in the Christian West have regularly taken on the pattern of that system. While it may no longer be in vogue to publish books titled *Systematic Theology,* both the training in seminaries and much of the lay discussion of doctrine in Western Christian churches follow the basic systematic theological structure.

Significantly, the great textbook of Orthodox theology, St. John of Damascus's *The Orthodox Faith,* does not follow this approach. For those trained in and expecting the pattern of Western Christian systematic theology, the Damascene's text at first seems remarkably disorganized; only later does one who exercises a little creative sympathy and continued engagement begin to discern a different impulse in the structuring of the book. St. John of Damascus—and, with him, the Eastern Christian tradition, both before and since his time—had no such confidence in humanly constructed systems of thought for the presentation of God's message to humanity. Orthodoxy has been unwilling to subject that message to whatever organizational pattern of human thought is currently the intellectual fashion. To do so, in their estimation, would be to endanger the Christian message with being ossified within a structure of thought which, when it passes beneath the sea of change, would drag the Christian message along with it.

Thus the typical Western Christian approach would be more likely than the Eastern Christian one to lead to the rigid ossification in doctrine which many in the Christian West think to have discerned in Orthodoxy. Again, an Eastern Christian could turn the charge back against Western Christianity and be able to produce a rather strong argument for this case. Moreover, the Western Christian approach to doctrine has been repudiated by the Orthodox, who have discerned in it an uncritical adoption of pagan approaches to thought. That leads us to the consideration of the third reaction commonly found among Western Christians to Eastern Christianity.

"Assimilated to Pagan Greek Thought"

The third common reaction against Eastern Orthodoxy is that it is suffused with the Greek philosophical thought of the ancient world. In past generations some scholarly works written by respected pioneers in the study of the history of theology took this attitude,[8] and these works have influenced the assessment of much contemporary scholarship, which has uncritically passed on that judgment. Subsequently, this attitude has been imported from these scholarly resources into some of the popular Western Christian literature that refers to Eastern Christianity. According to this third reaction, Orthodoxy can be characterized as a baptized version of some form of ancient Greek thought—most often Neo-Platonism. Consequently, Orthodoxy deserves to be rejected since it is so suffused with this ancient pagan approach that it cannot claim to offer a clear presentation of the Christian message.

This response might seem warranted in view of the argument in the previous chapter that Eastern Christianity has been shaped by its cultural milieu. Building upon this, the argument could be made that pagan Hellenic and Hellenistic mindsets were absorbed by Eastern Christianity and have had a profound impact on the structures of its thought. However, drawing the argument in this way requires the assumption that Eastern Christians were uncritical in their interaction with their surrounding intellectual culture and that such pagan thought passed unpurged into Orthodox teaching.

It is undeniably true that the leaders of Eastern Christianity during antiquity were intimately acquainted with their pagan intellectual milieu. They had been trained within it and knew it well. However, they were also sharply critical of that pagan intellectual culture. They sought to appropriate whatever within it could be rendered serviceable to the presentation of Christian truth, but they also recognized that it operated on bases that could not be assimilated within Christianity.

This was a basic concern from early in the development of Eastern Christianity. During the late second and early third centuries, Clement of Alexandria and Origen struggled with these questions. Their efforts were ground-breaking, but the resultant synthesis of what they saw as the best of the pagan philosophical tradition—namely, Platonism—with Christianity came under fire, both in their time and subsequently.

Among their sharpest critics were the Cappadocian fathers of the fourth century: St. Basil the Great, St. Gregory of Nyssa and St. Gregory Nazianzen (known as "Gregory the Theologian" within Eastern Orthodoxy). They developed a stance toward their pagan intellectual culture more critical and cautious than that of

[8]Johann Gottfried Herder (1744-1803) was the first Western Christian scholar to posit this view (Ernst Benz, *Die Ostkirche im Lichte der protestantischen Geschichtsschreibung von der Reformation bis zur Gegenwart* [Munich: Verlag Karl Alber, 1952], p. 130). Herder was followed in this estimation by Adolf von Harnack, whose impressive dogma-historical scholarship in so many other regards has assured that many subsequent Western Christian scholars have adopted this view.

Clement and Origen. The Cappadocians made a serious attempt to utilize the best of the ancient Hellenic and Hellenistic philosophical tradition in the service of Christianity, indeed, but they were also highly critical of and selective about that ancient pagan thought. They sought to purge it of all that would tend toward the corruption or confusion of the Christian message.[9]

Of course, the Cappadocians used the terminology of the intellectual world in this endeavor; they had no other choice. Even so, they sought to fill the vocabulary and concepts with content consonant with Christian teaching. Further, they challenged the bases of thought in Neo-Platonism, as well as other systems of pagan thought. The Cappadocian fathers repudiated foundational assumptions upon which such thought had been erected,[10] insisting instead on Christian ones.[11] The Cappadocian fathers saw all this as a necessary task; with it the church could responsibly and relevantly communicate the Christian message, making judicious use of whatever could be found serviceable in the prior intellectual heritage.[12] Using what could be appropriately assimilated from that pagan culture was, in the analogy used by St. Gregory of Nyssa, following the biblical precedent of plundering the Egyptians for the beautification of the tabernacle of God.[13]

More thorough acquaintance with the thought of the Cappadocian fathers, which Orthodoxy has so closely followed, would exorcise the common Western Christian accusation of syncretism with Greek philosophy. However, Christian scholarship in the West has never become as familiar with the Cappadocians as their historical importance within Eastern Christianity warrants: they played a role within the Christian East that would parallel the role of St. Augustine in the Christian West. Our Western Christian lack of acquaintance with the Cappadocian fathers has provided the soil in which this third reaction could grow.

Indeed, the reaction under consideration is a caricature that cannot be defended by anyone who has read much in the way of Eastern Orthodox doctrinal literature or church history. It is not too much to say that this third reaction man-

---

[9]In speaking about the proper use of the products of the intellectual culture available in his day, St. Gregory Nazianzen urged, "we should collect whatever advantage we can from them, . . . while avoiding their dangers, . . . as the divine apostle says, 'taking every thought captive to obey Christ' [2 Cor 10:5]" (*Oration* 43.11).

[10]St. Gregory of Nyssa declared, "Profane education is truly barren; it is always suffering the pains of labor, but without giving birth" (*The Life of Moses* 2.11).

[11]"If our course of education involves the study of profane teachings, we must not cut ourselves off from the nourishment of the Church's milk" (*Life of Moses* 2.12).

[12]In an allegorical exposition, St. Gregory of Nyssa argues, "The foreign wife [Moses' Egyptian wife] will follow him, for profane education offers some things which should not be rejected as we seek to produce righteousness, . . . provided that this union introduces no foreign defilement" (*Life of Moses* 2.37).

[13]*Life of Moses* 2.115-16.

ifests ignorance of that literature and history, not insight into it. In addition to the works of the Cappadocians, several other significant points can be adduced to support this assessment. First of all, at the fifth ecumenical council (Constantinople II, 553) many of Origen's views were condemned as heretical (without, to be sure, Origen being directly named and condemned). In addition, the council anathematized Evagrius Ponticus for adopting and popularizing such syncretistic views. Eastern Christianity thus officially and definitively rejected the synthesis between Christianity and pagan intellectual perspectives evident in the work of these otherwise gifted leaders.

Subsequently, the great shapers of Eastern Christian theology, St. Maximus Confessor and St. John of Damascus, building on the heritage of the Cappadocians, definitively articulated Orthodoxy's views. It is significant that they regularly did so by pointing out the contrast between the Christian views that should be embraced, on the one hand, and the views of Origen and Neo-Platonism, on the other. This orientation continued to shape Orthodox perspectives throughout the Byzantine period: among others, this can be seen during the high Byzantine era in the perspectives of the renowned scholar and patriarch of Constantinople, St. Photius,[14] and in the orientation of St. Gregory Palamas, archbishop of Thessaloniki and outstanding theologian during the late Byzantine period.[15] Indeed, throughout most of the Byzantine era, Byzantines referred to themselves as "Romans" (in Byzantine Greek, *romaioi*) or as "Christians," but not as *hellenes*—the Greek word for "Greek."[16] In so doing, they demonstrated their recognition of the corrupting power of ancient pagan Greek thought and sought to oppose its synthesis with the Christian message. During the twentieth century, the theologians who have sought to make Eastern Orthodoxy understandable to Western Chris-

---

[14]In his first tenure as patriarch of Constantinople (858-867), St. Photius wrote a letter to Boris, the recently converted khan of Bulgaria, in which he set forth the Christian faith, in part by pointing out significant decisions of the ecumenical councils. In the fourteenth section of the letter he commented on the fifth ecumenical council (553): "It also condemned and anathematized Origen, Didymos, and Evagrios, ancient plagues of the faithful, *men who contentiously strove to introduce Greek mythology into the Church of God*" (Despina Stratoudaki White and Joseph R. Berrigan Jr., trans., *The Patriarch and the Prince: The Letter of Patriarch Photios of Constantinople to Khan Boris of Bulgaria* [Brookline, Mass.: Holy Cross Orthodox Press], p. 47, emphasis added), an assessment which issued into a summary of various ways that ancient Greek philosophy had tainted their teachings.

[15]In *The Triads,* he declared, "Greek wisdom is demonic" (1.19), but he went on to indicate that, if one carefully cut away perspectives that would lead one away from God, it could be properly used by Christians (1.20). Cited from Nicholas Gendle, trans., *Gregory Palamas: The Triads* (Mahwah, N.J.: Paulist Press, 1983), pp. 27, 28.

[16]Robert Browning, *The Byzantine Empire,* rev. ed. (Washington, D.C.: Catholic University of America Press, 1992), p. xiii.

tians have stressed the distinctions between Orthodox thought and the Greek philosophical thought of the ancient world.[17]

In summary, it needs to be emphasized that Orthodox teaching has been consciously molded in contradistinction to, rather than in continuity with, pagan Greek philosophical thought. Admitting this does not require the conclusion that the Cappadocians or subsequent Orthodox theologians eliminated every trace of pagan thought or achieved a perfect assimilation of what could be utilized from it into Christian teaching. The significant point is that Eastern Christianity, from early in its history, has shown itself to be aware of the danger of uncritical assimilation of pagan thought and has vigorously opposed it.

Again, an Eastern Christian might turn this third reaction around and use it against Western Christians. Were one to analyze the influence of Greek thought on Eastern and on Western Christianity, respectively, one could hardly escape concluding that, historically, ancient Greek philosophical thought has been more uncritically embraced and has had a far more profound and lasting influence in Western Christianity. During the ancient period and much of the medieval one in Western Christianity, Neo-Platonism shaped the piety and practice of Christianity, both within the monastic world and in the life of the church outside it. No less a figure than St. Augustine—who has more profoundly shaped the whole of Western Christian theology, both Roman Catholic and Protestant, than any other figure—was committed to Neo-Platonism as the philosophical framework for his theologizing. Subsequently, Western Christianity's wholesale adoption of Aristotle's works as the basis of educational curricula during the Middle Ages, together with the virtually uncritical assimilation of his structure of thought for the development of theological teaching—both by Roman Catholicism as shaped during the medieval period and the Counter-Reformation epoch and by Protestants during the period immediately after the Reformers as well—indicates an incautious assimilation of ancient pagan Greek thought within Western Christianity. Many insightful critics from within Western Christianity have drawn attention to various negative effects of this uncritical appropriation of Aristotle over the centuries.

As with the first two reactions, the point of these last considerations has not been merely to allow Eastern Christians to return fire; it has been to suggest that Western Christian theologizing may need to take the log out of its own eye before denouncing specks in the eye of Orthodoxy (Mt 7:4-5). At the least, this should call Western Christians to listen thoughtfully to and appreciate the Eastern ap-

[17]John Meyendorff and Vladimir Lossky have both emphasized and elucidated these distinctions in their books.

proach to the Christian faith, which has continually kept before its eye the need to avoid contamination from Greek philosophical thought.

With these misperceptions answered, we should be better able to approach Orthodox teaching with openness and the expectation of benefit. To prepare for that, we also need to consider the Eastern Orthodox approach to doctrine, in order to compare it with the common Western Christian approach with which we are more familiar. That will be the final preliminary step we take before embarking on our examination of Orthodox distinctives.

3

ORTHODOXY'S APPROACH TO DOCTRINE

AS EASTERN ORTHODOXY HAS PASSED THROUGH THE CENTURIES, it has been marked by a consistent attitude toward Christian doctrine. The implications of that perspective for Orthodox views on various topics will be treated in subsequent chapters of this volume; in this chapter, we will consider fundamental characteristics of this common Eastern Christian perspective.

Orthodoxy "does" doctrine in a different way than Western Christianity. Both Eastern and Western Christianity build, of course, on the Scriptures and the experience, individually and collectively, of life in Christ within the church; even so, the approaches to Christian doctrine on the parts of Western Christianity and of Eastern Orthodoxy are significantly different. A good way to get hold of the contrast, in a preliminary fashion, is to consider the divergent connotations ordinarily assigned by Western Christianity and Eastern Orthodoxy to a term highly prized by both—*orthodox.*

THE MEANING OF *ORTHODOX*

For both Western and Eastern Christianity, the word *orthodox* is reserved for what is especially prized in Christian faith and practice. The term itself is a combination of two Greek words: *orthos,* meaning "upright" or "proper," and *doxa,* which means both "opinion" and "glory." In Western Christianity, the term *orthodox* is used for *right opinion.* This Western Christian usage intends both solid teaching and doctrinal precision. Consequently, *orthodox* is also used to identify groups and individuals known for their concern to maintain strict doctrinal positions. In Western Christianity, *orthodox* focuses on doctrinal precision; the term is rarely used with other significations.

Orthodoxy picks up on the other meanings of the Greek words that are combined in the term. In Eastern Christianity, *orthodox* is used for that which gives *proper glory* to God. The Eastern Christian usage includes solicitude regarding true teaching, but that is not the paramount concern; teaching is a necessary ingredient, but is not itself the focus. Eastern Christianity uses *orthodox* to describe a style of life and worship that is faithful to the Christian message. Such faithfulness—which requires but is not limited to concerns for truthful teaching—gives "proper glory" to God.

While it should be obvious that there is no absolute difference between the two connotations assigned in Western Christianity and in Eastern Orthodoxy to the term *orthodox,* it must also be clear that the emphasis falls differently in the two usages. In its own way, this difference between Western and Eastern Christian usage is a telling one: it indicates that the two traditions differ in their respective expectations regarding doctrine and the role it plays. We can now move on to compare them a little more closely.

"Doing" Theology

Whatever differences in doctrinal viewpoints and ecclesiastical affiliations otherwise separate them, Western Christians belong to that large segment of Christianity which has been influenced over the centuries by Western European heritage and culture. With that background, Western Christians have come to share a common perspective not only in their focus on questions of legal standing before God but also in their attitude toward theology. In the face of all the denominational divisions and differences in doctrinal emphases found in Western Christianity, similar patterns prevail throughout it concerning doctrine and its assumed role. Belaboring that common perspective point by point would be tedious (and unnecessary for our purposes); the common perspective can be approached more simply. We can unpack the shared Western Christian attitude by considering a tension that is rooted in the common perspective and found throughout Western Christendom.

When Western Christians speak about doctrine, they eventually end up mentioning a contrast between the *head* and the *heart;* put in other words, the conflict is between *doctrine* and *life.* In this contrast, *head* (or *doctrine*) has reference to what can be intellectually assimilated about Christian teaching, with *heart* (or *life*) pointing to an existential appropriation of the teaching in the lifestyle of the person. Almost always, the contrast is played out to the detriment of the head/doctrine component, although rarely would the intellectual appropriation be totally disparaged. What is intended with the contrast is a summons to press beyond merely becoming intellectually acquainted with the teaching to embracing it in one's personal depths so that the teaching profoundly affects the life of the one who "knows" the doctrine. This contrast appears on virtually every Western Christian theological menu; few believers in the West will have missed a steady fare of this contrast in sermon, book and discussion.

Given this pattern, it may be startling for a Western Christian to discover that this head-heart distinction which so often bedevils Western Christian theologizing is foreign to Orthodoxy. This does not imply that Eastern Christianity has no problems in doctrine or living it out; rather, it means that this particular tension, so prevalent within Western Christendom, is simply unknown to Orthodoxy. The chief reason for this is Orthodoxy's different sense of what *theology* is all about.

A large part of that difference is the strict sense in which the Orthodox understand the term *theology*. The word comes from two Greek words, *theos*, "God," and *logos*, "word." Thus, etymologically, *theology* means "talking about God"—not talking about various other doctrines also presented in divine revelation. In Eastern Christianity, *theology* retains that specific focus of speech *about God;* other doctrines are dealt with under appropriate specific designations. To be sure, Western theologizing recognizes the etymological distinction in its academic parlance: while *theology* can be and often is used with the generic sense of treatments of various doctrines, "theology proper" is the specific designation for doctrinal treatment that focuses on God. Even so, the common practice among Western Christians—in the academic setting or in the sanctuary—is to use the word *theology* in the broad sense.[1]

This might appear, at first glance, to be nothing more than a quibble about words; however, it is far more than that. As will be seen more fully below,[2] Eastern Christianity views talking about God as a hazardous enterprise. Since God has revealed himself in human language, we can speak of him; since he has summoned his people to proclaim him to the nations, we must do so. Even so, no human talk about God can fully express him, for human language cannot transcend its created capacities, which are incommensurate with the One of whom we are speaking. God will always remain beyond the best attempts to set him forth in our words. Orthodoxy, faithful to its own cultural background, has little confidence in human reason when it begins to speak about God.

---

[1]The Western pattern has allowed for the term to be used in even broader ways that, from an Eastern Orthodox perspective, sound bizarre—with books on the *theology* "of man," "of sin," "of the environment," "of welfare," "of the state," etc.

[2]See the treatment in chap. 4.

This has not led Eastern Christianity to a lack of interest in knowledge of God. To the contrary, Orthodoxy manifests a deep desire to know God, but in the biblical sense of what it means to *know* someone. In both the Old and the New Testaments, *know* is regularly used to refer to intimate communion, and not just in the sense of intellectual familiarity. When Scripture declares that "the man [Adam] *knew* his wife Eve, and she conceived and bore Cain" (Gen 4:1), it points, not to cognition but to the intimacy of marital union. When God assures Israel, "You only have I *known* of all the families of the earth" (Amos 3:2), he is not admitting to ignorance of other nations, but is stressing the exclusive and intimate relationship he had granted only to Israel. When Jesus Christ confessed in prayer to his Father in heaven, "This is eternal life, . . . [to] *know* you, the only true God, and Jesus Christ whom you have sent" (Jn 17:3), he pointed beyond mere intellection to ultimate life with God. Orthodoxy has stressed this: *knowing God* means having an intimate relationship with him, not just a wealth of data about him.

For Orthodoxy, to know God in this way is necessary for all theology and theologizing. Knowing God thus requires much more—and yet, paradoxically, much less—than mastering a wealth of revealed information about God. Knowing God in this sense means communion with him, living in openness toward and wonder before him. Knowledge of God in this way entails fellowship between the Creator and the creature—a fellowship that does not bridge the chasm between them but yet draws them together in intimacy. Such knowledge is not achieved by mastering data but by submitting to the God to whom the data point. Knowing God in this sense means *loving* God without reservation. Such knowledge of God reaches far beyond the processes of the mind, to the innermost depths of the one who would *know* God.

In Eastern Christian practice, from antiquity to the present, meditation and contemplation are the paths to knowledge of God. Divine revelation offers a foundation for all such meditation and contemplation, of course, but the Orthodox emphasis falls not on speech about but on silence before God and his revelation. The person who would know God must drink deeply of, and not just analyze, what God has made known about himself and his ways toward humankind; one must be saturated with it through wonder rather than seek to connect its elements in curiosity. The teaching offered within Orthodoxy inevitably manifests its mystical roots: indeed, a recent spokesman has styled Orthodox theology as *mystical*.[3]

[3]Vladimir Lossky, *The Mystical Theology of the Eastern Church* (Crestwood, N.Y.: St. Vladimir's Seminary Press, 1976); for a work that embodies this approach, see Bishop Kallistos (Timothy) Ware, *The Orthodox Way*, rev. ed. (Crestwood, N.Y.: St. Vladimir's Seminary Press, 1995).

In the history of Orthodoxy, a life given to meditation and contemplation, rather than the accomplishment of a prescribed course of academic study of Christian teaching, has been understood as both the root and the evidence of knowing God. For Eastern Christianity, living in mystical devotion to God is the only pathway to knowing God, and knowing God in this sense is a necessity if one is acceptably to speak about him. Evagrius Ponticus encapsulated this perspective memorably in an epigram often cited within Orthodoxy: "If you are a theologian, you will pray truly. And if you pray truly, you are a theologian." This maxim does not even mention academic learning about God, although such learning is not proscribed, of course. For the Orthodox, a life lived open to God is the prerequisite and authentication of a theologian.

From the Orthodox perspective on theology, the head-heart dichotomy which has plagued Western Christian theologizing does not arise. Unless a theologian's teaching has been so imbibed as to shape that theologian's life and give evidence of appropriately offering proper glory to God, Eastern Christians would be unwilling to offer it a hearing. This has not been an idle or only ideal expectation; it has been the pattern within Eastern Christianity throughout the centuries. We can appreciate the significance of this insistence within Orthodoxy—and the rigor with which it has been expected—when we see what has been required of a candidate for the office of bishop during most of the history of Orthodoxy. In order for a person to be considered for possible elevation to that office—the highest level of ecclesiastical responsibility and the one specifically charged with the church's teaching—he had to be (or to have been) a monk.

The Role of Academic Training

By comparison with Western Christian theologizing, Eastern Orthodoxy has manifested less confidence in human reason's capacities to talk about God and less curiosity to explore the possibilities about God which speculation might suggest. This has entailed no lack of profundity in Eastern Christian teaching about God—quite the contrary! However, the profundity which is the hallmark of that teaching bears the unmistakable marks of its source in meditation and contemplation. Eastern Orthodoxy is no less interested than Western Christian theologizing in speaking truth about God. However, Eastern Christianity has manifested little of the confidence Western Christianity has shown regarding academic training in doctrine.

Given the virtually universal endorsement of academic study of doctrine within

Western Christianity in the present day,[4] the Eastern Orthodox hesitation about such an approach to doctrine may well seem strange to Western Christians. However, Western Christendom was marked by that same hesitation during Christian antiquity and the early Middle Ages. Many of the leaders of ancient Western Christianity had practiced a life of meditation and contemplation themselves. During the ancient period and well into the medieval era, the link between mystical meditation and valid theologizing was recognized and honored as essential to the theological task.

However, with the development of universities during the eleventh and twelfth centuries, a new confidence in the potential of human thought arose in the Christian West. The mastery of available data offered in the universities' curricula, together with the thoroughness of analysis made possible by Aristotelian logic, spawned a vigorous intellectual curiosity and confidence among those involved in the new scholastic enterprise. In due course, such confidence in human reason spread out from the realm of the liberal arts toward the teaching of Christian doctrine. With it came the assumption that it should be possible to develop an intellectual expertise in doctrine through the application of the tools of logic and human reason, apart from the necessity of meditation and contemplation. This led to a bitter controversy over how theology ought to be learned and taught.[5] Eventually, a compromise was reached: theology was to be taught by clerics, but it would be taught as courses within the structure of the universities and not, as before, via meditation and contemplation in monasteries. Thus, the pattern from Christian antiquity and the earlier medieval period lost its previously unchallenged leadership; theology was taught as an intellectual discipline rather than as a mystical one. With the growing importance of academic training in Western European civilization during the high and late Middle Ages, on through the Reformation era and down to the present day within Western Christianity, the model that has prevailed for theological study has been that of the academy.

---

[4]There are, of course, wide divergences in the training offered and expected of prospective ministerial candidates within the various segments of Western Christianity. Even so, the basic pattern is similar: whether in a three-year Bible college program, some other form of training institute or a seminary education following upon the completion of a university degree, Western Christianity relies on classroom instruction which moves through various required courses, including some on doctrine. These courses progress through books or training manuals and are completed by passing academic examinations. Whatever the variation, it builds on the basic approach to theological education which was laid in the Christian West during the Middle Ages.

[5]The best-known part of this controversy was the conflict between St. Bernard of Clairvaux and Abelard. Although Bernard won that battle, his perspective lost the war: see the treatment in G. R. Evans, *Old Arts and New Theology: The Beginnings of Theology as an Academic Discipline* (New York: Oxford University Press, 1980), pp. 79-90.

To the monastic opponents of the medieval change in theological models, it would come as no surprise that this approach has resulted in the problem of the divorce between head and heart noted above. Indeed, that was the kind of problem those opponents prophesied would arise from the change. A distinction between what a facile intellect can grasp and an immature heart can absorb seems almost unavoidable. Beyond that, an intellectualist approach to mastering doctrinal details and their relationships can hardly be expected to wait for each learner to assimilate the material into the depths of his or her spirituality before moving on to the next topic. The head-heart dichotomy, resulting from (or at least, influenced by) this introduction of professional theologizing,[6] has continued to characterize Western Christianity. During the eras of the late Middle Ages, the Protestant Reformation, Pietism, the Great Awakening and on to the present day, this head-heart dichotomy has been a critical concern within Western Christianity.

This academic approach to training in doctrine has not fit well into Eastern Orthodoxy, which has always emphasized a way of knowing God that entails meditation and contemplation much more than intellection. Indeed, it is often said that Orthodoxy is "half teaching, half experience." Even this description, however, misses the genius of the Eastern Orthodox approach. Within Orthodoxy, study leads to wonder and, thus, to meditation; those who engage in such mystical contemplation come to know the one of whom the Christian faith speaks, and yet—paradoxically—the one whom it cannot adequately express. The knowledge of God that issues from such encounter is rooted in the revelatory data, to be sure, but the fruit it bears certainly tastes different than what hangs on the vine of an academic study of doctrine. Within Orthodoxy, the doctrinal leaders have historically been monks, not academic scholars. From a Western Christian standpoint, a certain depth of intellectual profundity may be missing at times in Eastern Orthodox teaching. However, an undeniable profundity of another sort—a somehow deeper and richer sort, accessible to the common Christian in ways that academic theology so often is not—pervades Orthodox teaching.

To be sure, the need to respond to the challenges of Western Christians scholars extensively trained in the theological disciplines has forced Eastern Christian-

---

[6]Nothing in this is intended as either an indictment of or a judgment on the role of professional theologians or seminaries; the argument is trying to make sense of how Western Christian theologizing has become so different from both its Eastern Christian counterpart and its own ancient and early medieval precursors.

ity to establish academic institutions to train its clergy.[7] In both the historically Orthodox countries and among the Orthodox immigrant communities in North America, seminaries are now to be found.[8] Even so, to this day within Orthodoxy, it is expected and demanded that theologizing be rooted in meditation and contemplation rather than in intellection. The accepted pattern is a well-steeped integration of doctrine in which the life of the teacher is itself evidence of and argument for his teaching.

Two significantly different senses of knowing are involved in the contrasting Western and Eastern Christian practices in and expectations for training in doctrine. These differences can be further seen in the divergent ways Western Christianity and Eastern Orthodoxy deal with the great monuments they share from Christian antiquity: the doctrinal decrees of the ancient ecumenical councils.

THE ROLE OF THE ANCIENT CONCILIAR DECREES

Both Eastern and Western Christianity build on the doctrinal decrees of the ancient ecumenical councils—the Nicene Creed of 325, elaborated at Constantinople in 381 (and known as the Nicene-Constantinopolitan Creed), plus the further refinements issued in subsequent ecumenical councils. However, these two Chris-

[7]During the seventeenth century, attacks by Roman Catholic scholars in Poland (then ruling much of the former Kievan Rus' state and, with it, many Orthodox) led the ecclesiastical leader in Kiev, Peter Mohyla, to set up an Orthodox academic institution. By then, the vigor of the Counter-Reformation and a renewed scholasticism had outfitted Roman Catholic spokesmen with considerable intellectual sophistication—a sophistication which the Orthodox needed to match and counter if they were to defend and teach Orthodoxy (Paul Robert Magocsi, *A History of Ukraine* [Toronto: University of Toronto Press, 1996], pp. 189-91; see also Ihor Ševčenko, "The Many Worlds of Peter Mohyla," in *Ukraine Between East and West: Essays on Cultural History to the Early Eighteenth Century,* by Ihor Ševčenko, [Edmonton: Canadian Institute of Ukrainian Studies Press, 1996], pp. 166-68). As has often been noted, though, this situation led the Orthodox to adopt much of the approach and attitude of their opponents, thus forcing Orthodoxy into a mode of thought and teaching influenced greatly by the scholastic models and arguments of its opponents; this led to a recognizable "westernizing" of Eastern Orthodoxy at the time. This approach to education—and especially its westernized results—has been vigorously criticized by leading Orthodox scholars: cf. the comments in Alexander Schmemann, *For the Life of the World: Sacraments and Orthodoxy* (Crestwood, N.Y.: St. Vladimir's Seminary Press, 1973), pp. 135-36 (and his citations there).

[8]Over the last three centuries, Russian Orthodoxy has had such institutions for priests but has struggled to find a way of training that would coincide more closely with the basic approaches of Orthodoxy; that struggle still goes on: see the assessment by Hieromonk Hilarion (Alfeyev), "The Problems Facing Orthodox Theological Education in Russia," *Religion in Eastern Europe* 19 (1999): 1-28. In North America, two leading seminaries are Holy Cross Greek Orthodox School of Theology (in Brookline, Mass.) and St. Vladimir's Theological Seminary (in Crestwood, N.Y.). In both, a rigorous academic program is required, but diligent efforts have been made to assure fidelity to Orthodoxy's basic approach to doctrine. It remains to be seen whether this venture will be able to retain that approach, or whether—like its predecessor in Kiev in the seventeenth century (cf. n. 7 above)—it will alter it.

tendoms appropriate and use those decrees in dissimilar fashions in their respective approaches to doctrine. While there are significant divergences within Western Christianity on this score—from those who assert "No creed but Christ (or, the Bible)," through those churches which explicitly endorse the ancient creeds[9] and have adopted subsequent confessional documents—the same basic attitude nevertheless prevails. According to this attitude, Western Christianity sees doctrinal statements issued on controverted questions as distinguishing what is declared from opposing viewpoints, on the one hand, and as defining (or explaining) the truth, on the other. Within Eastern Christianity, ecclesiastical pronouncements on matters of controversy also are seen as distinguishing truth from error. However, Orthodoxy rejects the notion that these statements define (or explain) the truth. The Eastern Christian consciousness of the limitations of even believing human reason, when confronted with the mysteries of the Christian faith or their divine source, prohibits that notion. Since all Christianity is built on the foundation of the ancient conciliar decrees, this East-West divergence is significant.

Whether all Christians are conscious of it or not, the doctrinal positions of all Christianity, Western and Eastern alike, affirm and build on the doctrinal decrees promulgated by the ancient ecumenical councils. What is confessed in these doctrinal declarations is foundational to Christianity: they deal with the Trinity and with the person of Christ. To be sure, many Western Christians may not be aware of the controversies leading to the ancient ecumenical councils that produced the creeds that repudiate the heresies and confess the Trinity and Christology; even so, in affirming those doctrines, Western Christians embrace the teaching of those ancient doctrinal deliverances. Many Western churches do impart an awareness of the ancient creeds to their members and utilize those creeds to some extent in their services of worship; within Eastern Orthodoxy, the Nicene-Constantinopolitan Creed is regularly confessed in worship. Even so, while the whole Christian church embraces these creeds, the West and the East display different approaches to and expectations about the doctrinal decrees of the ancient ecumenical councils.

[9]Terminological divergence between Eastern and Western Christianity often confuses discussion somewhat in this regard; Eastern Orthodoxy recognizes only one creed, the Nicene-Constantinopolitan Creed (called simply, within Orthodoxy, "the Nicene Creed"); Western Christianity also recognizes the Apostles' Creed and the Athanasian Creed. Within Western Christianity, it has become common to refer to "the ancient creeds," a usage foreign to Eastern Orthodoxy. Both Christendoms affirm the decisions of the ecumenical councils subsequent to Constantinople in 381 (such as "The Symbol of Faith" of Chalcedon in 451). Western Christians sometimes refer to these, inexactly, as "creeds," whereas Orthodoxy sees them as defenses of the creed. In the treatment here, I will follow the usage of each segment of Christendom in discussing their respective views of the role of the ancient conciliar decrees.

Western Christianity's attitudes toward doctrine lead to expectations of clarity and explanation in doctrine. It is not surprising, consequently, that Western Christians commonly view the ancient creeds as the first significant postapostolic steps in the process of defining Christian truth. The Western cultural emphasis on law comes into play here: the ecumenical councils are understood to be ecclesiastical authorities which define the faith to be believed. From this perspective, the creeds laid the foundation for the structure of Christian doctrine by setting forth the relationships of the persons of the Trinity and by analyzing the relationship between the divine and the human natures of Christ. The ancient creeds are seen as articulating the teaching found in Scripture, but they did so as the first step in a long journey of further doctrinal and confessional statements. On this Western Christian assumption, the need to defend the faith against aberrations and controversies in the history of the church led to further appropriations of the doctrinal resources deep within scriptural teaching, which resulted in further developments in understanding. This led to subsequent creedal/confessional declarations dealing with other doctrines. From this perspective, fuller creedal teaching is found in later confessions of the respective churches—the Thirty-Nine Articles for the Church of England, the Augsburg Confession and Formula of Concord for the Lutherans, the Westminster Confession of Faith and Catechisms for Presbyterians, the Three Forms of Unity (the Belgic Confession, the Heidelberg Catechism and the Canons of Dordt) for Reformed churches of Dutch background, and the Canons and Decrees of the Council of Trent for Roman Catholics, to note a few examples.

In this Western Christian approach, the ancient creeds initiated a process of ever more elaborate doctrinal articulation—not that anyone in the Christian West would explicitly claim that the ancient creeds actually or fully explain the Trinity or Christology. Even so, those creeds are viewed and dealt with in the Western Christian approach as part of a process leading to ever more explicit declarations of Christian teaching. Indeed, some Western Christian scholars who have written about the history of Christian doctrine have presented that history as the ongoing march toward more precise explanatory statements of doctrine,[10] in which the ancient creeds were the initial steps.

In the Christian East, quite a different attitude prevails with regard to the ancient conciliar decrees. For Orthodoxy, the ecumenical councils were manifesta-

[10]See J. Gresham Machen, "The Creeds and Doctrinal Advance," in *Scripture and Confession: A Book About Confessions Old and New,* ed. John H. Skilton (Nutley, N.J.: Presbyterian & Reformed, 1973), pp. 149-57; see also Louis Berkhof, *The History of Christian Doctrines* (London: Banner of Truth Trust, 1969), pp. 23-24.

tions of a Spirit-inspired unity in the faith, not legal institutions for defining doctrine. The councils met to discern how best to protect the faith, not to explain it. With this, in Orthodoxy, the ancient conciliar decrees are not understood as offering maps for those who would wish to explore the doctrines of the Trinity or of the person of Christ. Rather, the creed and the subsequent conciliar decrees function as "No Trespassing" signs, warning against a variety of heresies that would mislead one about who God is and who the Savior is. In the Eastern Christian tradition, the ancient creed and the decrees are not seen as instruction leading to further such elaboration of doctrine, but as ruling out error. Beyond that, they confess the truth but do not attempt to explain it, according to Orthodoxy. The emphasis for Eastern Christianity is not on explanation but on mystery—on adoration of truth rather than its clarification.

From the Orthodox viewpoint, all the controversies with which the ancient ecumenical councils had to wrestle arose from attempts to explain how God was both three and one, or how Christ was both God and man and yet one Savior. However, in each case, the explanations offered were found wanting, since they undercut the basis of the Christian faith. The ancient ecumenical councils were called to deal with these dangers, but they did not do so by offering explanations themselves. The creed and decrees they produced were not composed to be technical discourses; they were written to protect the church then and thereafter from such teachings as would destroy the doctrine of salvation.

According to Eastern Christianity, then, the creed and the conciliar decrees—which summon us to worship and to humility before the God whom we cannot possibly understand and certainly cannot explain—serve to protect the apostolic heritage, not to prepare for future doctrinal developments arising from it. Correlatively, Orthodoxy does not approach the subsequent doctrinal history of the church with the expectation of ever more explicit explanation; rather, for Eastern Christianity, that subsequent history must be a standing with the church of all ages in the basic message of the Christian faith "once for all entrusted to the saints" (Jude 3). The goal is not explanation of the Christian faith, but faithful adherence to its mysteries.

Concluding Observations

These divergent approaches have born dissimilar fruits in Western and Eastern Christianity. It can hardly be disputed that the Western approach has, among other things, led to increasingly refined doctrinal positions. Since the declaration and defense of these are essential to orthodoxy (in the Western Christian connotation), it is not surprising that churches in the West have polished and refined their doctrinal emphases, becoming distinctive over increasingly arcane points of doctrine and interpretation. The history of churches in the Christian West has been marked by divisions; these have been followed by further divisions over what appear—except for the excited participants in the conflicts—to be less and less significant matters of doctrine. This process has caused many in the West to wonder what provokes such ecclesiastical and theological masochism. Some of it, at least, has to do with the Western Christian view of doctrine, its understanding of what it means to be orthodox and its confidence in human reason to explore the things of God.

In the Christian East, that has not been the pattern of the history of the church; churches within the pale of Orthodoxy have not split over points of doctrinal disagreement. Unless a doctrinal point led to unquestionably more faithful life and worship—that is, unless it measured up to what was demanded of true teaching—it would not be embraced by Eastern Christians. If a teaching manifested a confidence in or reliance on human reason more than the church's liturgical interpretation of the faith, or if it entered too readily upon explanation of what are mysteries, it would not be embraced by Eastern Christians. Consequently, Eastern Orthodoxy has not been fertile ground for the seeds of doctrinal schism to be sown; the Western Christian preoccupation with explanation meets no warm welcome within its circles.

The Orthodox approach to doctrine has not led it to explain and argue, but to seek to worship and to stand in the apostolic faith alongside brothers and sisters in the faith through the ages. Orthodoxy expects not clarification but adoration, not teaching but praising. Orthodoxy has had its own historical problems, but splitting over refined doctrinal definitions has not been one of them. This outworking of the Eastern Orthodox approach to doctrine is undeniably inviting for Western Christians who have grown weary and frustrated with the results of the Western Christian penchant for explanation and doctrinal definition. Surely this approach is one that such Western Christians can respect and, as they are able, try to assimilate in a relevant fashion.

This chapter completes the necessary preliminaries for our study of Eastern Orthodox distinctives. We can now responsibly move on to consider some specific doctrines, attitudes and practices of Orthodoxy which distinguish it from Western Christianity. As we embark on these investigations, Western Christian readers should recognize from what we have considered that Orthodoxy does not conform to our Western preconceptions about doctrine. However, as we will see, profundity of another sort is evident in the distinctives of Orthodoxy.

4

Talking About God

Talking about God is basic to Christianity. The Christian faith presents God as the Creator of the universe, the one who preserves all that exists, the one against whom humanity has sinned, and the one who has had mercy on the undeserving. God is and must be at the heart of all Christian discourse, every doctrinal consideration and each ethical question. Christianity cannot be itself without talking about God at every intersection of life. What Christians say in talking about God is thus foundational to understanding what Christianity is all about. However, talking about God is precarious: on what basis do Christians claim to speak appropriately about him?

Christians affirm that human talk about God depends on God first revealing himself to us. In dealing with and speaking about the one who is the maker and sustainer, the lord and judge of all, we human beings need to give rapt attention to what he has said before daring to speak ourselves. Christians affirm that God has spoken to us in creation, in the Scriptures and in the incarnate Son of God. Because God has thus made himself known, we are enabled to speak about him and have the hope of doing so in responsible fashion.

Preliminary Considerations

As introduction to the rest of this chapter, it would be helpful to indicate what Eastern and Western Christians have in common in what we say about God. Doing so will enable us to focus on the distinctives of Orthodox talk about God against the backdrop of that commonality.

All Christians believe that God is triune: the Father, the Son and the Holy Spirit are one God. This confession was hammered out during the course of controversies in the first four centuries of the church's history. Through Scripture and ecclesiastical practices passed down since the time of the apostles, the church came to recognize the necessity of confessing that God is one but exists in three persons.

No church father taught, though, that the doctrine of God as triune was open to comprehension. Faithful to the ancient confession, both Western Christianity and Eastern Orthodoxy embrace the doctrine of the Trinity.

This commonality did not, however, preclude differences in presenting the doctrine, and from these differences a doctrinal division arose between the two segments of Christendom. Already by the fourth century, two contrasting approaches of setting forth trinitarian doctrine had developed. Eastern Christianity followed the Cappadocian fathers, who started with the three persons and moved to the oneness of God. By contrast, Western Christianity took the path of St. Augustine, who began with the oneness of God and moved to the threeness of the persons. The Eastern Christian approach allowed for a straightforward affirmation of the confession in the Nicene-Constantinopolitan Creed of 381 that the Spirit "proceeds from the Father." In the Christian West, though, Augustine's approach ended up viewing the Holy Spirit as proceeding "from the Father *and the Son*"—in Latin, *filioque*.[1] While this "fit" with the approach taken in Western Christian teaching about the Trinity, it was impossible from the Eastern Christian one. In the Cappadocian fathers' teaching, followed by Eastern Orthodoxy, God the Father is the source of being for both the Son and the Holy Spirit. This entails no subordination, since the Son and the Spirit each receive divine being from the Father: eternal, divine being knows neither beginning nor end, no greater or less. For Orthodoxy, "sharing" the procession of the Spirit between Father and Son is impossible, so *filioque* is an impossibility for Orthodoxy. The Christian West's subsequent unilateral insertion of *filioque* into the creed during the Middle Ages sealed a divergence of teaching and confession that has endured through all the intervening centuries. Frequently addressed in dialogues and councils, the controversy over the *filioque* phrase has never been resolved; it continues as a main doctrinal difference between Western Christianity and Eastern Orthodoxy.[2] Even with this divergence, though, Eastern Orthodoxy and Western

[1]See Jaroslav Pelikan, *The Emergence of the Catholic Tradition (100-600)*, vol. 1 of The Christian Tradition: A History of the Development of Doctrine (Chicago: University of Chicago Press, 1972), p. 293; see also Otto W. Heick, *A History of Christian Thought*, 2 vols. (Philadelphia: Fortress, 1965), 1:248.

[2]The controversy flared up in the ninth century, in the conflict between Pope Nicholas I and St. Photius, Patriarch of Constantinople; since then, the controversy has waxed and waned in intensity, but the divergence remains. For a concise Orthodox presentation, see John Meyendorff's summary in *Byzantine Theology: Historical Trends and Doctrinal Themes*, 2nd ed. (New York: Fordham University Press, 1979), pp. 91-94; for a somewhat fuller treatment, see Jaroslav Pelikan, *The Spirit of Eastern Christendom (600-1700)* (Chicago: University of Chicago Press, 1974), pp. 193-98, 275-78; for a vigorous presentation of the Eastern Orthodox perspective, see Vladimir Lossky, *In the Image and Like-*

Christianity both embrace the doctrine of the Trinity confessed in the Nicene-Constantinopolitan Creed.

Similarly, in both Western and Eastern Christendom, Christians believe that God is incomprehensible, incomparable and ineffable. God cannot be "enclosed" within our understandings; no analogy in all of creation adequately reflects him; it is beyond our ability to express in human language who he is. Christians believe and trust in God, but they do not claim either to comprehend him mentally or to describe him fully. We believe in him whom our minds cannot fathom and our words cannot capture.

Again, this commonality has not precluded differences between Eastern and Western Christendom. Here, though, the divergence is not in doctrine but in the degree to which Western Christianity and Eastern Orthodoxy respectively emphasize divine incomprehensibility, incomparability and ineffability. In Western Christian teaching, these serve as foundational cautions against intellectual hubris but are not particularly prominent in doctrinal treatments. By contrast, Orthodoxy emphasizes these at virtually every turn, as we will see in the following treatment.

As a final preliminary consideration, we should realize that talk about God is foundational to everything else in Christian discussions of doctrine. As foundational, though, our views about God may not necessarily be self-consciously articulated or even particularly clear to us in their details and implications. We have learned to deal with topics about God in certain ways and with certain assumptions. We build on these patterns, but we have not necessarily examined them assiduously. Since we share these perspectives with others in our particular Christian tradition, we are often unaware of the somewhat different ways taken and assumptions held by other Christians as they talk about God. Encountering ways and assumptions that diverge from our own can be disconcerting and disorienting, and sometimes we react to them rather than reflecting on them. We can recognize this pattern in some of the ways we within Western Christianity differ in our views about God,[3] even though we all share the basic Western Christian approach to talking about God. As we move into the following treatment, we need to be ready

---

ness of God, ed. John H. Erickson and Thomas E. Bird (Crestwood, N.Y.: St. Vladimir's Seminary Press, 1985), pp. 71-96; for further treatments, consult the bibliographical data offered by Pelikan, pp. 308-10. For a concise Roman Catholic presentation, see *Catechism of the Catholic Church,* 2nd ed. (New York: Doubleday, 1997), sec. 246, p. 73.

[3]E.g., while Western Christians confess that God is sovereign, they argue—often with more heat than light—over what that means in regard to grace and election. Also, viewpoints on the possibility of continuing divine revelation and of miraculous manifestations generate intense argument within much of Western Christendom.

to reflect on the way Orthodoxy talks about God, which differs in some striking regards from our Western Christian pattern.

More is involved in this than the difference in Western and Eastern Christian uses of the term *theology* itself.[4] As suggested above, since these differences are foundational, they may strike us as disconcerting and disorienting—even more so than the other Orthodox distinctives treated in subsequent chapters of this volume. Considering Orthodoxy's way of talking about God will be a challenging enterprise, both intellectually and spiritually. If we will reflect on the way Eastern Christians talk about God, though, we will have much to ponder and to enrich our own approach to and understanding of the doctrine of God.

"Positive" and "Negative" Theology

The first key difference to note is that Eastern Orthodoxy divides theology into two categories, "positive" and "negative" theology. These terms play no particular role in Western Christian discourse about God,[5] but they are foundational to Orthodoxy's treatment of theology. In Eastern Orthodoxy, "positive" (also called "cataphatic") theology and "negative" (or "apophatic") theology designate two ways of "doing" theology. Positive theology and negative theology speak in dissimilar ways about God, but those ways are intimately related in Eastern Christianity's teaching about God. Since negative theology assumes and builds on positive theology, we should consider first what positive theology is, according to Eastern Christianity.

Positive, or *cataphatic,* theology teaches about God through affirmations. It deals, thus, with what can be understood, clarified and set forth about God in propositions. Building on what God has revealed about himself, positive theology seeks to articulate what *can* be affirmed about God and communicated in statements to others.

This sounds much the same as what any Western Christian would recognize as theology. Indeed, in the Christian West, positive theology has so dominated the theological stage that the adjective is neither necessary nor understood. Teaching in clear and orderly form what should be believed—that is what theology in Western Christendom has been all about. Since the general approach of Western Christianity to theology is virtually what Eastern Orthodoxy intends with positive

---

[4]As was pointed out above (chap. 3, p. 59), Orthodoxy reserves the term *theology* for talking about God, as over against a common Western Christian practice of using *theology* generically to refer to doctrinal discourses on a variety of topics.

[5]To be sure, medieval theologians in the Christian West showed keen interest in Pseudo-Dionysius's works, in which negative theology received pronounced emphasis. Apart from some mystical strains, though, that interest has long since dissipated in Western Christianity.

theology, we do not need to pursue cataphatic theology more closely—except for one point. That point is an important one, though: it shows that Eastern Christianity has more modest expectations of positive theology than does Western Christianity; this point also indicates why, according to Orthodoxy, negative theology is necessary.

Within Christianity, we talk about God with confidence since he has revealed himself and has commanded his church to tell about him. In Western Christendom, we have been especially concerned to set forth that revelation in explicit teaching. Western Christianity recognizes, of course, that no one can fully state all the implications of Christian doctrine and, more specifically, that no human being can "explain" God. Even so, in talking about God, Western Christianity has emphasized teaching and clarification as much as possible—in accordance with its general approach to doctrine. As we have seen, the Christian East has not sought explanation. Eastern Orthodoxy stresses the importance of accepting God's truth, and it encourages vigorous reflection on the various disciplines of doctrine, including theology. Even so, this emphasis fits into the whole package of Eastern Christian thought differently than the correlative emphases do in the Christian West. This is manifest in the Orthodox attitude toward divine revelation in Scripture.

All Christians rely on Scripture to enable us to speak truly about God. Thus, Scripture is foundational to the theological task everywhere in Christendom, both East and West. That common attitude has not precluded arguments among Christians, though, about Scripture as divinely inspired, as revelation or as culturally bound, and various positions have been articulated on these questions. Eastern Orthodoxy brings another concern to the consideration of Scripture, a concern basic to the Orthodox approach to talking about God: Eastern Christianity stresses that even Scripture does not—indeed, cannot—say all there is about God. While Western Christian theologians would affirm this as well, this affirmation carries special significance for Orthodox talk about God.

Eastern Christianity emphasizes that God has condescended to human beings to reveal himself to them.[6] In this, the Orthodox faithfully follow the path of the Greek church fathers. This revelation is of a God who is great, unfathomably beyond us.[7] Since he is God, there is no way that we as mere human beings, as his

---

[6]Western Christian thought recognizes this as well, of course. However, Western Christianity has stressed it far less than Orthodoxy has. Western Christianity's greater confidence in human intellection to deal with revelatory data and its penchant for explanation probably account in large part for the less prominent role this consideration plays in Western Christian thought.

[7]"The divine nature cannot be apprehended by human reason; we cannot even represent to ourselves all its greatness" (St. Gregory Nazianzen *The Theological Orations* 2.11).

creatures, can understand him.[8] There is no "suprahuman" language that God could use to communicate with us—and even if there were, we would not be able to understand it. God has accommodated himself to us and our limitations,[9] using human language and human experience of the world to tell us about himself and his relationship to us.[10] In all this, God speaks truly as he reveals himself to us, but he does not speak exhaustively and penetratingly, such that we could comprehend him.[11] Thus, God's revelation in Scripture is true, although it does not say everything about God. It is adequate for God's purposes and for our needs, but not sufficient to enable us mere limited human beings, his creatures, to obtain discursive knowledge of him.[12]

According to Orthodox perspectives, Scripture must be accepted as God's true revelation to humanity, adequate for his purposes toward us. We mislead ourselves, though, if we think that through Scripture we come to comprehend God. Through divine revelation we come to know God truly, but not discursively. This requires us to avoid, at all costs, the assumption that we can explain God. He has utilized things from created reality to indicate who he is to us and for us, to show his relationship to the world and his direction of it, and so forth.[13] Indeed, everything God tells us about himself is placed within the mold of created reality, using our human words and referring to our experience of the creation. Such revelation is true, but it cannot capture the fullness of who God is in himself.[14]

Thus, we must not merely nod our heads to divine incomprehensibility. According to Orthodoxy, we need to keep it constantly in mind as we talk about God. The God to whom we relate is with us, but he is always beyond us and our understanding. If even Scripture is thus delimited in its presentation of God, positive theology must be as well.[15] For Orthodoxy, this approach is no disparagement of Scripture; rather, it is a recognition of what Scripture is. Similarly, to insist upon

---

[8]"God cannot be measured by the heart, and he is incomprehensible by the mind" (St. Irenaeus *Against Heresies* 4.19.32).

[9]"God has not left us in utter ignorance. . . . He has revealed knowledge of himself to us in accordance with our capacity" (St. John of Damascus *The Orthodox Faith* 1.1).

[10]"The treasure of divine wisdom is hidden in the baser, crude vessel of words" (Origen *On First Principles* 4.1.7).

[11]"The Deity cannot be expressed in words" (St. Gregory Nazianzen *The Theological Orations* 4.17).

[12]"He has revealed to us what we needed to know, but he has withheld what we were unable to bear" (St. John of Damascus *The Orthodox Faith* 1.2).

[13]"The inspired book teaches us through metaphors" (St. Gregory of Nyssa *The Beatitudes* Sermon 2).

[14]"The Holy Trinity far transcends every comparison and analogy" (St. John of Damascus *On Heresies* 103).

[15]"[In talking about God], we have to set forth in human terms what transcends the human order" (St. John of Damascus *The Orthodox Faith* 1.2).

the limitations of cataphatic theology—to hesitate about claims of even gifted, sanctified minds to set forth and explain any doctrinal truth fully, and especially truth about God—is only to recognize the limitations we have as God's creatures, limitations from which even divine revelation in Scripture does not deliver us.

So, Orthodoxy affirms the importance of positive theology: we must teach all we responsibly can about what God has revealed to us in Scripture in order to understand what we can and enable others to understand as much as they can too. But Eastern Christianity also recognizes the limitations of cataphatic theology. A leading Orthodox spokesman put it well when he wrote, "All that we affirm concerning God, however correct, falls far short of the living truth. . . . Having made an assertion about God, we must pass beyond it: the statement is not untrue, yet neither it nor any other form of words can contain the fullness of the transcendent God."[16] Positive theology can neither set forth God in his transcendence nor overcome the finitude of its human practitioners, no matter how much academic training theologians receive or how godly they become. In Orthodoxy, this awareness impinges on all doctrinal affirmation, and especially on all talk about God. As an outstanding Romanian Orthodox theologian has declared, "The consciousness of God's mystery is simultaneously implied in the things which are known about God."[17]

This is the necessity and justification for *negative,* or *apophatic,* theology. It proceeds in the opposite direction from positive theology: instead of affirmations, apophatic theology makes negations about God, that is, saying what is not true about him.[18] This is more than just recognizing and declaring that anything evil or sinful is unworthy of God and cannot be attributed to him, though. Negative theology attempts to peel away not only what would be sinfully unworthy of God,

---

[16]Bishop Kallistos (Timothy) Ware, *The Orthodox Way,* rev. ed. (Crestwood, N.Y.: St. Vladimir's Seminary Press, 1995), p. 14.

[17]Dumitru Staniloae, *The Experience of God—Orthodox Dogmatic Theology: Revelation and Knowledge of the Triune God,* trans. Ioan Ionita and Robert Barringer (Brookline, Mass.: Holy Cross Orthodox Press, 1994), 1:109.

[18]Those familiar with ancient philosophy will recognize that Plotinus and the Neo-Platonists posited a "negative way" to ascend to the Ultimate, a way in which the boundaries of human thought must be transcended in order to achieve union with the One. As with other elements of their ancient intellectual milieu, so also here the Greek church fathers appropriated but profoundly transformed the concept of a "negative way" to the One—God, in Christian teaching. As over against Neo-Platonism, the Greek church fathers denied that union with God involved reabsorption into the essence of the One; rather, according to their teaching (followed in subsequent Orthodoxy), God will remain everlastingly transcendent and inaccessible in his essence to his creatures, and as his creatures we will always remain distinct from God. For fuller discussion of this question, see Lossky, *In the Image and Likeness of God,* pp. 14-15; see also Vladimir Lossky, *Orthodox Theology: An Introduction,* trans. Ian and Ihita Kesarcodi-Watson (Crestwood, N.Y.: St. Vladimir's Seminary Press, 1978), pp. 24-25, 31-32.

but all mere creaturely concepts. Since all such concepts arise from experience of creation or are produced via the cognitive processes of mere creatures, they are inevitably inadequate to present God as God. Apophatic theology invites us to transcend the limitations of creaturely experience and human thought. This is necessary, according to Orthodoxy, if theology is to be as responsible as it can be in talking about God. This orientation was put well by St. Gregory Nazianzen long ago when he urged, "How do you describe God's essence? Not by stating what it is, but by rejecting what it is not."[19]

According to Eastern Christianity, it is safer to say what God is not than to try to assert what he is. *Saying what he is* must run afoul of what God is, since our human thoughts and words cannot contain or define him. However, *saying what God is not* allows us to rule out what cannot capture him, opening us thus to the indescribable greatness of who God is—apart from and beyond our reason, even reason aided by divine revelation. Of course, apophatic theology does not deny the truth of the revelation God has given, but it emphasizes that even this revelation can only speak of God via human concepts and experience. Because this is so, even the concepts used in divine revelation are inadequate to "contain" God. Unable therefore to "capture" him fully, even these concepts must be transcended.[20] While they speak truly of God, they could not possibly present him exhaustively. Therefore even they must be negated in the sense that we recognize they cannot present God discursively. Who he is remains beyond human expression at its most eloquent and human thought at its loftiest; this is expressed in Eastern Orthodoxy through negative theology.

Apophatic theology points beyond human thoughts and words, but it can only be expressed in those thoughts and words. It reaches out beyond itself and its limitations. A few examples may make this somewhat more accessible.

One of the prayers offered by some Orthodox in the morning includes the request that the day may be peaceful so that they can offer "hymns to you, the Father and the Son and the Holy Spirit, the only God, who is *more than without beginning* and Creator of all."[21] These words push beyond human understanding to praise God in prayer. In accord with this, St. Gregory of Nyssa declared, "It is impossible for [the divine nature] to come within the scope of what we can comprehend. But we have gained one advantage from our examination: we have succeeded in form-

[19]St. Gregory Nazianzen *Theological Orations* 3.11.

[20]St. Gregory of Nyssa urged, "Inspired by God, the Scriptures reveal wonderful things about the transcendent nature. But what are they, in comparison with that nature itself? Even if I could understand everything Scripture says, what is pointed to is still more" (*The Beatitudes*, Sermon 7).

[21]Excerpted from a morning prayer of St. Basil the Great to the Holy Trinity (emphasis added).

ing an idea of the greatness of what we have sought simply by being unable to perceive it." Almost playfully but with consummate apophatic precision, he also urged, "The characteristic of the divine nature is to transcend all characteristics."[22] The sixth-century church father known as Pseudo-Dionysius continues in this vein when he affirms, "He [God] exists beyond being and is known beyond the mind."[23]

Since all our thoughts, ideas, insights and speech about God are and must remain creaturely, what is left to us, then, from this perspective? According to Eastern Christianity, we are not thereby abandoned to doubt or skepticism; instead of this or any other such despairing response, we are called to go in confident hope beyond our reason, into contemplation of him who is far beyond all creaturely limitation. As St. Gregory of Nyssa affirmed, "The divine is *there* where human understanding cannot reach. . . . The divine nature . . . transcends every cognition and representation. It cannot be likened to anything humans know."[24] Apophatic theology invites us to God, into a fellowship with him that transcends our human capacities:

> The apophatic way of "unknowing" brings us not to emptiness but to fullness. Our negations are in reality super-affirmations. Destructive in outward form, the apophatic approach is affirmative in its final effects: it helps us to reach out, beyond all statements positive or negative, beyond all language and all thought, towards an immediate experience of the living God.[25]

Drawn beyond cognition and thought by negative theology, we are not left with uncertainty, but with fellowship with the God who has spoken truly to us. We are also left with humility before this God who is too vast for us, who nevertheless loved us so much that he gave his only Son that whoever believes in him might have eternal life (Jn 3:16).

Thus, negative theology does not undermine positive theology; rather, negative theology builds on positive theology. According to Orthodoxy, cataphatic theology is necessary to apophatic theology: positive theology not only sets forth what can be said and should be learned and confessed by Christians propositionally, but it also serves as the taking-off point from which Christians proceed on to the worship and honor of the one who is still beyond our loftiest and most exalted thoughts, even those built on Scripture itself: "[By] apophatic theology . . . [we]

---

[22]St. Gregory of Nyssa *The Beatitudes,* Sermon 1; *The Life of Moses* 2.234.
[23]Letter 1.
[24]St. Gregory of Nyssa *The Life of Moses* 1.46-47.
[25]Ware, *The Orthodox Way,* p. 15.

rid ourselves of concepts proper to human thought, transforming them into steps by which we may ascend to the contemplation of a reality which the created intelligence cannot contain."[26]

Thus, in Orthodoxy, theology—"talking about God"—done rightly leads to silence before God, to serene contemplation of God. This mysticism is not avoidance of or escape from Scripture, but reverence and awe before the God who has so graciously condescended to reveal himself to us at all in Scripture. This God, our God, is beyond all talking, description and every attempt of ours to understand him. Yet he has made himself known to us, truly though not discursively, and we can rely on what he has said and revealed. But as we do, Orthodoxy emphasizes, we must pass on from concept to contemplation. According to the Christian East, theology should not issue into doctrinal wrangling and argument, but into silence, awe, mysticism and worship.

God is incomprehensible, indeed. While Western Christianity teaches this, in Eastern Orthodoxy divine incomprehensibility is heavily underlined and receives its full *theological* due. Eastern Christianity stresses that our words, our theology, cannot capture God, and that our ideas—no matter how vast or profound—cannot surround him. He is truly beyond all our talk about him. Apophatic theology does not deny or destroy a concern for careful theology; according to Orthodoxy, it is theology at its most careful.

ESSENCE AND ENERGIES

A second significance difference between Eastern Orthodox and Western Christian talk about God is in their respective ways of describing how God relates to his creation. Both segments of Christendom recognize that we must distinguish between the intratrinitarian relationships and the relationships of the triune God to creation. In the past, failures to do so have ended up blurring the distinction between Creator and creation and introduced doctrinal error. In Western Christianity, the two are distinguished as God's works *ad intra* (the intratrinitarian relationships) and those *ad extra* (how God relates to his creation). This distinction is recognized as important in technical theological discourse in Western Christianity, but it serves more as background qualifier than as constitutive of theological teaching.

The situation is quite different in Eastern Christianity, where the distinction plays a decisive role in virtually every facet of doctrinal teaching. This was already

---

[26]Vladimir Lossky, *The Mystical Theology of the Eastern Church* (Crestwood, N.Y.: St. Vladimir's Seminary Press, 1976), pp. 45-46.

the case among the Greek church fathers, who distinguished between God in the divine being and God in his relationship with his creation. At times, those Greek church fathers used the terms "essence" and "energies" to make this distinction. Later, in the fourteenth century, St. Gregory Palamas focused on this pair of terms as articulating a necessary distinction, which honors God's genuine transcendence while celebrating God's intimate immanence. From Palamas, building on earlier patristic emphases, Orthodoxy has come to express that distinction as one between the divine *essence* and the divine *energies.* The divine *essence* is God *in his being,* and the divine *energies* are God *in his actions.* This seems straightforward enough, but it is anything but simple.

In the first place, to speak of God's *essence* or his *being* already runs us up against Orthodoxy's apophatic emphasis. As humans, we need to speak about God in distinction from us and from all the rest of creation; we thus end up talking about God as God. However, the only way we can do so is to use our human terminology, words that reflect our experience of the creation and our limited thought. In the structures of that thought, we recognize that all sorts of things have existence in creation, that they *are*—and so we speak of them as having *being.* Rocks, dogs, clouds, trees and humans "have being." We also recognize that God *is,* and we consequently speak of his *being.* But is "being" a category into which divine existence can be subsumed? Is not God's *being* so utterly beyond anything we can imagine or experience that it belongs *outside of* any *category* of "being"?

To pursue this point, when we humans speak about what is common to certain types of creatures, we may use various terms from biology (phylum, genus, species), but we will eventually speak more broadly, about the common *nature* the respective creatures share. The most obvious manifestation of this in Christian doctrinal terminology is when we speak about *human nature.* We recognize that all humans have this nature, and we confess that in the incarnation the Son of God took on human nature. We know that we cannot encounter human nature in the abstract, for we only encounter people—all of them individuals who share human nature. We "abstract" that nature from the individuals we encounter and thus develop some understanding of that shared nature. Even so, we speak with confidence of such shared common *natures*—whether human or of some other creaturely sort. We also speak about the divine *nature*—but Christian teaching excludes all thought of God being one of a number of beings who fit in the category of *divine nature* and from whom we abstract an understanding of that divine nature. According to the Christian faith, there is only one God; the *divine nature* is not "shared" with other divine beings. Thus, whatever we may know about the divine nature tells us about God in himself.

But the problem in our terminology and understanding extends beyond what we have considered so far: is it appropriate to lump together what we have abstracted mentally regarding various categories of creatures under the designation *natures* and use the same term to speak about the *divine nature*? Can the *divine nature* be subsumed into the broader category of *natures* by which we speak generically about various forms of existence? The answer is as clear as the consideration is challenging: God cannot be included as another "nature" within our thought processes. We cannot avoid speaking about the *divine nature,* at least as distinct from all other (creaturely) *natures,* since we have to distinguish God from creation. Likewise, in speaking about the incarnate Son of God, we end up having to speak of his divine and his human natures. Even so, all talk about the *divine nature* is speech about something utterly beyond the furthest reach of our mental category "nature."

So, when Orthodoxy posits the distinction between the *divine essence* and the *divine energies,* and we note that it is the distinction between God in his being and God in his actions, we should recognize that we are only setting boundaries to the different kinds of things we must say about God; we are not exploring charted waters. The divine essence is God in his being, in his nature—in himself as God, apart from and beyond any contact with his creatures. We believe, as taught by Scripture and the church, that the one God exists in three persons—the Father, the Son and the Holy Spirit. The relationships among the three persons of the Trinity are within the oneness of God; each of the three persons equally shares the divine being, with none of them subordinate in nature to either of the other two. Thus, we affirm that the divine essence is one and absolutely unique. As the being of God himself, though, it is utterly beyond us, both in this life and in the life to come. According to Orthodoxy, we must confess the *divine essence* and speak about it as that which the Father, the Son and the Holy Spirit share as God. However, we cannot claim to understand the divine essence in any regard. As St. John of Damascus urged, "It is clear that God exists. But what he is in essence and nature is utterly unknowable and beyond understanding."[27] According to Eastern Christian teaching, that will not change even in the eternal state; God is and always will remain utterly and absolutely beyond us in his essence.

---

[27]St. John of Damascus *The Orthodox Faith* 1.4; cf. the Damascene's related comment: "He [God] cannot be numbered among 'beings,' not because he does not exist, but because he transcends all beings and even being itself. If knowledge has to do with beings, then what transcends knowledge certainly transcends essence—and what transcends essence transcends knowledge" (ibid.).

But God also has acted toward his creatures—in the work of creation itself, in his sustaining them in existence and in the salvation he graciously brings to a fallen creation. These activities are God's deeply intimate, intensely involved relationship with all he has made and loves. Orthodoxy teaches that all this involvement with creation takes place through the *divine energies.* These divine energies are not effects that God has on creation or descriptions for what he does with creation; the divine energies are God. They are not "actions" or "activities" in which God engages his creation "at arm's length," as it were; they are God. All God's actions vis-à-vis his creation—the act of creation itself, maintaining creation in existence, revealing himself to his creatures, and the salvation he works for them—are in the divine energies. Orthodoxy teaches that all these activities are God himself, in action toward his creation, and not "merely" divine influences upon or effects within us.

In clarification, the Orthodox stress that the divine energies are not *effects* that flow out of the divine essence as their *cause.* If they were, that would make the energies something produced by God—and, thus, part of creation (even if a highly exalted part of it). According to Eastern Christian teaching, the divine energies are not created; they are fully God, but not as or in the divine essence. A leading Orthodox theologian stated that the divine energies are "the outpourings of the divine nature which cannot set bounds to itself, for God is more than essence. The energies might be described as that mode of existence of the Trinity which is outside of its inaccessible essence. God thus exists both in His essence and outside of His essence."[28] The divine energies are God: they are nothing less or other than God, but God in action with and for his creation.

Orthodoxy thus teaches that there is an ineffable distinction within God, a distinction according to which the one God remains both inaccessible and transcendent (in the divine essence) and yet also communicable and immanent (in the divine energies).[29] According to Eastern Christian perspectives, "God is transcendent in His essence, . . . but God proceeds outside His essence. He continually bursts forth from this hiding-place, and this bursting forth . . . [is] a mode of existing in which the Divinity can communicate itself to created beings: they [the divine energies] are an immanent aspect of God, His manifesting descent."[30] In the divine energies, the God who is utterly beyond us nevertheless is at the same

---

[28]Lossky, *Mystical Theology of the Eastern Church,* p. 73.

[29]Cf. the statement by Ware, "The essence signifies the whole God as he is in himself; the energies signify the whole God as he is in action. God in his entirety is completely present in each of his divine energies" (*The Orthodox Way,* p. 22).

[30]Lossky, *In the Image and Likeness of God,* p. 40.

time intimately involved with us. The God who is indescribably other is also the God who is love (1 Jn 4:8).

With this distinction between the divine essence and the divine energies, Orthodoxy has found a way to affirm on the one hand the absolute and uncompromised transcendence of God as over against his creatures and on the other hand the equally absolute and undiluted immanence of God with and in his creatures. According to Orthodox teaching, apart from this distinction, either the divine activities with creation would end up blurring into the divine essence and issue into some sort of pantheism, or else the divine essence would be at such a remove that we would have no contact with God at all. This distinction, which may seem initially speculative or abstract, is anything but that; it is the foundation for deeply personal experience of God.

PERSONAL EXPERIENCE

A third distinctive of Eastern Orthodox talk about God is the emphasis on personal experience. To be sure, all Christian teaching, East and West alike, affirms that believers have a genuine relationship with God as their Father, Savior and Sanctifier. Within Western Christianity, some groups focus much of their attention on the way to obtain a "personal relationship" with God. So, a stress on personal experience is not unique to Eastern Christianity; what is distinctive is the way in which the Orthodox construe it. In their teaching, personal experience is closely tied in to their distinction between the divine essence and the divine energies. Indeed, that distinction was adopted within Orthodoxy as a way of defending the reality of personal experience between believers and God.[31] Also, the emphasis on personal experience shows the goal of negative theology.

Apophatic theology calls us to negate our intellectual conceptions and rise above them, and thus to open ourselves to God who is unutterably beyond us and all our thoughts and words, and to experience him intimately. This is necessary, according to Eastern Christianity, not only because we are finite; it is also necessary because God is transcendent. He is absolutely *beyond* us in his essence. But the Christian faith also teaches that God loves us, that he is near his people. According to Orthodoxy, the corrective and purgative value of negative theology prepares us to experience God beyond thought and explanation in the communion of divine love.[32]

---

[31]Ibid., pp. 53-54.

[32]"The apophatic way does not lead to an absence, to an utter emptiness; for the unknowable God of the Christian is not the impersonal God of the philosophers" (Lossky, *Mystical Theology of the Eastern Church*, p. 43).

Our relationships with spouses or close friends may help us process this challenging teaching. In our deepest personal relationships, we find fulfillment not in intellectual comprehension but in a love which cannot be explained and beggars our words. We "know" (as "positive/cataphatic" information) much about our spouse or close friend. In that close relationship, such information serves as the foundation for another "knowing" (of a "negative/apophatic" sort), in which that other human person is and remains mysterious but compelling. This all issues into a deep relationship of commitment and love that neither needs nor welcomes explanation. We *experience* that intimate personal relationship. In that sense—beyond description or explanation—we "know" the other person beyond knowledge and relate to them in love.

In the divine energies, we experience this communion with God. We are not drawn to or put into communion with the divine essence—always an impossibility for mere creatures, according to Eastern Christianity. In the divine energies, though, God is intimately involved with his creatures. As we have seen, the divine energies are not effects within us caused by the divine essence; rather, the divine energies are God himself acting not at a safe distance, but in the closest possible immanence with us. According to Orthodoxy, God's closeness to us in the divine energies enables us personally to experience the love of God—or, better put, personally to experience God as love.

This is not just or even first of all an individual experience, though. The God who in his energies intimately relates to his creatures especially loves and cares for the people he has called his own—the church.[33] This divine intimacy is for them all; he manifests and administers it in the church. This divine intimacy is also for individuals, but it is never individualistic. The corporate dimension of Christian experience is fundamental to Orthodox understanding of the experience of God's love in his energies.[34]

However, we do not always sense the fullness of this experience. Although God's immanence never flags, our alertness to God and our experience of intimacy with him often fluctuates. The experience is not ours to command. Devotion to God is required of us, but we depend on the largesse of God to break through our manifold distance from him and allow us to experience him in his energies. This experience is beyond our capacities: it is "an experience which tran-

---

[33]St. Paul's letters typically begin with a specific address to a church (e.g., "To all God's beloved in Rome, who are called to be saints" [Rom 1:7]), to whom he declares God's loving blessing ("Grace to you and peace from God our Father and the Lord Jesus Christ" [Rom 1:7]).

[34]See the treatment below, chap. 10.

scends both the terms of affirmation and of negation that express it."[35] And yet in the depths of our being we experience intimacy with him "in a sensible and conscious manner,"[36] with a certainty that beggars argument and conclusion. This personal experience is a direct one, in which we sense the mystical presence of God within us in an intimacy that sweetly engulfs us in God's love and draws us into yet deeper intimacy with him. According to Eastern Christian understandings, this is what humanity was created to receive and what is communicated to us in salvation in Christ.[37]

Personal experience is requisite to any valid talk about God, from an Orthodox perspective. Such mystical experience of God in the divine energies not only draws us to God, it also confirms within us the appropriateness of both positive and negative theology. We must speak about God because we are Christian; but we must also rise above these concepts, because God is transcendent. Personal experience of God draws us into union with him about whom theology speaks. Without that experience, any such talk about God is vacuous and presumptuous, according to Orthodoxy.

CONCLUDING OBSERVATIONS

Eastern Christianity's approach to talking about God differs strikingly from the Western Christian approach. With Orthodoxy, Western Christianity recognizes that God is incomprehensible, but our Western Christian confidence in doctrinal exposition forces that recognition "to the back of the theological room," as it were. In contrast, in Eastern Christianity, divine incomprehensibility fills the room. Orthodoxy never loses sight, not only of our finitude but also of God's transcendence. The structures of Orthodox talk about God make room for the cataphatic theology which we in the Christian West also practice, but Eastern Christianity has emphasized the inevitable limitations of all our propositional affirmations about God. Orthodoxy has adopted as a basic element of talking about God an apophatic approach to theologizing which is virtually unknown in Western Christianity. Further, the Eastern Christian distinction of divine essence and divine energies has no parallel in Western Christian teaching. Because of all this, even the emphasis on personal experience—an emphasis vigorously asserted within Western Christianity—takes on colors in Eastern Orthodox theology not found on the Western Christian palette. The differences are striking, given our fundamental agreement in confessing the triune God.

---

[35]Staniloae, *The Experience of God,* 1:111.
[36]Ibid., 1:112.
[37]See the treatments below, chap. 6, pp. 105-6; and chap. 8, pp. 142-44, 146-52.

In the face of all this divergence, is it possible for Western Christians to benefit from what we have seen of Orthodoxy's approach to talking about God? A few points can be suggested in this regard. In the first place, Western Christians can learn a more measured respect for "positive" theology. We must diligently and vigorously seek to understand all we can of divine revelation, of course—however, that diligence and vigor have already marked Western Christianity. Reflection on Eastern Christianity's approach to talking about God might introduce a welcome sense of humility into our expositions of the faith. It might be salutary for us in the Christian West to remember more self-consciously that we are dealing with a revelation from God in which he descends from an unimaginable height and accommodates himself to our limited capacities in order to let us know who he is. We could also learn to remain intensely aware that we are expounding only what God knows we can handle, and not ultimate verity as it is in him. Embracing these emphases would not require us to be less concerned for careful cataphatic theology, but it would lead us to a greater appreciation for the insights of those who approach God's revelation from other vantage points than we do, and are thereby able to discern other facets of the jewel of divine revelation than we are. This would result in a greater ecumenical openness as we learn from and with other brothers and sisters in Christ who also seek to understand God's gracious self-revelation.

A second potential benefit to us, closely related to the first, is that we might sense the futility of some of our Western Christian wrangling about Scripture. In it, according to Eastern Christianity, God has communicated truth which must lead and guide us, but he has not made a full disclosure of himself. What we find in it is true, but it does not present the fullness of God or ultimate veracity. If truth resides in God alone, and if God in his essence is beyond our grasp, then we should be considerably less assertive about our particular ways of reading his revelation. This need not lead to carelessness regarding truth or indifference to God's Word, but it might disable some of our propensity for claiming absolute standing for our viewpoints and interpretations. Too often some Western Christians have identified their way of reading Scripture with God's very intent in his self-revelation. By keeping in mind that Scripture serves God's purposes and not our curiosities or intellectual vanities, we might gain a greater humility in appropriating Scripture—a humility that embraces in joyful and confident faith what God has said but recognizes how much he has left unsaid in stooping to our finitude and giving us a glimpse of his transcendence.

Third, if Western Christians could appropriate negative theology in some measure as it is practiced within Eastern Orthodoxy, we would end up with a richer sense of who God is, on the one hand, and a greater humility for what we say about him, on the other. The recognition that he transcends not only what we can say but all we might imagine, and that even Scripture cannot possibly present him thoroughly and discursively, might work within us a spiritually healthy and holy silence. Apophatic theology undercuts the presumption that we limited human beings—via reading Scripture, studying doctrine and using our minds—have become experts in talking about God because we have mastered the data of revelation. We do not have, and must not act as if we have, "God in a box," whether that box be denominational or doctrinal. Beyond what we claim to know and understand, beyond all our limitations, is our God—who invites us to leave behind our considerable intellection and to encounter him beyond our capacities.

Doing that would lead us, in the fourth place, to the heart of the personal experience emphasized in Orthodoxy. In much of our Western Christian discussions of personal relationship with God, we give attention to what we can and should do to achieve and maintain that relationship—repenting of sin and believing in him, reading the Scriptures, praying and living in faithful obedience to his commands. While all of this has its place, according to Eastern Orthodoxy, personal experience of God takes place beyond our intellect and our efforts, in the direct encounter with God in his energies. This is a mysticism of openness to God which welcomes his presence and yields itself to his love. Experiencing God in this fashion frees us up to celebrate his love and helps us put the rest of our talk about God into perspective. We Western Christians could use more of that.

If we could appropriate even some of the Orthodox approach to talking about God, we in the Christian West would be drawn to greater wonder before him and less wrangling about our various views. It would also lead us to greater humility and a responsible silence, in place of the chatter and argument that so often bedevil our talk about God. Humility and wonder should mark any response to God and his revelation; if we can learn that from our brothers and sisters in Eastern Orthodoxy, we will have learned a great deal.

5

THE CREATOR AND THE CREATION

IN THE NICENE-CONSTANTINOPOLITAN CREED, Christians confess faith in "God the Father Almighty, Maker of heaven and earth, and of all things visible and invisible." There is no divergence between Western and Eastern Christianity in this affirmation; according to both, God has created all things. However, in view of what we have already treated of Orthodox understandings, it is not surprising to discover that Eastern Christianity has given its own turn to this common confession. The difference between this and Western Christian perspectives boils down to the great stress Eastern Orthodoxy lays, in several ways, on the distinction between the Creator and the creation. That distinction, in turn, shapes the way in which creation itself is understood.

DISTINCTION BETWEEN CREATOR AND CREATION

The distinction between the Creator and the creation is foundational in Eastern Orthodoxy. While Western Christian theology also recognizes the difference, Eastern Christianity has freighted it with greater significance, not only for teaching about creation and its relationship to God but also for much of the rest of Orthodox doctrine. Further, where Western Christian theologizing has allowed for a variety of approaches to the unlikeness between God and the creation, some amounting almost to a denial of that unlikeness,[1] the Orthodox manifest a common emphasis that knows subtle shadings but allows for no transgression of the distinction.

[1]As an example from popular approaches to theology, whenever God is treated with human beings as another member (even if the most exalted) in a common situation (in the chain of being, of being bound by the laws of logic, etc.), the qualitative difference involved in the distinction between Creator and creation is traded for a quantitative one, and the distinction is forced into the background, where it does not function. From the realm of academic theology, Process Theology offers another example: in it, God is so enmeshed in the evolution and historical development of the creation (physical, social and cultural) that the distinction between Creator and creation is virtually obliterated.

For Orthodoxy, the importance of this distinction becomes clear as we consider our human inability to conceive of and speak appropriately about God in his relationship to the creation. In pondering creation, the Christian comes to the first words of Scripture: "In the beginning God created the heavens and the earth" (Gen 1:1 RSV). Like all the rest of Scripture, this passage assumes the existence of God. But when human beings attempt to think or speak about the existence of that God who created all things, we inevitably end up using categories bounded by our intellectual capacities—to be specific, in the question of creation, we make use of time concepts which human thought cannot transcend. Our existence as creatures is ineluctably bounded by time; we can neither conceive of nor speak about an existence unbounded by time. But time has no necessary existence; it came to be as part of God's creation. Only God has existence in and of himself, and his divine being is not bounded by time. Even so, it is not uncommon to hear someone speak about God existing "before" creation, although time itself came into existence with creation. There could be no "before" before creation. All we can responsibly say about God "before" creation is that God *is*.

Beyond specific time limitations in our thought, our discussions about God and creation often indicate that our rationality cannot escape being bounded by the existence of the creation itself. In speaking about "before" creation, we cannot properly say that there was "nothing else." To speak in that fashion already assumes the creation in which the anything "else" came into being. Again, we cannot say that there was nothing "outside of God"—speaking in this way also assumes the presence of the created. There was neither darkness nor light, neither void nor anything else "in addition to" God. Even to say that "only" God existed "before" creation is misleading; speaking in that fashion also assumes the existence of the creation with which we are familiar.

These considerations reinforce what was presented in the preceding chapter about human intellectual limitations in thinking and speaking about God. Our human words, our thought processes, our whole intellect is bounded by our creatureliness, and when we attempt to overstretch that—in this instance, by trying to speak of "eternity past" (itself an indication of our difficulty) in which God existed "before" creation—we cross the limits of our ability to understand.

Awareness of these limits to our understanding and our speech is not the private preserve of Eastern Orthodoxy; it can be found in Western Christian discussions about God and the creation too. What is distinctive about Orthodoxy is how great a stress is laid upon these limits. Western Christian theologizing affirms but does not particularly dwell on the inescapable limitations of humans to think and speak appropriately about God and creation; Orthodoxy never strays from this awareness.

Beyond this, Orthodoxy emphasizes that there is an absolute chasm between the God who created all things and the all things which he created. What God made is something *radically other* than himself. Better put, God is *radically other* than what he created. God cannot even be "placed" with created beings in a shared category of "being." Indeed, even using the same term "being" violates truth, for God and all the rest of what exists cannot be reduced to elements in a common quantification. Divine being is beyond all categories of "existence"; there was no "category" of "being" in "eternity past" into which God "fit." Divine being is *sui generis,* totally other than any understanding of being which any of his creatures can devise. Creator and creation, according to the uniform teaching of Orthodoxy, are absolutely, totally and eternally distinct. There is no "chain of being" which somehow includes both God and his creation. The Creator is totally other than his creation.

NATURE AND WILL

The distinction between Creator and creation shapes the Eastern Orthodox understanding of the relation of the creative act to God. Orthodoxy emphasizes that God created by free choice, not from some necessity of the divine nature. This choice was not, of course, in conflict with his nature, but God did not have to create in order to be God. Whatever exists does so because of divine volition, and not because of the divine nature itself.

According to Eastern Christianity, there is thus a profound difference between the relationship among the three persons of the Trinity and the relationship of God to his creation. According to the Christian faith, Father, Son and Holy Spirit are one in nature. All three persons are from eternity; there is neither before nor after with the three persons of the Trinity. The Son did not begin to be at some point in the depths of eternity, with the Spirit somehow following upon that: all three persons of the Trinity are from eternity. The triuneness of God is not the result of choice but is who God is. Triuneness belongs to God's nature; it is not the outworking of divine volition. In stark contrast, the creation is not an element of or derivative from God's nature, but is the result of God's will.

For Orthodoxy, this is of the utmost importance. There is, consequently, no "bridge" between the being of the Creator and created being.[2] While some Western

[2]Orthodoxy teaches that in the incarnation God established a bridge between humanity and deity, for the Son of God became man, uniting himself to created being. However, there was no such bridge in creation itself, and none appeared until the incarnation took place. For a consideration of the Orthodox understanding of the significance of the incarnation, see below, chap. 7.

Christian thought has argued that the "divine ideas" according to which God created the cosmos offer such a bridge for human intellect to traverse,[3] Eastern Orthodoxy argues that there is no point of contact between created natures and the divine nature in any such divine ideas. The divine thoughts that issued into creation were not "rooted in" or "part of" the divine essence; they were God's free choices which brought into existence beings radically other than himself. God's creation is not, in some sense, suffused with evidence of the "divine ideas" which give access to the mind of God and, thus, offer approach to his essence. Rather, the creation shows what God willed to create. Given this, it is not surprising to discover that Orthodoxy urges that creation is not filled with little portions of the divine, nor is the divine nature somehow diffused throughout or sprinkled within that creation in some fashion. Uniformly, Orthodoxy insists that God's nature, the divine being, is and remains distinct from the creation which he brought into being.

Thus, in creation we are not confronted with the divine nature, but with the divine will. The patterns we discern in creation do not give us access to eternal ideas in God as elements of his divine nature; rather, those patterns indicate what God freely chose to do in his act of creation. In creating, God has manifested those choices, and from the creation humans are to discern his eternal power and deity (Rom 1:20). However, those divine choices were free choices, not necessary options dictated by particulars within the divine nature.[4]

ESSENCE AND ENERGIES

While God's being remains eternally distinct from all that he created, it is also true that God himself created. This is the point at which the distinction between "essence" and "energies," discussed previously, becomes relevant in the discussion of Orthodoxy's views on the relationship of the Creator to the creation. According to Eastern Orthodoxy, God created all that is by his energies.

Creation came into being through the divine energies—which are no less God

---

[3]During the Middle Ages in Western Europe, much of scholastic theology involved arguments based on the assumption of these divine ideas and their consequent importance for human understanding of the world (since human beings were made in the image of God and, presumably, had the impress of these ideas in their own intellects). In later scholastic theology, this perspective (called "realism") was challenged by another scholastic perspective (called "nominalism") which pointed out that no one could know for certain that these divine ideas were in God's mind or, if they were, that they were imprinted on human minds. In subsequent centuries, Roman Catholic and Protestant theologians have often championed modified forms of the realist position.

[4]English versions of the New Testament frequently include the word "nature" in their renderings of Romans 1:20; however, the Greek term for nature, *ousia,* is not found in the verse. This is itself an indication of the looser way Western Christianity has of speaking about the divine nature, in comparison to the Orthodox strictures presented above.

than the divine essence. In the divine essence, God remains eternally incommunicable, incomprehensible, indescribable, ineffable. In the divine energies, however, God created the cosmos. God himself created "all things, visible and invisible," giving them existence; he did this by his energies.

In making the creation, God brought into existence that which had no previous existence: he created *ex nihilo.* The resultant creation received its existence. It did not, however, receive a necessary existence. Only God necessarily exists; the creation exists in constant dependence on him. God honored what he made by giving it genuine existence, but neither creation as a whole nor any created being is ever self-sufficient. In his energies, God upholds the creation's existence.

Thus, according to Orthodoxy, God is never distant from his creation. He is not the divine clockmaker of deist thought, contentedly observing his well-ordered handiwork functioning predictably from afar. Instead, with St. Paul, Orthodoxy affirms that "we live and move and have our being" in God (Acts 17:28). From moment to moment, God sustains his creation in existence: it depends on him for that existence. Thus, while God is utterly transcendent in his essence, he is absolutely immanent in his energies.

This does not mean, for Orthodoxy, that there are no structures in the creation, as if God were keeping a jumbled lot of creatures existent in chaotic disorder. However, the axioms of mathematics, the laws of nature and the rules of human behavior do not exist in and of themselves. God maintains them, as he does all the rest of creation—by his energies.

Thus, by his energies, God is near to his creation. In terms of his energies, he created. Via his energies, he maintains that creation. And through his energies, he communicates and has communicated with his creation. Through the divine energies, the one true God has acted to create and to reveal himself to his creation. But while God himself communicates to and relates with his creation, he does so not in his essence but in his energies—which are no less God than his essence. Thus, the grace, mercy and providence of God which Scripture praises are, for Orthodoxy, not merely effects which God has on us and the rest of his creation, but are God himself, in his energies. God thus deals in faithful love with that creation which he freely chose to create and continues to uphold, a creation that is utterly and entirely outside of himself and yet receives him unceasingly in his energies.

Eastern Orthodoxy versus Greek Philosophy

The Eastern Orthodox distinctives noted so far about God and the creation do not comport with the emphases found in ancient pagan philosophy. As discussed in chapter two, the common Western Christian attitude that Orthodoxy offers only a baptized version of uncritically assimilated pagan Greek thought is simply wrong-headed. In fact, Eastern Christianity has consciously and deliberately structured its teaching about God and creation as alternative, both to ancient Greek thought and also to early attempts to accommodate Christian teaching to ancient philosophy. The Greek church fathers who shaped the Orthodox understanding of creation were aware of what had been taught about the cosmos, both by Hellenic and Hellenistic philosophers, and by some earlier exponents of Christian teaching. However, those church fathers articulated their views about God and the creation in opposition to the regnant assumptions of ancient pagan thought. Orthodoxy has followed the lead of these fathers. This can be seen in their responses to the teaching of the Gnostics, of the great Hellenic philosophers, and of Clement of Alexandria and Origen. Further, it is manifested in the Greek patristic (and Orthodox) understanding of change in the creation.

As over against Gnosticism, a movement which sought to adapt Christian teaching to ancient pagan philosophy, the early shapers of Eastern Christian teaching emphasized that the creation around us did not arise from emanations or developments out of the divine being. The common Orthodox perspective—originally articulated by the Greek church fathers—is that the nature of all of created reality is other than the nature of God (as we have seen above). As over against any attitude that would posit a chain of being between the Creator and the creation, Orthodoxy emphasizes the radical distinction between them.

In addition, the Greek church fathers—and Orthodoxy with them—decisively repudiated a foundational element of pagan Hellenic teaching about the cosmos. In reflecting on the cosmos, the ancient Greek philosophers had pondered the significance of continuity and change, and in the face of other significant differences in teaching among themselves, they had come to a common perspective. For his part, Aristotle recognized that everything that one could experience was susceptible to change, but he urged that the cosmos itself must be eternal. While the appearances change, the matter out of which everything is formed has always existed. In that way, what appeared transitory actually had the unchanging constancy that he and most other Hellenic philosophers prized. For Plato also, what one experiences in the cosmos is constant change. However, to him, flux showed the weakness or decay of the material cosmos. According to Plato, the good and true must be eternally unchanging, unaffected by the vicissitudes of flux and time. Thus, the good and the true are not to be sought in the material cosmos; they can only be found in another realm—in the intellectual realm of pure and unchanging ideas. In the face of their opposing attitudes toward the material cosmos itself, Plato and Aristotle agreed that the unchanging had ultimate value as genuine being.

In sharp contrast to Hellenic philosophical attitudes on this question, the Greek church fathers reserved unchangeability for God alone. With those fathers, Orthodoxy affirms that only with God is there "no variation or shadow due to change" (Jas 1:17). For his creation, including any supposed "realm" of pure ideas, it is a different story. According to Orthodoxy, all that is—the cosmos which our senses can perceive and any idea we could possibly entertain—came into being through God's creative fiat. Anything and everything outside of God, sensible and intellectual alike, only began to have existence at creation—none of it is eternal.

In the late second and early third centuries, some Christian teachers tried to accommodate Christian teaching to the ancient Hellenic perspective on change and constancy—a perspective which had been adopted by Hellenistic philosophies as well. Although Clement of Alexandria and his student, Origen, had fought against Gnostic teachings, they both tried to assimilate Christian doctrine to the reigning attitude toward change and constancy. Origen's speculative proclivities found special outlet in this regard. In his doctrinal teaching, the ancient pagan philosophical demand for the unchanging profoundly affected his presentation of Christian truth. However, subsequent leaders of Eastern Christianity rejected these attempts. Indeed, the Greek church fathers developed their views on creation as deliberate counters to Origen's teaching.[5]

In diametric opposition to the Hellenic and Hellenistic views about change, and as alternative to Origen's attempted accommodation of Christian teaching to those views, the Greek church fathers taught that God made the cosmos to experience flux and change. This experience of flux is not a flaw or a fault in the creation; quite the contrary, it is the divine intention for creation. Orthodoxy has built its understanding of the cosmos on the teaching of these Greek church fathers. For Orthodoxy, the change or movement that we find in creation is a necessary, good, divinely intended given for all created natures; they are and are made to be dynamic. God made a universe of things outside of himself to be continually changing and developing.

Against ancient Hellenic and Hellenistic philosophy, Eastern Orthodoxy underlines the difference between the Creator who is eternal and his creation which is bounded by time, from beginning to end. The divine nature is eternal and un-

---

[5]John Meyendorff, *Byzantine Theology: Historical Trends and Doctrinal Themes* (New York: Fordham University Press, 1976), p. 129.

changing, but created nature is neither—nor was it meant to be. God made it not to reflect a static purity, but to engage in a constant dynamism of change and development.

THE DYNAMISM OF CREATION

God's Word brought all things into existence. According to Genesis 1, God spoke and the heavens and earth came into being and took shape in the respective days of creation. As St. John opens his gospel, he indicates that the "Word" that brought all things into being is the one who, incarnate, is known as Jesus Christ (Jn 1:1-3, 14). Eastern Orthodoxy has given special consideration to the way the apostle speaks about the Word and the creation.

The word he used for "Word" is the common Greek term *Logos.* By the time the apostle wrote, this term had been used in Hellenistic philosophizing about the cosmos,[6] but he countered a basic element of that teaching when he declared that the Logos "became flesh" (Jn 1:14)—an affirmation utterly repugnant to the philosophical perspectives of the day.[7] According to the apostle, this Logos was the one who created all that exists—including that humanity which he would later assume in the incarnation. The Logos of God brought all things into existence, and they continue to exist in and because of him: "in him was life" (Jn 1:4).

This Logos—who was "with God" and "was God" (Jn 1:1)—is the second person of the Trinity, one of the three who share the divine essence. According to Orthodoxy, in the divine energies this Logos created the cosmos. He thus brought into existence all that exists, creating beings totally other than the divine being. But these beings were not created to be estranged from God, although they would be totally other than God. Rather, they were formed to enjoy communion with God. According to Orthodoxy, this communion with God is not some "spiritual" or "religious" addition to created reality; it expresses the deepest meaning of creation. Deeply implanted within all that the Logos created is a dynamism that calls every nature, and each individual that embodies every nature, toward God.

The term used for this Godward-directedness is also *logos* (plural, *logoi*)—which points out the close relationship, in the divine energies, of the Creator to his cre-

---

[6]The Stoics had spoken of a *Spermatikos Logos,* a "germinating word," which had shaped the material cosmos into the various forms to be found in it.

[7]Both Hellenic and Hellenistic thought posited a radical distinction between the material and the immaterial realms; to affirm that the eternal immaterial had taken on the material was preposterous, on the bases of ancient philosophical thought. Even the Stoics, who could allow that the *Spermatikos Logos* had shaped the cosmos, could not entertain the idea that that Logos would ever assume materiality and, in the words of the apostle, "*become* flesh."

ation. This term had also been used in Hellenistic philosophizing about the cosmos, but Eastern Christian teaching transformed its meaning.[8] According to Orthodoxy, the creaturely *logos* expresses what each created nature ultimately is and is more fully to become in God's creative intention. Thus, the creaturely *logoi* are the thoughts of God for and about the various created natures—the thoughts according to which he chose to create them. The Logos expressed God's will for creation in what he made; the Logos thus implanted the appropriate *logos* in each of the distinct created natures. This did not result in an "essential" or "natural" connection of any creaturely *logos* to its Creator: the divine Logos created all things by the divine energies, not out of the divine nature. Even so, by the act of creating, the Logos expressed the divine will for each created nature and implanted that will deep within it, and every individual that embodies each of those natures receives it. There is a distinctive *logos* for trees, flowers, dogs and human beings, and each individual representative of each created nature has that *logos* within himself, herself or itself. This divinely implanted *logos* defines each created nature and each individual creature, and this *logos* indicates what the ultimate purpose of that individual ought to be. This *logos* is God's will for that created nature and his call to each individual that has that nature. Thus, the *logos* is both gift and vocation. The *logos* of each creature implies and requires movement and development for that creature as God's design for it.

The dynamism of creation is purposive: it intends a development toward greater communion with God—to his glory and the benefit of the creature. This development toward him, different as it would be for the various created natures, is God's will for all of these natures. From the perspective of the various created natures (that is, from what is in them), this *logos* entails its own distinctive "energy" in which that creature is to live out or live up to its divinely implanted *logos*. As the divine nature acts by its energies, so too created natures express themselves by their energies.

As the divine Word, the Logos expresses who God is. As the one through whom the Father created all things, the Logos expresses the divine love and delight in the creation he made. In his energies, God made the creation, and he made it for fellowship with himself in his energies. Dependent on God for existence, the creation was to turn to God for communion with him, a communion appropriate to each of the respective created natures.

---

[8]In Stoic teaching, *logoi* referred to the eternal essences which lay behind what one finds in the various forms found in the cosmos. As will be readily understood from the presentation in this chapter, such an understanding could not be acceptable to Orthodox thought. The Greek church fathers imparted quite a different connotation to the term, and Orthodoxy has followed their usage and understanding.

Thus, the creation was not made to be a static entity, glorifying God in its unchanging beauty. Instead, it was to be dynamic, developing as it passed through time in an increasing communion with God in his divine energies. Flux and change are not, thus, evidence of decay or weakness in the cosmos; indeed, they are what God intended for creation. Without them, creation would not have been good.

THE GOODNESS OF CREATION

The creation was good, as Genesis 1 repeatedly informs us. Its goodness did not exclude or merely tolerate the materiality of the creation, as would have been the case from the perspectives of ancient Hellenic and Hellenistic philosophies. Instead, the goodness of the creation assumes the materiality of that creation. God made matter, and he declared it good. According to Eastern Orthodoxy, this perspective is fundamental for Christian thought. When sin intrudes upon God's creation in due course, the fault does not lie in the material realm, but in Adam's spiritual unfaithfulness, which misuses the material cosmos. Further, for Orthodoxy, spirituality does not entail escape from the material world to ethereal realms of immaterial bliss, as in Plato's yearning to be rid of the prison house of the body through death, in order to arise to a privileged status of disembodied existence. The Christian hope is the resurrection of the body to life eternal in the new heavens and new earth. A proper perspective on the goodness of the creation must include a ringing affirmation of the material cosmos, according to Orthodoxy.

Another aspect of the goodness of creation was that it was in conformity to God's intention: it certainly could not have been good otherwise. However, this initial goodness was not the goodness of ultimate development and perfection. Further development of creation was intended by God and expected. Created reality was not made perfect in the sense of being at its final goal; it still had to develop in the direction of ultimate perfection. The original creation was itself the beginning realization of the full embodiment of God's purpose for creation. Because of that, God said at the conclusion of the work of creation that it was "very good" (Gen 1:31).

According to Orthodox understandings, the goal of that development was communion with God, in keeping with the intended possibilities of each created nature. Eastern Christian thought has given a special term to that ultimate goal toward which each created nature is driven by its *logos*: that purpose or goal is called the *skopos* (plural, *skopoi*). The *skopos* of each created nature, and of all the individuals in which that created nature is actualized, is not contemplation of the divine essence, which will always remain inaccessible to all creatures. Rather, the *skopos* of each created nature is communion in the divine energies; that is, each created nature is increasingly to dwell in and be transformed through communion with God.[9] While this communion would be differentiated according to the respective created natures, and while those differences would continue even in the further development of creation, all of creation was impelled toward communion with God. In this way, all creation glorifies God and praises him. Thus, from an Orthodox perspective, the rocks, the mountains, the trees and the rivers do praise God and give glory to him. Biblical statements to this effect in the psalter and elsewhere are not exaggerated metaphors but expressions of truth, the truth intended and secured by God in creation.

At this point, it is worth noting that in the Orthodox understanding of creation there is no dualism between nature and grace. Nature does not exist as a time- and matter-bound realm, above which a realm of immaterial grace is to be understood, and from which God intervenes for spiritual purposes.[10] According to Orthodoxy, there is no such supratemporal, immaterial realm of grace. God himself, in his energies, is ever immanent in his creation. Thus, nature is the abode of grace, and grace suffuses nature.

In that divine grace, all created natures were to live up to their respective *logoi* and attain their appointed *skopoi* of communion with God. In its development toward that goal, every created nature and every individual always would depend on God and live by his grace. This dependence on divine grace was not a remedial provision made by God in view of the fall into sin; rather, this was the case for all created natures in God's good creation. While this was true of the entire original creation, it was to find its highest expression in humanity, created in the image of God.[11] From the first moment of creation, all that God made was de-

---

[9]This communion will include contemplation of the economy of salvation, the mystery of God and the wonder of divine love—in the Liturgy of St. John Chrysostom, used in Orthodox churches on most Sundays during the church year, God is addressed twelve times as "Lover of humanity." However, as noted above, this is not an attempt to contemplate *the divine essence,* which will be forever "beyond" all creatures, even in the final state.

[10]In much Western Christian thought, the realms of nature and grace are viewed as distinct. This pattern, found in the medieval scholastics, attained lasting significance in the form given it by St. Thomas Aquinas and ultimately became the approved orientation on the question for Roman Catholic thinkers. Even though Protestants do not accept Thomas Aquinas as a necessary authority, the same basic perspective is also commonly found among them. The prevalence of this perspective can be appreciated by recognizing that the term *supernatural,* used commonly among Protestants to describe God's special works for salvation or in answer to prayer, assumes this distinction.

[11]We will not give special attention here to the creation of human beings, or to their fall into sin; those questions are dealt with in chap. 6 below.

pendent on the divine energies; that situation has not changed because of the sin of Adam and Eve.

THE IMPACT OF THE FALL

The fall of our first parents into sin broke the harmony of God's good creation. Human sin introduced more than disruption, though, with all its unfortunate consequences. The Fall was a cosmic catastrophe. The whole creation suffers now because of humankind's sin. As St. Paul puts it, in the era after the Fall, "the whole creation has been groaning" (Rom 8:22). Why is this? According to Eastern Orthodoxy, the cosmos groans because the "natural energies" which conform to the divine plan (that is, the *logoi*) are in struggle with the destructive forces of death unleashed in God's good creation by human sin. Desiring in its respective *logoi* to serve the Creator faithfully, the creation suffers because of the defaulted leadership of Adam and Eve and the host of their progeny. Without the faithful superintendence of the divine image-bearers, the rest of the creation has not only lost its appointed leadership but now endures the effects of human sin.

All this occurred because Adam—to whom God entrusted control over his creation—turned away from his *logos,* which was to subject himself to God. In the midst of God's good creation, however, Adam chose to subject himself to the creation[12] rather than to God. In so doing, Adam bound himself to mere creation, which has no absolute existence in itself. Thus, Adam chose death rather than life, with consequences for the whole of creation. That creation now groans, but the Christian faith promises the assured hope for the groaning cosmos that "the creation itself will be set free from its bondage to decay and will obtain the freedom of the glory of the children of God" (Rom 8:21). The bonds of sin and death will ultimately be broken, both for the children of God and for the rest of the creation, and all will everlastingly live up to their respective *logoi* and attain their *skopoi.* God's will *will* be done, in heaven and on earth—in the entire creation he has made—because he himself has entered history to redirect it to himself.

The Word became flesh (Jn 1:14); the incarnate Logos came as "the last Adam" (1 Cor 15:45; Rom 5:12-21). He constantly and faithfully turned toward God, which was, as true man, his *logos.* As the last Adam, he subjected himself freely to death, which had no claim upon him. By his resurrection, he has broken the power of death, has liberated humanity from it, and now leads his church and the rest of

---

[12]Within Orthodoxy, there have been differences of opinion as to whether this subjection was to the suggestion of the serpent or to the supposed potential of the fruit. In either case, Adam subjected himself to creation rather than to his Creator.

creation toward the full realization of their *skopoi,* their original created purposes—namely, communion with God. Thus, in Christ, God's original intended purpose is achieved. All creation is reclaimed through the work of the Redeemer. He is now "making all things new" (Rev 21:5), leading that creation toward its ultimate goal, the new heavens and the new earth, where righteousness dwells, where all of creation communes faithfully and fully with the divine energies.

Concluding Observations

This Eastern Orthodox understanding of creation and of its relationship to the Creator offers Western Christians intriguing perspectives on how creation was good, how it was to develop and how the redemption of Christ relates to the creation. Eastern Christian teaching reminds us of the tremendous gulf between the Creator and his creation, emphasizing his utter transcendence in powerful fashion. At the same time, it points out the Creator's absolute immanence in and with his creation in its every aspect, from the beginning of creation, through all the vicissitudes of time and all development and change, and unto the full manifestation of the new heavens and the new earth. There is much in the Eastern Orthodox understanding of the relationship of the Creator and his creation that can enrich our Western Christian perspectives about God and his relationship to the creation of which we are part and in which we live.

In addition to this general stimulation, the distinctive Orthodox perspectives presented in this chapter open up possibilities for helping Western Christians in some of the difficulties we encounter in our discussion of the relationship of the Creator and the creation. There are doubtless several ways in which these Orthodox distinctives might offer such assistance. The three suggestions that follow are meant to be suggestive, not exhaustive, of the Orthodox resources in this regard.

For one thing, the Orthodox emphasis on our human inability to conceive of and speak about God and creation together could help us escape the sometimes acrimonious "creation versus evolution" arguments that so often have bedeviled reflection on the creation among Western Christians over the last century or so. From the perspectives of Orthodoxy, the first chapters of Genesis do not *explain* creation. Creation was God's act, and no amount of human intellectual ingenuity could ever account for it, nor any human words capture it. The terse affirmations made in Genesis 1–2 do not amount to explanations or even descriptions, from an Orthodox perspective; they confront us with the declaration that all that is came from God. In presenting the entire universe as God's creative handiwork, Orthodoxy excludes all thought of an evolutionary process operating outside of God, to be sure. Equally, it precludes any arrogant claim to comprehend from the first chapters of Genesis how God brought everything into existence. What Scripture presents is the declaration that God made all that is, without any attempt to clarify how all came into being. The opening chapters of Genesis present what must be wondered at, not what can be fathomed. They offer stimulation for common praise by all those who believe in him, not material with which we should browbeat fellow believers whose ideas about the way in which God may have accomplished that work differ from ours.

Further, even if God had explained it to us, could we have understood it? What language could God borrow to explain to mere creatures the act of creation so that we could comprehend it? If his ways and thoughts are beyond ours (Is 55:8-9), should we not offer humble praise for his creation and what he has told us about it, rather than fighting among ourselves as to who best comprehends how God brought all things into existence? Is the beginning of Scripture intended to satisfy our intellectual curiosity about "how," or is it to invite us to celebrate "what" and "who"? Western Christians could learn a bit more humility in speaking about creation and God from their brothers and sisters in Eastern Orthodoxy—and perhaps, as a result, learn better how to appreciate our brothers and sisters in Western Christianity too.

As a second point, the Orthodox distinctives we have considered in this chapter invite us to deepen our recognition of the chasm that separates all of creation—even human beings—from God. Too often in Western Christian thinking, God has become another member in some category of thought—although the most exalted member, to be sure. Whether it is in a chain of being or as one bound by some laws (of logic, morality or whatever), we too often subsume God into a category with creatures. He is not bound by what binds us. Were we to keep that constantly in mind, we would unquestionably speak more humbly about him and avoid many problems provoked by our own careless thought. This would not result in an unpredictable tyrant being unleashed in the realm of our discussions: Orthodoxy reminds us that the one who is absolutely distinct from us is ever near us in an immanence we cannot begin to fathom. We live and move and have our being in him—the one who sustains us in every moment because of his love for his creation. Rather than another member to include in sophisticated discussion and subject to our theodicies, God is our Creator who loves us and calls us unto himself.

As a final point, is it not spiritually challenging and theologically stimulating to think, with Orthodoxy, that turning to God is more than a religious option for creation, human beings included? How might it change our attitudes—in verbal witness to the gospel message, in addressing contemporary social and ethical problems, in responding to the needs of others and in numerous other regards—to begin our thoughts with the conviction that we and all the rest of creation are made for communion with God? That is where our sisters and brothers in Eastern Orthodoxy begin—we could do far worse than to follow their lead.

6

HUMANITY AS CREATED AND FALLEN

IN SETTING FORTH ITS UNDERSTANDING OF HUMANITY, Eastern Orthodoxy has relied on the same biblical information used by Western Christianity—preeminently Genesis 1–3, with subsequent scriptural instruction about what God originally intended for human beings and about what has happened to them since their creation. Not surprisingly, both segments of Christendom have given considerable attention to the place of humanity within the story of creation and to what transpired in and because of the fall of our first parents. Within Orthodoxy, reflection and teaching have led to perspectives that, in some significant regards, differ profoundly from perspectives commonly held within Western Christianity. These differences can be found in Orthodoxy's views both on humanity as created and on humanity as fallen.

AS CREATED

Eastern Christian doctrine about humanity as created was shaped by the common elements of teaching on the issue as found in the Greek church fathers of the first few centuries. In the seventh century, St. Maximus Confessor sought to set forth the consensus in teaching and connections in thought in the teaching of the earlier church fathers.[1] In so doing, he ended up leaving his own distinctive mark on that teaching. One of the areas in which this is unmistakable is his presentation of patristic teaching on creation, to which this chapter is indebted. He set forth the four main elements outlined below. While some of the church fathers included additional elements beyond them, and while contemporary Orthodox authors might

---

[1]During the eighth century, St. John of Damascus continued this endeavor, building on the prior work of St. Maximus. These efforts were so well received that the Damascene's *The Orthodox Faith* continued to serve for more than a millennium as the best presentation of Orthodox teaching.

suggest the value of additional considerations beyond these four shared patristic emphases, any such additional teachings and suggestions have not commanded universal assent among Eastern Christians. The following four points have commanded such assent; they constitute the common teaching of Eastern Christianity on humankind as created by God. Not surprisingly, each of the points works together with the others, making for a well-integrated doctrinal perspective on humanity as created.

The human being as microcosm. Eastern Orthodoxy emphasizes that the human being, as originally created, was a microcosm of the whole of created reality. On the one hand, this understanding builds on the Nicene-Constantinopolitan Creed's affirmation that God created "heaven and earth, and all things visible and invisible"; on the other, it accepts the ancient insight that there is an undeniable division within reality between what belongs to the realm of the senses and what belongs to the immaterial realm. Thus, as Orthodoxy explains, the creation God brought into being exists on two levels: there is the intellectual or spiritual or nonmaterial realm, and there is also the material, physical, tangible or bodily realm. Angels and spirits belong in the first realm, as does any idea or thought that reason can produce. In the second belong the stars, planets, vegetable and animal life—all the material stuff found in creation. For Orthodoxy, these two realms are distinct and operate on different bases. However, as against the common teachings of ancient pagan philosophy, they are not in opposition to each other in some kind of dualism of matter and spirit. They are the two parts of the creation God brought into being.

According to Orthodox teaching, everything in creation belongs to either one or the other of these two realms, *except humanity.* Only human beings were created with both spiritual and material components. Thus, only human beings partake of both realms of creation. Because of this, according to Orthodoxy, humanity is a microcosm—the whole of creation in small, the unique partaker of both realms.

Nothing else in all creation shares this privilege: the most powerful beast of the jungle is unequipped to function in the intellectual realm, and angels experience the privilege of the spiritual or intellectual realm but cannot partake of the material or physical one. In being both formed out of the dust of the ground and also receiving spiritual/intellectual life by the breath of God (Gen 2:7), human beings came to share in both realms. In this, according to Orthodox teaching, humanity is greatly privileged. By God's creative intention, human beings—and only human beings—are microcosms of the whole of creation.

Human beings participate in both realms at once, and in both equally. There is in Eastern Christian thought no Platonic preference for or exaltation of the intellectual or noetic at the expense of the bodily or the material. Rather, a human being is seen as a whole, composed of both the bodily or material and the spiritual or immaterial together. That is how God created humanity, and only human beings participate in both realms. This privilege gives human beings a distinct, unique and exalted position within the whole of creation. Indeed, for Orthodox thought, this raises humankind above the status of angels, who—however exalted in their spiritual/intellectual situation—nevertheless participate in only one of the realms of creation.[2] Humanity was greatly honored by being the sole microcosm of all of creation, for everything in creation was thus summed up in humanity, according to Orthodox teaching. Thus, human beings were created to be, in their faithful integrity before their Creator, the ones in whom the divergent realms of creation held together.

The human being as mediator. Beyond this, humankind was privileged in yet another way by its Creator: humankind was created to serve as mediator within creation. The divine command to be fruitful, multiply, fill the earth, subdue it and have dominion over it (Gen 1:28) entailed humanity's special role for and with the rest of creation. Sometimes called the "cultural mandate" in Western Christianity, this divine command set humanity in the role of mediator in the midst of creation. Human beings were to work with the world and offer it back to God for his praise. Human beings were thus to serve in a "natural priesthood,"[3] that is, they were so to deal with the rest of creation that all created things would be enabled better to live up to their various *logoi* and thus commune with God.

Given the dynamism of creation, as discussed in chapter five, humanity's mediatorial activities within it would have entailed bringing forth its full potentiality, developing the possibilities within the whole of creation to the glory of God. Almost everything that we take for granted in life had yet to be developed under human dominion and culture: the Garden of Eden offered Adam and Even neither schools nor tools, neither encyclopedias nor scientific understanding, neither music nor art, neither traffic regulations nor farmers' markets. God put everything at their disposal, but our first parents—and all those who were to descend from them—were to serve God by developing the wherewithal of creation, in all its multitudinous possibilities in both the material and the intellectual realms. This

---

[2]This can be seen via a comparison of what St. John of Damascus teaches about angels and human beings; cf. *The Orthodox Faith* 2.3 and 2.12.

[3]The Romanian Orthodox theologian Dumitru Staniloae uses this designation in his (not yet translated into English) *Teologia Dogmatica orthodoxa,* 3 vols. (Bucharest: Editura Institutulni Bibic si de Misiune, 1978), 2:232.

immense task was their divine calling, a calling to serve God and the rest of creation by living up to the role of mediator within creation.

As mediator within creation, humankind was to help each creature live up to its *logos* and attain the *skopos* held forth for it in God's creation. All of creation was good in God's eyes (Gen 1:31). As we have seen, that goodness did not preclude but rather assumed further development and change into a fuller manifestation of God's creative intention for everything within creation—including humanity—and for all of creation as a whole. This was to occur through human labors: human beings were to lead all of creation to become all that God intended it to be. This was humankind's responsibility as God's vice regents on earth. For itself, humanity was also to grow in the fulfillment of its *logos,* to seek its *skopos* and to attain that fullness of communion which was held forth for humanity as God's faithful servants.

The human being as personal being. The third distinctive element in Orthodoxy's understanding of humanity as created is the emphasis on humankind as personal beings. All Christians recognize, of course, that Adam and Eve were persons, but Eastern Christianity has especially emphasized the personhood of the original man and woman. According to Orthodoxy, God had a special purpose in this: human beings were created as persons to enjoy communion with the three persons of the Trinity. Privileged as microcosm, called to be mediator, human beings were especially blessed by being made as persons themselves to experience intimacy with the divine persons of Father, Son and Holy Spirit. Exalted as the angels were by being in the divine presence, they were nevertheless unable to enjoy the fullness of intimacy with God as persons; only humankind held this unique privilege. Adam and Eve were personal beings, distinguishable from each other. Their descendants were to continue in this privilege, knowing both communion with the three persons of God and with the distinct persons of other human beings.

While created as persons, however, humankind was not created to be individuals, separate from each other or from God; that is, human beings neither were nor were intended to be autonomous or self-sufficient, islands unto themselves. Human beings were made by God for social interaction with other human beings; they were made especially for communion with God. The human *logos* or natural dynamic was toward God; humankind, as created, tended spontaneously toward God, and also toward other human beings. The call to love God with all one's heart, soul, strength and mind, and to love one's neighbor as oneself (Mt 22:37-39) expresses the *logos* with which God created human beings. Created as persons, humankind was to develop relationships, structures for society, and all that would be necessary for human beings to interact with each other, God and the rest of creation in ways that were rooted in an all-encompassing love.

Even so, God created humanity with both the responsibility and the freedom to continue to decide for communion with God and with others, or to choose against it. Orthodoxy stresses that, as persons, human beings were created by God with personal will. Their *natural* will was directed toward God in love and, in God, toward all other human beings (and, indeed, toward the totality of creation). However, Orthodox teaching emphasizes that God did not intend for human beings to live up to this as machines. Rather, God created human beings as persons, freely able (and responsible) to choose to love God and others, but also freely able to choose otherwise. Following St. Maximus Confessor's articulation, Orthodoxy styles this *personal* will as the *gnomic* will—the will in which each human being either follows or repudiates his or her *natural* will to turn toward God. Every human being is responsible to use that personal will to turn toward God—who leaves each person with the freedom to choose to do so or not to do so. Thus, Adam had a "free will": by nature and by the will which resides in human nature, he tended toward God, but in his personal or gnomic will, Adam had the freedom to choose whether to follow his *logos* or not.

The human being as image of God. The final element in Orthodoxy's understanding of humanity as created deals with the understanding of what it means for humankind to have been made "in God's image." Within Christendom at large, this biblical teaching (Gen 1:27) has spawned considerable discussion. It received a great amount of attention in ancient Christianity, in both the East and the West. Since then, Western Christianity has continued to ask the question where, specifically, the image of God might reside in human beings[4] and whether it has continued in humankind after the fall of our first parents into sin.[5]

In contrast, Orthodoxy has usually steered away from attempts to try to locate or pinpoint where the divine image resides in human beings. Early on, the Greek church fathers came to the conclusion that such a quest was not the way to discover how humanity is image of God.[6] Their hesitation to ask this question has

[4]The most common answers in Western Christianity have urged that the image is found in the intellect, the ability to choose freely, in righteousness or in some combination of these.

[5]Within Roman Catholicism, the standard perspective has been that the image of God remained unaffected by the fall into sin; by contrast, classic Lutheranism has taught that the image of God was lost in the fall; Reformed Protestantism has urged that the image was damaged but not totally eradicated by the Fall. Within each of these traditions, there have been teachers who have urged various refinements or modifications of the received perspective as well.

[6]Vladimir Lossky, *The Mystical Theology of the Eastern Church* (Crestwood, N.Y.: St. Vladimir's Seminary Press, 1976), pp. 115-16.

become the common approach within Eastern Christianity. However, this has not meant that Orthodoxy has neglected to consider what it means that human beings were made in the image of God. Quite the contrary, Eastern Christianity teaches that this image is essential to human existence; no one can be a human being without also having the image of God.

What, then, is involved in the image of God, according to Orthodoxy? The answer may at first appear simplistic, even a way of avoiding the question. However, on further reflection, that answer suggests a humble profundity that is challenging. According to Eastern Christian teaching, the *imago Dei* is whatever and all that distinguishes humankind from all the rest of creation. This, in its entirety, constitutes the image of God in humanity, for it is the image of God that distinguishes humanity from everything else in creation, nothing of which bears that image. In the Orthodox understanding, God has thus even more highly exalted humanity than he did in making humankind the sole microcosm, for God has made human beings in his own image. Humankind not only bears the imprint of both realms of creation; human beings also bear the image of the Creator.

Thus, Orthodoxy refuses to limit the *imago Dei* to the immaterial parts of humankind. While Eastern Christianity recognizes that God is spirit (Jn 4:24) and has no body, that has not led to any disparagement of either the physical portion of creation or to the denigration of human materiality in favor of some disembodied component of a human being (which would be, therefore, somehow more appropriately related to God). Instead, Orthodoxy affirms that God made human beings body and soul, and that the integrality of the human being as God's creation entails that we acknowledge the human being is God's image-bearer.[7]

Thus, the body is included in the concept of the image, not as a "part" of the image, but as essential to the particular creation which God blessed with the privilege of bearing his image. According to Orthodoxy, the physical body of humans is a visible form that uniquely matches the invisible divine glory (although God has no body). In this lies the dignity of the body in biblical thought: the body in its physical outwardness is as much the "person" as are the inward and intangible constituents of human personhood. As persons formed for communion with God, men and women—in both body and soul, and in the totality of their beings as persons—bear God's image. This is a given for humanity, according to Orthodoxy.

This understanding of humankind as image of God does not, however, view the image as a static condition, true of human beings in the abstract. As we have

---

[7]This is closer to the Hebrew concept of the whole human person as *nephesh* than is the Greek notion of *psyche*, which tends to emphasize only the immaterial self.

seen in the Orthodox understanding of creation, all creation is suffused with a dynamism that energizes it and impels it to move toward God's intended purposes. The image of God in humankind partakes of this dynamism as well: while human beings bear the *image* of God through God's creative act, they are to acquire *likeness* to God through communion with and living unto him.

Thus, Eastern Christian interpretation of the divine counsel regarding the creation of humankind almost always distinguishes the *image* of God from *likeness* to God (Gen 1:26): the former is gift; the latter is calling. Thus, for the Orthodox, image and likeness are not parallel terms. Rather, humanity has received the image of God and, through communion with God and growing in his grace, is to acquire likeness to God. Each human person bears God's image and is to grow into God's likeness. This was God's calling to Adam and Eve and, through them, to all those who would descend from them. By walking in God's ways, Adam and Eve, together with their descendants after them, would become ever more like God; acting in faithful obedience to him, out of love for him, they would have increasingly acquired likeness to him who is holy, righteous, love, glorious and eternal. Without ceasing to be creatures, they would have become more and more like the Creator. They would have become ever more fully holy, righteous, loving, glorious, and they would have received life everlasting in communion with God.

Our first parents bore the image of God and were to become ever more like him, receiving eternal life in their faithfulness to him. This not only would have been their privilege, but that of all their descendants as well. That, however, was not the way things turned out.

AS FALLEN

The four emphases set forth above reflect Eastern Orthodoxy's understanding of humanity as created. What does Eastern Christianity say about humanity as fallen? In this, too, Orthodoxy has taken its own path within Christendom. Building on the same biblical revelation studied by Western Christianity, Eastern Christianity has articulated perspectives that are in several regards significantly different from—at times, even opposed to—those found in the Christian West. And yet those Orthodox approaches are legitimate interpretations of biblical revelation. Moreover, they mesh with the other elements of Orthodox teachings about God, creation, humanity and salvation. There are six elements involved in the Eastern Christian consensus concerning fallen humanity.

The original sin. Adam and Eve were formed as persons for communion with God. They naturally tended toward that communion in their human *logoi,* but they had the freedom as personal beings to continue to turn toward God or to choose to do otherwise. They were called to live out of, with and for God. They were to acquire likeness to God through divine grace, by communing faithfully with God and relying on him at all times, in everything—including the path toward ultimate likeness to God. Surrounded by the bounty of the Garden of Eden, commanded by God to abstain from the fruit of only one tree in the garden, Adam and Eve had neither example of nor excuse for looking elsewhere than to the way God had laid out for them to follow. Even so, as persons they had the option of choosing another path, and that is precisely what the serpent invited and enticed them to do.

According to the Orthodox understanding of what transpired in the temptation of our first parents, the serpent offered a shortcut to the goal Adam and Eve were to achieve. He offered them another way to be "like God" (Gen 3:5)—namely, eating the very fruit God had forbidden to them. The temptation they faced did not invite them entirely to abandon God's purpose for them; indeed, it set the same purpose before them. However, the alternative path offered by the serpent involved turning from God and the faithful communion with him which they were called to practice. Thus, from an Orthodox perspective, the serpent's temptation was especially insidious: he offered the inexperienced another simpler way to achieve the goal God had for them. Thus, the poisonous denial of God's veracity ("You will not die" [Gen 3:4]) and of his generosity ("for God knows that when you eat of it your eyes will be opened" [Gen 3:5]) was disguised with the honey of an easier route to God's intended goal for humanity ("you will be like God" [Gen 3:5]).

However, the path God had set before Adam and Eve involved unceasing communion with God, so that they could attain the goal of likeness to God. In this communion they would love God and depend on his love toward them. In taking and eating the forbidden fruit, Adam and Eve chose instead to become "like God" by a different path. In so doing, they freely chose to disobey the divine command, "going their own way." Thus, Adam and Eve violated the communion they had previously known with God and rebelled against their Creator.

In this tragic original sin at the beginning of human history, our first parents traded their dominion over all the rest of creation, under God, for submission to that creation, instead of to God. In yielding to the suggestion of the serpent, Adam and Eve were led by something in creation, rather than leading it. In following the word of the tempter, Adam and Eve foolishly expected to acquire likeness to God by disobedience to God and eating willfully that which God had forbidden. The folly is manifest further in that Adam and Eve thus expected to receive from the creature that which could be received only from the Creator. Indeed, they turned from the Creator to the creature and exchanged the glory of God for that of a creature (Rom 1:23). In this original sin, Adam and Eve turned from reliance on God to reliance on the creation to attain the development they were to pursue. In so doing, however, our first parents turned to that which has no ultimate life in itself—the creation which depends on God for its existence. They thus forfeited life.

Death as consequence. The consequence for Adam and Eve, and for humanity descended from them, was the death of which God had warned them when he forbade them to eat of the tree of the knowledge of good and evil (Gen 2:17). Western Christian teaching commonly speaks of God's curse because of human sin. However, according to Eastern Orthodoxy, what befell Adam and Eve was less curse than consequence. While the serpent was cursed (Gen 3:14-15), and the ground was cursed because of human disobedience (Gen 3:17-19), God did not place a curse upon humankind.[8] To be sure, our first parents were punished in what befell them because of their sin, and God did expel them from the Garden of Eden (Gen 3:22-24). However, the emphasis in Genesis 3 is not on curse but on grace to the undeserving. God promised alleviation of the consequences of their death-bringing choice: they would still have children (Gen 3:16) and would be able, through heavy toil, to provide for them (Gen 3:17-19). Even though they would die (Gen 3:19), God would not leave his image-bearers in the serpent's thralldom: God promised a deliverer who would ultimately destroy the work of the serpent (Gen 3:15).

Without in any way minimizing the horrendous effects of the original sin—for Adam and Eve themselves, their descendants and the rest of creation—Orthodoxy emphasizes the love of God for humanity in his response to that sin. Death came upon Adam and Eve, not so much as curse but as consequence of turning from him who alone is life to that which has no life in itself. Thus, according to Eastern Christian teaching, death was the result of turning away from him who is life. In so choosing, Adam and Eve chose against the *logos* of human nature, which naturally moves toward God, and thus set their feet and the feet of their descendants on a path which—moving away from him—inevitably leads to death.[9] Mortality

---

[8]In presenting God's response to human sin, St. Irenaeus of Lyons pointed out that the curse fell on the ground and on the serpent, but that "God pronounced no curse upon Adam" (*Against Heresies* 3.23.3).

[9]Thus St. Athanasius urged: "Since they rejected things eternal and, by the devil's counsel, turned to the things of corruption, humankind became the cause of their own corruption in death" (*On the Incarnation of the Word* 5.1).

has befallen humanity; God's warning about the result of eating the forbidden fruit (Gen 2:16-17) was shown to be true.

Subsequent humankind, descended from and in solidarity with Adam (Rom 5:12, 15, 17), now must die as well. Orthodoxy contends that humanity suffers, ever since Adam and Eve, from the "cosmic disease" of death: we have all caught it from Adam. Mortality came to reign among those created for life, for our first parents turned from life to that which has no life—that is, they turned to death, and all their descendants turned with and in imitation of them.

The question of guilt. The sin of our first parents brought death upon them and upon subsequent humanity, descended from them. By yielding themselves to that which has no life in itself, Adam and Eve turned to death, and death has enslaved them and all their descendants. St. Paul emphasized that sin came into the world through Adam, that death entered through that sin, and that death has spread to all humanity descended from Adam (Rom 5:12). Because of all this, all subsequent humanity dies—indeed, death has dominion over humankind because of Adam's sin (Rom 5:15, 17).

Does this render subsequent humanity guilty of Adam's sin? Is Adam's transgression imputed to his descendants? That is, do human beings now bear the guilt of Adam's sin? Western Christian teaching responds affirmatively to those questions; while there are differences of emphasis and explanation of the guilt inherited from Adam, Western Christianity shares the general conviction that God has imputed the sin of Adam to all his descendants and that they all are guilty of that sin. In Eastern Christian teaching, however, these questions receive a negative answer. According to Orthodoxy, the human race does not share in or inherit the guilt of Adam's sin, although it unquestionably suffers the effects of that sin. There is, thus, no imputation of Adam's sin to his descendants. This idea requires some explanation.

In Eastern Orthodox teaching, guilt before God depends on one's own sin; put another way, no one can be guilty of another's sin. One might suffer the consequences of another person's sin—through family ties, friendships or some other form of interpersonal connection. However, Orthodoxy teaches that God does not hold us guilty of someone else's sin. Thus, while all humankind since Adam and Eve suffer the death-bringing consequences of their sin, no one else but Adam and Eve are guilty of their original sin. Nevertheless, we have been profoundly affected by it. An example might clarify this somewhat: if the parents in a family decide to move from a farm to the city, or from one country to another, the entire family is affected by that decision. The little children in the family, living at the time of the decision or born subsequently, will be affected by that decision, but no one would give them either the credit or the blame for that decision. Similarly, Adam and Eve made their horrendous choice in the Garden of Eden; the guilt is theirs alone, but the effects extend to all their progeny. According to Orthodoxy, no one inherits Adam's guilt.

The question of corruption. A further question arises: if the fall of Adam and Eve did not result in guilt for their descendants, did that original sin result in corruption for humanity? Again, Western Christianity answers in the affirmative: corruption came upon all humankind because of Adam and Eve's transgression in the Garden of Eden. Eastern Christian thought, from its earliest beginnings, has taught that corruption has been transmitted to subsequent humanity from that original sin. That corruption, however, is differently construed than it is in Western Christian thought.

Orthodoxy recognizes and argues that physical corruption—that is, death and all that leads up to it—is passed on to us from Adam and Eve. We have all caught the "cosmic disease" of death from them. Thus, corruption has passed, in that regard, to the descendants of the first couple. Eastern Christianity says as well that human beings are the products of and are influenced by the accumulated history of humanity's subsequent failures to turn to God. Therefore, since culture, civilization, society and all things around us have been corrupted, we are inescapably surrounded by corruption and, inevitably, influenced by it. Bad patterns, evil examples and the sinful milieu in which human beings find themselves shape them and predispose them to sin. In this manner, humans imbibe wrong attitudes and learn to choose wrongly. In this regard, too, subsequent humanity has suffered corruption because of the sin of our first parents.

Orthodoxy posits another element in the corruption transmitted to subsequent humanity through Adam's sin; this element is not found in Western Christian teaching on the subject. According to Eastern Christianity, the relationship between sin and death is not only a work/wages one (Rom 6:23): death also *leads* human beings to sin. By this, Eastern Christian teaching intends "death" in a broad sense—not only actual death itself but the fleeting transitoriness of life in all its ramifications that has descended upon us with and because of sin. Being enmeshed, engulfed and immersed in an existence that bears every indication of being limited and ending in frustration, disappointment and death is a heavy burden for humanity. In that awful situation introduced by Adam's sin, human beings opt for what may be temporarily satisfying rather than what would be conducive to everlasting life with God, in communion with him. That is, human beings sin because of death (Rom 5:12).[10] The corruption that surrounds and pervades human life thus draws human beings into sin.

The question of depravity. In Western Christian teaching, one of the horrendous aspects of the corruption that humanity has inherited from Adam is the depravity of human nature. Among different groups of Western Christians are wide differences about the extent and impact of that depravity. For some, depravity is understood to be *total*—intending by that not that people are as bad as they could become, but that every element of human nature is infected by depravity. Thus, depravity is total in the sense that nothing in human nature has escaped the depravity that has been inherited from Adam. According to other Western Christians, human nature is depraved in serious ways, with the result that people are sinners. However, common popular Western Christian assumptions (and some explicit teaching) exempt various elements of the human being from that depravity—for example, reason and the human will. While Western Christians may argue whether such depravity is total or somewhat restricted, they all begin from the assumption that human nature has been depraved because of Adam's sin.

To a Western Christian, consequently, it is startling to discover that Eastern Christianity denies that our human nature is depraved. Orthodox teachers can agree that the human nature has been defaced or tainted by sin, in the sense that sin has overlaid our human nature with defilement. But the sin cannot reach into or affect our human nature itself. In Eastern Christian thought, the concept "nature" is reserved for what God made, and "human nature" refers to human beings as God constituted them. As God's creation, "nature" remains good. Sin has no power to destroy what God has made or to alter his creation. Though all of creation, and humanity within it, has suffered from and been tarnished by sin, the creation still belongs to God. *Nature,* thus, cannot be turned into its opposite by human transgression, and *human* nature cannot be depraved.

According to Orthodoxy, sin is not an act of nature, but of a person. This correlates with the Eastern Christian understanding of creation: each nature created by God, and each individual which embodies that nature—whether human, animal, plant or whatever—bears within it a *logos* which impels it to God's service. Further, even after the fall of our first parents into sin and the horrific conse-

---

[10]English versions of this verse typically treat the Greek phrase ἐφ' ᾧ as a causative conjunction, resulting in the translation "and so death spread to all because all have sinned." The phrase may also be construed as a relative clause, resulting in the rendering, "and so death spread to all, *because of which* [referring back to 'death'] all have sinned." See the brief discussion in John Meyendorff, *Byzantine Theology: Historical Trends and Doctrinal Themes* (New York: Fordham University Press, 1974), pp. 144-45.

quences that arose from it for human beings and for all the rest of creation, each created nature—and thus each individual that embodies that nature—still carries within it that dynamic *logos* which calls it to its appropriate divine service.

Consequently, for an Eastern Christian, it is impossible to speak of a "corrupt" or "depraved" or "sinful" human nature, since nature comes from God's hand. Individual persons may (and do) sin, but the sin is the work of a person, not of human nature. If a person chooses by her personal (gnomic) will to turn from God, this is not the choice of her human nature or its will; the natural will, rather, impels us to turn in service to God. Sin is the fault of and is rooted in persons, not in nature.

However, Eastern Christianity is under no fond illusions about humans choosing rightly and serving God. Only one has ever done that perfectly, and he was God incarnate. Nevertheless, Orthodoxy argues that human beings freely choose their own paths; they do not always choose wrongly, but they do choose wrongly. All such wrong choices are sins, in which human beings fail to live up to their *logoi*, and it must be said of humankind that "all have sinned and fall short of the glory of God" (Rom 3:23). But none of us bears or suffers from a depraved, corrupt or sinful human nature, according to Orthodoxy.

We all stand in the situation of Adam and Eve, with our human nature and its natural will impelling us toward God but with our personal wills allowing us to choose for or against him. Since our first parents' original sin, however, human beings suffer from the terrible disadvantage that humankind has a long history of mortality, sin and disobedience. That mortality itself has influenced men and women to seek their fulfillment in the transitory things of creation rather than in the Creator. We thus freely but inevitably fail to live up to our *logos*—and so fail God. Mortality entices us to turn away from God, flawed patterns in society and culture pull us toward conformity, and too often—like our first parents—we choose forbidden fruit. Occasional choices in the opposite direction do not break the pattern or free us from death. But neither our faults nor the responsibility for them can be foisted upon our human nature. We have made the wrong choices, sinning against God, and we are responsible for our own sins, not for those of others—including that of our first parents. From the Eastern Christian perspective, the concept of a *depraved* human nature, in any sense, is inconceivable. Thus, according to Orthodoxy, Adam's descendants are neither guilty of nor depraved by his sin.

Cosmic consequences. Up to this point, we have considered what Eastern Christianity sets forth as the consequences of the fall of our first parents for humanity itself. Orthodoxy also teaches that beyond but inescapably related to these were consequences for the rest of creation. Given humanity's place and responsibility within the cosmos, human sin could not but have wide-ranging and devastating implications. However, since the present chapter is a treatment of *humanity* as fallen, we will not enter into these questions in particular depth. They can be dealt with more summarily by briefly considering the impact of the human fall into sin on the place and responsibility of humankind within creation as set out above.

In the first place, as *microcosm,* humanity's fall has introduced sin into both realms of creation; both realms have thus been defiled. Instead of standing at the pinnacle of created privilege, glorifying God in both realms, humankind has fallen away from God and, as microcosm, taken the rest of creation along with itself. However, neither the visible nor the invisible realm rebelled against God. Cursed by God for human sin, the rest of creation now endures futility, being kept from purely glorifying its Creator at present, but it eagerly awaits divine restoration (Rom 8:19-21). Until then, it is defiled and suffers because of human sin.

Second, because of humanity's position as *mediator* for creation, the original sin entailed devastating consequences for creation. Not only has sin entered both realms of creation, now both realms have also lost their divinely appointed leader. Human beings were to work with the creation, to bring out all its potentialities for the glory of God. Humanity was to do this in loving service of God and devoted care for all of creation. Turned from their Creator, human beings cannot resign their mediatorial role within creation; they inevitably still work with and use the creation. However, as a result of the human fall into sin, our involvement with the rest of creation has often failed to respect it as God's. Rather than make stewardly use of it, we have exploited it; instead of manifesting its potentialities for divine glory, we have dealt with it as a resource for our own temporally limited purposes. The development of culture, in all its manifestations, has continued despite human sin; human beings remain the mediators of creation. Attracted to the transitory, though, short-sighted human beings have abused the creation for ourselves. In so doing we have ineluctably made use of the wherewithal God himself built into creation. In our sin, however, we have failed to do this faithfully for God, to his glory. In this, human beings have failed God; we have also failed the creation.

In the third place, humankind's status as *personal beings* has suffered horrific results from humanity's fall into sin. As will be recognized from the treatment above, the great privilege of personal communion with the persons of the Trinity has been forfeited. In addition, sin has disrupted human relationships. This was evident in the way Adam responded to God's challenge to him in the Garden of Eden after Adam had sinned: rather than standing united with Eve in the indissoluble love in which God had united them (Gen 2:22-24), Adam laid the blame for his sin on her (Gen 3:12). All the alienation, hostility, resentment, aloofness and every other manifestation of interpersonal distance which human beings have ever endured—whether as individuals or as social groups—arose from the sin of those made to be, in God's good creation, *personal beings.* The whole bloody history of warfare, strife, tension and maltreatment of all sorts—physical, emotional, psychological, whatever—had its start in the fall of our first parents into sin.

Fourth, as *image of God,* human beings have not only failed to achieve likeness to God, they have also failed to portray God within creation. All the consequences of sin noted immediately above show that humanity, as the leader of creation, has presented a false face to that creation. Under God, humans were to be the vice regents of creation; they were to be, on a creaturely level, the lords of creation, ruling lovingly over it for the well-being of creation and the glory of God. By yielding themselves to the supposed power of the forbidden fruit, Adam and Eve placed themselves under the creation. In addition to falling thus into death, they put themselves under the power of creation. In the Garden of Eden, humankind began looking to the rest of creation as its hope for the future and the present. From that have flowed all the idolatries and addictions humanity has known.

Orthodoxy asserts that all these cosmic consequences of the fall of our first parents into sin arise from humanity's place and responsibility within creation. While human beings failed God, themselves and the rest of creation, they did not become something other than human beings. More particularly, human failure did not result in God modifying the human place and responsibility within creation. According to Orthodoxy, humankind became inferior to its privilege and vocation, but God did not change his plans.

Even so, in Eastern Christian teaching, since human beings still have within them the implanted *logos* and their natural will toward God, they can live up to what God intended to some degree: the course of history has not been one dark tunnel of evil. In part, human beings have lived up to God's intention for them as microcosms, mediators, personal beings and image-bearers of God. From these efforts come all the good results of culture, society and historical development. Even so, human sin has pervaded humanity's involvement within creation. That has meant cosmic consequences because of human sin; divine mercy has countered all this, though, and brings hope for humanity and all the rest of creation.

Concluding Observations

The differences between Western and Eastern Christian teachings on both created and fallen humanity, given their common basis in Scripture, are dramatic and extensive. A Western Christian has much to ponder and, probably, to question as he or she considers the Eastern Orthodox view of humanity—especially of fallen humanity. Considering how Orthodoxy's perspective enables it to deal with two related issues may give enough pause to invite us to appreciate the Eastern Christian viewpoint in the face of its significant differences from the views with which we in the Christian West are familiar.

In the first place, Orthodoxy's position accounts readily for the "good" done by those who do not profess faith in or seek to obey God. Its repudiation of the depravity of human nature because human nature remains God's handiwork—with its declaration that individuals freely choose whether to follow their *logos* or not—allows Eastern Christianity to account for such anomalous "good." We can only compare this responsibly to Western Christianity if we distinguish majority and minority streams of understanding in the latter, since they adopt significantly divergent views on the question.

In much Western Christian teaching, human beings can do good, despite suffering from a depraved human nature.[11] Tainted by sin, defiled in all parts, the faculties of a human being can still function responsibly before God and others to some extent. Thus, while sinful, humans can nonetheless exercise their free wills to choose rightly, and so can do what is good, without divine assistance. Such good does not contribute toward their salvation before God—but as his creatures fallen human beings retain their basic capacities. Dimunition and distortion of those capacities characterize the depravity of fallen human beings.

This Western Christian approach allows for the "good" which Orthodoxy also acknowledges fallen humans accomplish. To an Orthodox, this arises from our human nature as God created it: although fallen, we remain his creatures and are thus free to choose by our gnomic wills to turn toward God and the good or not. Our human nature remains God's good creation. The Western Christian attitude is subtly different, but in an important way. Human nature is depraved, although it remains God's creation. Sin is thus situated deep within human nature itself, which—to an Orthodox understanding—impugns God's good creation and thus mitigates the personal responsibility we bear for what we do that is not good. The Orthodox understanding invites those who hold this Western

---

[11]The following teaching, in various modifications, summarizes the perspectives offered in Roman Catholicism, Lutheranism, Pentecostalism and much of evangelicalism.

Christian approach to consider anew what it means that their human nature, which they receive from God as his good creation, is depraved.

A minority position within Western Christianity, but a significant one, holds that because of our first parents' sin, human nature is depraved and turned from God so that it cannot do good in his sight.[12] The approach does not allow for free will somehow to transcend the pull of depravity, except by divine assistance. This orientation understands human will as the will of the sinner, twisted and driven by depravity, and so only truly "free" to be a sinner. From this perspective, what is left of depravity if one can do good in his or her own power?

How, though, does this approach account for the reality that those who are in rebellion against God nevertheless do the sort of things he commands for neighbors, friends, relatives, in society and so forth, while being sinners themselves? Once the depravity of human nature is assumed in this fashion, accounting for the considerable "good" done by people throughout the world and over the course of its history becomes at least difficult. The usual response from these circles is an affirmation of what is called "common grace"—divine involvement that is "common" to both the rebellious sinful and the Christian faithful. This "common grace" allows fallen humans to transcend their depravity and do some of what God intended for his image-bearers. The anomaly in this response, though, is that human society throughout the world is thus awash in *common* grace, even though such Western Christian circles typically restrict the use of the term to *saving* grace.

By contrast, the Eastern Orthodox understanding of human nature, even after the fall of our first parents, readily allows for such "civic good" to be accounted for without special recourse to a use of the term *grace* that is not explicitly warranted by Scripture (always a strong concern in the Western Christian circles that embrace this minority position). Given how much civic good—caring for the poor, orphans, widows; seeking justice and promoting reconciliation; putting others' concerns ahead of one's own—has been done in the ages since Adam's fall (and in our own as well) by persons who do not profess faith in God, the Orthodox perspective deserves respect and appreciation as an insightful approach to this problem. It also challenges this significant minority position within the Christian West to find better ways of accounting for such civic good than it has so far.

Second, it may initially seem to a Western Christian that the Eastern Christian views on fallen humanity build on a superficial view of sin. The insidiousness of

---

[12]This position is held by "high Augustinians," including those in the classic Reformed and Presbyterian communions, and in some evangelical and baptistic churches which have embraced this Augustinian (or Calvinist) perspective.

sin is certainly in no doubt in Western Christian teaching; it has invaded and corrupted all of creation, including human nature, and leads God's image-bearers into sin. People constantly violate God's standards. Compared to this, Eastern Christian perspectives on sin initially seem shallow: is sin nothing more than what one consciously chooses? Are people really able to do what God wants even now, after Adam's fall, if they choose to do so?

In response, we should not underestimate the significance long recognized in Eastern Orthodoxy of the influence of examples, milieu, habit and life expectations in shaping a person's choices. Psychoanalysis has only begun to expose this tangle of impetuses residing deep within the human person; we choose freely, but always in context. Further, it would be judicious to reflect on what precisely sin is according to the Orthodox. In much of Western Christian teaching, sin ends up being presented as the infraction of a set of rules; since they are divine rules, sin is serious. In Orthodox teaching, sin is not so much the violation of rules—although it is that, of course. Rather, it is always the violation of a personal relationship with God—being unfaithful to him and rebelling against him, turning away from him. In the Orthodox understanding of what it means to sin, God remains in focus, and human responsibility is therefore all the more crushing.

The distinctive Eastern Orthodox view of humanity gives much for a Western Christian to consider. Since any Christian understanding of salvation must counter its correlative view of our first parents' fall into sin, it will not be surprising to note, by way of anticipation, that the Orthodox view of salvation's accomplishment varies significantly from Western Christian teaching. We turn to that divergence in the next chapter.

7

The Accomplishment of Salvation

IN THE APOSTOLIC WITNESS, THE SALVATION accomplished by Jesus Christ is presented as a multifaceted jewel, brilliant from many angles. According to the New Testament, he saved, redeemed, died for, delivered, offered himself as a sacrifice for, reconciled, shed his blood for, gave himself as a ransom for, and—to mention no others—liberated humankind. The titles accorded him in view of his saving work are numerous: among others, he is called Savior, Redeemer, Lamb of God, the Resurrection and the Life. Unquestionably, the work of Christ is many-sided and can be viewed from a number of perspectives. None of them exhausts the full meaning of what he did for a fallen creation. Indeed, the multiple vistas they open on the accomplishment of salvation show it to be an unfathomable mystery, beyond human comprehension.[1] It should not be surprising that the biblical imagery for what Christ did is so manifold: after all, the Scriptures present him as the center of all God's work with and for humanity and the rest of creation. As the need of fallen humans was great, so the work of Christ was varied; since he fulfilled the will of God in all its richness, Christ's work was inevitably multifaceted.

The abundance of apostolic imagery for the work of Christ presents a daunting challenge for the church's teaching: while it can rejoice in all he has done for it, its presentation of that work will inevitably be partial and limited. Even with the determination to proclaim the apostolic witness regarding Christ's salvation in all its fullness, some of that witness will fit better with the emphases of other churches or speak more directly to the culture in which the church finds itself than will other elements of that apostolic testimony. The proclamation of the church is, indeed, ineluctably shaped by the culture that has shaped its members and by the need to

---

[1]According to St. Peter, even the angels cannot comprehend the salvation wrought by Christ (1 Pet 1:12).

speak relevantly to it.[2] That culture thus helps to frame the church's approach to life and, consequently, its understanding of the fallen human predicament. The doctrinal perspectives it articulates from scriptural teaching on this question will predispose it to be most alert to those apostolic emphases regarding Christ's work that intersect with those perspectives. It must not become tone deaf to other emphases, but it may not be able to incorporate them readily into the music in which it sings the praises of its Savior. This is not unfaithful to the scriptural presentation; rather, it focuses on what addresses the problem as it has come to understand it. This pattern, though, can become unfaithful if the church—whether ignorantly or arrogantly—treats its song as the only one Christians could compose or should sing.

Western Christianity and Eastern Orthodoxy each have developed distinctive approaches to the work of Christ. Each approach reflects the culture and background in which the two main segments of Christianity developed, and each approach deals with the work of Christ in ways that fit their respective assessments of the human predicament. Both sets of emphases are biblical. Consequently, both Western Christianity and Eastern Orthodoxy can profitably listen to each other in considering what Christ accomplished in the way of salvation. To prepare for this chapter's consideration of the distinctive emphases of Orthodoxy on the accomplishment of salvation, it would be helpful to summarize the basic ones of Western Christianity.

The cultural milieu within which Western Christianity developed has been profoundly shaped by ancient Rome's preoccupation with law. Given that, it is not surprising that in Western Christianity most of our attention concerning the accomplishment of salvation has concentrated on the legal imagery in the biblical witness. We have traditionally focused on the justice of God, the question of humankind's guilt, the necessity of satisfaction, payment of debts, being justified, standing before God in his court and the like. In Western Christianity, that approach became dominant by the end of Christian antiquity and developed further during the Middle Ages; it received classic formulation and further elaboration by St. Anselm of Canterbury in his book *Cur Deus Homo (Why God Became Man)*. The Protestant Reformers of the sixteenth century continued in the same approach, and in subsequent centuries most of our Western Christian focus on the accomplishment of salvation has continued to look at these issues. For all the differences which have developed within Western Christianity, even in questions regarding the salvation of Christ, we share the orientation on law, human guilt be-

---

[2]See the discussion of this above, chap. 1, pp. 20-26.

fore God and the necessity of payment or sacrifice to achieve a right standing with God. In whatever ways Western Christians have worked out their various understandings about salvation, we all focus on Christ's work as a sacrifice, a payment for human sin, an enduring of the judgment of God so that human beings might be forgiven and accounted righteous in God's sight.

While these issues that we have focused on in the West are, unquestionably, part of the biblical presentation about the accomplishment of salvation, they do not exhaust the apostolic witness on the matter. By way of contrast, Eastern Christianity has only given limited attention to legal orientations but has focused on other elements of the apostolic teaching. As we have seen, Orthodoxy arose in a culture with different emphases than those of ancient Rome. We have also seen that Eastern Christianity understands the predicament of humanity after the fall of our first parents differently than we do in Western Christianity. It is not surprising, consequently, to discover that Eastern Orthodoxy's understanding of how salvation is accomplished is also distinctively other than that shared among Western Christians.

While Western Christianity typically understands humankind's problem in terms of our situation (as guilty, depraved, unrighteous before God), Orthodoxy sees the problem in terms of our enemies (sin, death and the devil), who hold us in their tyranny. In Eastern Christian thought, these are the powers which, since the primordial fall, hold humanity in bondage. As a result, the Orthodox understanding of the accomplishment of salvation is shaped by these biblical perspectives. In Western Christianity, Christ is seen as the one who suffers the punishment human beings deserve for their sin: Christ is seen as *victim.* By contrast, in Eastern Christian thought, Christ is the *victor:* he defeats those enemies and frees humanity from their bondage. How does he accomplish this? In the Eastern Christian tradition, there are four main elements to this answer.

THE INCARNATION

In the first place, Eastern Orthodoxy places great emphasis on the incarnation. For Eastern Christianity, the incarnation is not just the necessary preliminary or foundation for what Christ would subsequently do as Savior via his life, death and resurrection; rather, the incarnation itself is part of the accomplishment of salvation. According to Eastern Christian thought, humanity was created for life with God, in communion with him. Because of sin, humanity was bound over to death and cut off from divine fellowship. No mere human could reclaim life and restore communion with God. In the incarnation, however, God unites human nature to himself: what humankind could not do in its fallen condition God does in the incarnation. Since God is himself life, when "the Word became flesh" (Jn 1:14) he thereby restored and assured life and divine communion to human nature. In the incarnation, thus, the stranglehold of death on humanity is already broken. Much more needs to be done by the incarnate Son, of course. Even so, the incarnation itself is the foundation on which the saving work of Christ is established, and the assurance of things yet to come.

Furthermore, the compelling power of sin is broken in the incarnation. This victory has two facets. In the first place, according to Eastern Christian understandings, while Christ's human nature was sinless, it nevertheless shared all the weaknesses and disabilities which had arisen within humanity since the fall of our first parents. Thus, he endured all the frailties and faced all the temptations with which humanity has been burdened and confronted since the primordial fall. However, since the personal (gnomic) will of the person of Christ is the will of the second person of the Trinity, Christ does not and, indeed, cannot sin. Although enmeshed in human weakness, the Son of God never turns from God. Thus, the "hold" of sin on human nature is overcome.[3] While all persons preceding Christ had sinned against God, the incarnate Son never does. Finally, there is an exception to the sad observation "no one living is righteous before you" (Ps 143:2). However, this is more than simply a dictum about Christ: he is not just a stirring example or encouragement to turn from sin. Reflecting the Pauline emphasis on solidarity in Adam and solidarity in Christ (Rom 5:12-21; 1 Cor 15:21-22), Orthodoxy has emphasized that the victory of Christ in this regard is effective for all those who are "in Christ." The consequences of Adam's sin, including propensity to sin, passed upon all those in him; the consequences of Christ's righteousness also pass to all those who are in him—namely, life with and faithful communion with God.

Second, with the introduction of eternal life to human nature in Christ, humanity is no longer inevitably bound to death, as it had been since the fall of our first parents. In the Eastern Christian understanding of the effects of the primordial fall, being bound over to death led to humanity being attracted to the transitory things of this world. That is, since we were dying and had no lasting life, we turned, foolishly but inevitably, to find comfort in those things which, like us, were

[3]Vladimir Lossky expresses the Orthodox view succinctly when he writes, "Christ assumed our nature; He voluntarily submitted to all the consequences of sin; He took on Himself the responsibility for our error, while remaining a stranger to sin, in order to resolve the tragedy of human liberty" (*The Mystical Theology of the Eastern Church* [Crestwood, N.Y.: St. Vladimir's Seminary Press, 1976], p. 153).

passing. To turn in ourselves toward God was, while possible, something which humans did not do.[4] However, in the incarnation, human nature is enabled to aspire again to what is truly lasting—namely, life with God, communion with God, the goal of our intended existence.

Thus, from an Eastern Christian perspective, the incarnation is truly to be celebrated. More than in virtually all of Western Christianity, Orthodoxy treats the incarnation as part of the actual accomplishment of salvation. The incarnation itself contributes to our salvation from sin, death and the devil. While the incarnation is not enough to achieve salvation in Eastern Christian thought, as has sometimes been alleged by Western Christian scholars,[5] it is unquestionably true that the incarnation figures much more prominently in the accomplishment of salvation in Orthodoxy than it has in Western Christian thought.

THE LAST ADAM

A second key element of the Orthodox understanding of the accomplishment of salvation is "recapitulation" in Christ as the last Adam. This teaching, traced back to St. Irenaeus in the second century, was not something he claimed to be novel. Since he was taught by St. Polycarp, who had been taught by St. John, the heritage of the theory goes back very nearly to, if not all the way to, the apostles themselves. In any event, what Irenaeus urged, and what has been followed in the subsequent generations of Eastern Christian thought, is that Christ entered into history as the last Adam, in order to reverse the course the first Adam had taken and reclaim humanity and the rest of creation for their original created purposes.

As God's image-bearer—like Adam, specially brought into the world for God's purposes—the incarnate Son of God lived "by every word that comes from the mouth of God" (Mt 4:3), not only in the time of severe temptation (in a wilderness [Mt 4:1], not a verdant garden [Gen 2:8-9]), but throughout the whole of his life. Christ turned unreservedly and always toward God. Christ has recapitulated hu-

---

[4]According to Orthodoxy, it is possible for human beings, even after the Fall, to turn toward God: our *logos* orients us in that direction. But death holds us in bondage. We can (and sometimes do) turn toward God and do what is right and pleasing in his sight. But death captivates our attitudes and thoughts, and it turns us away from what leads to the life found only in him. Looking for what satisfies our fleeting desires and gives us temporary pleasure, none of us since the Fall has purely and faithfully turned to God.

[5]The redoubtable nineteenth-century historian of Christian thought, Adolph von Harnack, thus described the significance of the incarnation for Eastern Orthodox thought in this way: see his *What Is Christianity?* 2nd rev. ed., trans. Thomas Bailey Saunders (New York: G. P. Putnam's Sons, 1904), pp. 249-50. With his considerable influence, this misunderstanding has been frequently repeated and passed on in the works of subsequent Western Christian scholars.

man history as the last Adam: in him the gnomic will of the incarnate Logos always chose faithfully to move in the direction of the natural will of human nature, toward God and communion with him. By this perfect obedience the last Adam has displaced the first Adam's disobedience; as the last Adam, he now leads the creation—human beings and all the rest—toward God's original intended purpose. That is, as the Logos incarnate, he now leads all created natures in their respective *logoi* toward the *skopoi* God intends—namely, communion with him. Christ has thus redirected the course of history; he has reclaimed the whole of creation for God's original purpose. Thus salvation in the Eastern Christian tradition is not just for individuals, souls or human beings; it is for all creation. Even salvation itself serves the greater end of reorienting all creation to God's intended purposes.[6] In Christ the last Adam, all things are made new (Rev 21:5). In this recapitulation in the last Adam, all the dreary results of the first Adam's sin are overcome, not only for humanity itself but for all the rest of creation in which human beings were called to serve. Christ is the victor over sin.

This understanding of recapitulation builds on the faithful life of Christ as the last Adam, but it also affirms the necessity of both his death and his resurrection for the accomplishment of salvation. Since this last Adam, never having sinned, need not have died, death had no legitimate power over him (Jn 10:17-18; 14:30). However, he freely gave himself over to death, to overcome it by suffering it. He broke its bars by rising again from the grave. In so doing, he became, as St. Paul teaches, "the first fruits" of the general resurrection of the dead (1 Cor 15:20); Christ became the guarantee of the fulfillment of God's original creative purpose for all of creation[7]—namely, life with God forever.

The Death of Christ

In the third place, Orthodoxy has spoken significantly about the death of Christ and its part in the accomplishment of salvation. Western Christianity, of course, has emphasized the role played by the death of Christ too. However, Orthodoxy has treated that death in strikingly different ways than are common in Western Christianity.

For much of Orthodox teaching, Christ's death was a satisfaction indeed—but

[6] Vladimir Lossky sets forth the Eastern Orthodox view forthrightly when he writes, "After the Fall, human history is a long shipwreck awaiting rescue: but the port of salvation is not the goal; it is the possibility for the shipwrecked to resume his journey whose sole goal is union with God" (*Orthodox Theology: An Introduction* [Crestwood, N.Y.: St. Vladimir's Seminary Press, 1978], p. 84).

[7] Hence the striking formulations by St. John of Damascus: "Creation has been sanctified by the divine blood," and "Through the cross all things have been made right" (*The Orthodox Faith* 4.4, 4.11).

what it satisfied was the *truth* of God. While we in the Christian West often speak of Christ satisfying the *justice* of God and enduring the penalty of broken law for us, the Eastern Christian emphasis is somewhat different. Sometimes Orthodox refer to the death of Christ as a satisfaction of divine justice; more common is the teaching that the satisfaction in Christ's death was the satisfaction of God's truth.[8] The divine warning to our first parents that disobedience would result in death had come to pass; sin and death had passed on to all humanity; and the cycle of sin and death had continued.[9] Since Christ had never sinned, he did not have to die himself. However, those "in him" are and would be sinners for whom death must come as the consequence of sin. As the last Adam, the new head of a renewed humanity, Christ took on himself the death which should befall all those in him. In so doing, he satisfied God's truth. Because of the death of Christ, that truth is not violated when those who are sinners receive everlasting life. In this manner, the Eastern Christian tradition speaks of Christ's death as a satisfaction.

The death of Christ manifested the depths of his love for humanity. He has entered fully into our situation: not only did he take on a weakened human nature in the incarnation and live for us, but he also yielded himself for us to death, which had no legitimate claim upon him. By taking it fully into himself and enduring it, he plunged to the nadir of our situation because of his suffering love for us. In that love, he assumed our death into himself, but by assuming it he overcame it. The one hanging on the cross was the incarnate Logos, in whom is life (Jn 1:4). God cannot die; even so, as an ancient Eastern Christian liturgy declares about Christ, "One of the Trinity died in the flesh." But death could not possibly hold the incarnate Son of God in its power. By enduring death, Christ conquered it: as St. Paul declares, Christ *triumphed* in the cross (Col 2:15). In Orthodoxy, "Calvary is seen always in the light of the empty tomb; the Cross is an emblem of victory."[10] Christ is the victor over death.

Further, Orthodoxy emphasizes that he is the victor over the devil. The incarnate Son of God did "give his life as a *ransom* for many" (Mk 10:45). The idea of ransom entails paying a price for someone or something. By Christ's ransom for many, he paid the price to free them. We recognize this emphasis in Western Christianity too. Eastern Christianity, however, has examined the implications of

---

[8]One of the desiderata in scholarship on Orthodoxy is an examination of the liturgical interpretation of the cross, which is rich and multifaceted. I hope to turn to this as part of a subsequent monograph on the Orthodox understanding of salvation.

[9]See Gen 2:17; 3:19; Rom 5:12; 6:23.

[10]Bishop Kallistos (Timothy) Ware, *The Orthodox Church*, 2nd ed. (New York: Penguin, 1993), pp. 227-28.

this concept in another way than we are familiar with in the Christian West—specifically, by asking to whom the ransom was paid and exploring the implications of the answer.

Sometimes in the Eastern Christian tradition this ransom is understood as paid to God. That is, since God will be the judge of human sin on the final day, the ransom to free humankind from punishment is paid by Christ to God. This sounds quite similar to much Western Christian teaching. Often, though, in Orthodoxy the ransom is understood as paid to the devil.

Among many of the early Greek church fathers, and in subsequent Orthodoxy, the idea of a ransom paid to the devil is understood as Christ offering himself to Satan in place of humankind, over whom Satan had dominion. Satan had achieved this power over human beings through the deception of our first parents. In that primordial deception, he had taken humanity into his thralldom and since then had held them unjustly in his tyranny. Even so, Satan had achieved that dominion over them. God would not simply strip the devil of that authority, but would deal with it by offering a ransom for humankind. The incarnate Son of God proffered himself in exchange for the human beings Satan held in his grip. For the devil, the attraction of the ransom tendered by Christ was that he was pure, virgin-born and a worker of miracles—a much more attractive and glorious captive than the lot of fallen humankind in Satan's grip.

According to this understanding, the devil greedily focused only on the perfect humanity and willingly accepted the exchange. In accepting the ransom offered, the devil rose to the bait but was caught on twin hooks. For one, Satan overreached himself by grabbing at Christ, who was pure and sinless man: exceeding the boundaries of his rights, the devil lost them all.[11] For the other, the devil did not consider that accepting the ransom would involve him trying to keep God himself in his control. As an ancient Byzantine sermon asserted, "Hell received a body and encountered God; it received mortal dust and met heaven face to face."[12] As many in the Eastern Christian tradition have put it, "The deceiver was thus justly deceived." Through Christ's ransom, humanity is purchased from tyrannical bondage; in that ransom, the devil lost both humanity and the ransom himself. Christ is victor over the devil.

This understanding of the imagery of Christ's death as a "ransom" was an at-

[11]This approach is found in Pseudo-Macarius *The Fifty Spiritual Homilies* 11.10; St. Gregory of Nyssa *An Address on Religious Instruction* 22-26; St. Maximus Confessor *Ad Thalassium* 64; and St. John of Damascus *The Orthodox Faith* 3.1; 3.27.

[12]This is from a well-known ancient Paschal sermon, read in every Orthodox congregation during the Easter service.

tempt to explore the biblical teaching about the ransom of captives, about being redeemed, about Christ purchasing his people. The teaching that the ransom was paid to the devil is common but not universally embraced in Orthodoxy. No less a figure than St. Gregory Nazianzen (greatly revered among Eastern Christians as "Gregory the Theologian") scorned the idea that a ransom was paid, whether to God or to Satan. While the Cappadocian father acknowledged that Scripture describes Christ's death as a ransom,[13] he repudiated both the idea that God held humanity in bondage and the declaration that the devil had legitimate rights over humankind. According to St. Gregory, the biblical presentation of Christ's death as a ransom was intended to describe the deliverance of humankind Christ accomplished by his death. For Gregory, asking to whom this ransom was paid was wrong-headed, an attempt to explain too much what can only be celebrated. For him, "ransom" points to the wonder of spiritual freedom secured through the salvation accomplished by Christ; the church should revere Christ's death as humanity's ransom rather than analyze the particulars of the transaction.[14] In this concern to glory in the wonder of the accomplishment of salvation, all of Orthodoxy agrees with him. However, in his rejection of the idea that a ransom was actually paid—whether to God or to the devil—much of Orthodoxy has not followed his lead.

THE RESURRECTION OF CHRIST

In the fourth place, Orthodoxy lays great emphasis on the resurrection in the accomplishment of salvation. The Eastern Christian approach to the resurrection is strikingly different from the common Western Christian view of its significance. In Western Christianity, the basic understanding of salvation is that the work was finished in Christ's suffering and death on the cross. While Christ was buried and spent three days in the tomb, whatever may have gone on during that time had little of broad salvific significance.[15] In the resurrection—which, of course, Western Christianity celebrates on Easter and every Sunday of the year—Christ came back from the dead. However, apart from the affirmation that the resurrection of Christ showed that God had accepted the sacrifice Christ had offered on the cross and that salvation had thereby been achieved, many Western Christians—whether layperson, pastor or theologian—might well be somewhat stymied by the question of what contribution the resurrection itself makes to the accomplishment of salvation.

---

[13]"He redeems the world at a great price—the price of his own blood" (St. Gregory Nazianzen *Oration* 29.20).

[14]He expresses himself to this effect at *Oration* 45.22.

[15]Among Western Christians, widely divergent views are held about what Christ may have done in the three days; we need not explore them for the purpose of these considerations.

Orthodoxy sees humanity's problem as its bondage to sin, death and the devil. Salvation in its fullness is not completed until life is restored to Christ and those "in him": Christ's resurrection is a necessity to break the bonds of death. Only in this way, from an Eastern Christian perspective, can eternal life be granted and Christ be victor over our enemies. What is assured in Christ's incarnation, pursued in his life and reached for in his death—namely, eternal life, communion with God and victory over our enemies—is only achieved fully and completely when Christ rises from the grave. Thus, Orthodoxy celebrates Easter—the resurrection of Christ—more than our common Western Christian understandings of the accomplishment of salvation would lead us to do. In this regard, it is telling that during Passion week in Western Christianity, the heaviest emphasis falls usually on Good Friday, while Easter is celebrated as the assurance that salvation has been achieved. By contrast, in Eastern Orthodoxy, Good Friday is a necessary step of salvation, but Easter is celebrated as the great day in which salvation is assured and achieved. The Easter vigil service in an Orthodox church is an elaborate, overwhelmingly joyful celebration. Anyone who attends such a service will have no doubt about the primary importance ascribed by the Orthodox to the resurrection of Christ for our salvation.

Concluding Observations

Eastern Orthodoxy has not focused on the same facets of the biblical presentation of the accomplishment of salvation that Western Christianity has; instead, Eastern Christianity has appropriated other elements of the rich apostolic imagery and witness. The Eastern Christian tradition has stressed the significance of the incarnation, the role of Christ as last Adam, the victory of Christ on the cross and the resurrection of Christ. In keeping with its cultural heritage, Orthodoxy has focused on the dynamic story of the accomplishment of salvation, rather than its legal ramifications. Eastern Christianity has concentrated on Christ's victory over evil, issuing in the reclaiming of all creation and it now being led to its originally intended purpose. It has caught the drama of the apostolic emphases on ransom, freedom, victory and life.

The orientation on Christ as victor is apostolic and stimulating. For Western Christians familiar only with their own traditions' presentations on the accomplishment of salvation, the Orthodox view can kindle new wonder at the multifaceted accomplishment of salvation and the apostolic presentation of it. Eastern Christians could profitably appropriate Western Christian insights on that accomplishment, too, for the full biblical portrayal is richer than what has become the traditional orientation in either Western or Eastern Christianity.

For Western Christians, however, considering the Orthodox emphases on the accomplishment of salvation can engender new appreciation for the significance of the incarnation. As a way of opening to that appreciation, Western Christians might well ask themselves what significance *for the accomplishment of salvation* they see in the incarnation. If one comes to the assessment that it was only the necessary preliminary to the accomplishment of salvation, then he has much to profitably ponder in the Orthodox understanding of the incarnation. In addition, if a Western Christian has not reflected on the apostolic presentation that Christ was the last Adam, whose life, death and resurrection reoriented both humanity and the rest of creation to God's original purposes, then the Eastern Christian understanding offers rich insights into the ways of God for salvation. Further, if the Western Christian understanding of salvation has focused on personal spiritual standing but has relegated the broader significance of salvation for the rest of creation to the future, following Christ's second advent—as much of Western Christianity has—then the Orthodox affirmation that Christ's salvation also reaches out in the present age and claims the whole of creation and human service within it offers much to consider. In addition, the Orthodox view on Christ's death as a ransom offers a variant to the "satisfaction to divine justice" and "punishment from God" emphases traditional in Western Christianity and would thus help a Western Christian see other sides of the significance of Christ's death. Finally, the Orthodox stress on the resurrection of Christ offers Western Christians much to consider in comparison to the way they probably see that resurrection through the lenses of Western Christian teaching. This point warrants somewhat fuller explanation.

It needs to be forthrightly stated that the Eastern Christian view does more justice than the common Western Christian orientation to the Pauline presentation on the significance of Christ's resurrection. It is hardly possible to read the apostle's declarations about that resurrection attentively and come to the assessment that he viewed the resurrection primarily as a divine declaration that the death of Christ had been accepted by God as accomplishing salvation: "If Christ has not been raised [from the dead], then our proclamation has been in vain and your faith has been in vain. . . . If Christ has not been raised, your faith is futile and you are still in your sins" (1 Cor 15:14, 17). For the apostle, without the resurrection of Christ there is no salvation, whatever may have transpired on Good Friday. He goes on to declare, though, that Christ certainly has been raised from the dead, and that because of this all who believe in him have eternal life and the assurance of their own resurrection (1 Cor 15:20-22). If the hope of the gospel is eternal life (Jn 3:16), then Christ's resurrection to life is absolutely essential to the accomplishment of salvation.

The impoverishment of the way Western Christianity has viewed Christ's resurrection vis-à-vis the accomplishment of salvation can readily be recognized by considering how Western Christians' prayers refer to salvation. Typically, thanks are given to God that Jesus suffered and died for us, to accomplish our salvation, but—apart from rare exceptions—the resurrection of Christ is not mentioned, and if it is mentioned, it sounds more like an afterthought than an element in the actual accomplishment of salvation. The Eastern Christian view on the resurrection of Christ is dramatically different. For Orthodoxy, the resurrection of Christ is not merely the affirmation or assurance that the sacrifice offered on Good Friday was accepted. On the contrary, for Eastern Christianity, the resurrection of Christ is itself essential to the accomplishment of salvation. No resurrection, no life; no life, no gospel; no gospel, no hope—that is St. Paul's view of the significance of the resurrection for the accomplishment of salvation. This is the orientation Eastern Christianity has wholeheartedly embraced, and we in the Christian West should do no less as we ponder and give thanks for the accomplishment of salvation. In this, as in many other regards, we have much to learn from our Orthodox brothers and sisters.

8

The Application of Salvation

BOTH EASTERN ORTHODOXY AND WESTERN CHRISTIANITY affirm that the salvation accomplished in Christ is applied to human beings by grace, through the work of the Holy Spirit. Nevertheless, this commonality, rooted in scriptural teaching, does not preclude significant differences between the two Christendoms specifically on grace and the Holy Spirit[1] or more generally on the application of salvation. Indeed, the differences between Eastern Orthodoxy and Western Christianity on the application of salvation are striking. Orthodoxy views it as *theosis*—"deification" or "divinization"—a term that plays no appreciable role in the classic Western Christian perspectives on the application of salvation.[2] Western

---

[1]With regard to *grace*, see the treatment below in chap. 9; as for the differences regarding the Holy Spirit, in addition to the question of the *filioque* (on which, see the treatment above, chap. 4), see the concise treatment in Vladimir Lossky, *In the Image and Likeness of God* (Crestwood, N.Y.: St. Vladimir's Seminary Press, 1985), pp. 109-10; for a fuller discussion, see his *The Mystical Theology of the Eastern Church* (Crestwood, N.Y.: St. Vladimir's Seminary Press, 1976), pp. 156-73.

[2]Within Western Christianity, but outside its "classic" streams (Roman Catholic, Lutheran and the various branches of the Reformed), the holiness strand of the Wesleyan tradition and Pentecostalism stand as exceptions to this generalization. In their teaching, the application of salvation includes a transformation which is, at times, styled "divinization" and, in several regards, approaches Orthodoxy's doctrine of *theosis*. Even so, the Wesleyan/Pentecostal perspective does not include the sacramental component that is at the heart of the Orthodox teaching, so a significant divergence still obtains. Cf. Edmund J. Rybarczyk, *Beyond Salvation: Eastern Orthodoxy and Classical Pentecostalism on Becoming Like Christ* (Carlisle, U.K.: Paternoster, 2004). Beyond this, Finnish scholarship has urged that Martin Luther's (but not Lutheranism's) understanding of salvation can be understood as *theosis:* see Veli-Matti Kärkkäinen, *One with God: Salvation as Deification and Justification* (Collegeville, Minn.: Liturgical Press, 2004); T. Mannermaa, *Christ Present in Faith: Luther's View of Justification* (Minneapolis: Fortress, 2005); and R. Saarinen, *Faith and Holiness: Lutheran-Orthodox Dialogue 1959-1994* (Göttingen: Vandenhoeck & Ruprecht, 1997). As this book was going to press, I learned about another relevant title which had just been published but which I was unable to consult: Nancy J. Hudson, *Becoming God: The Doctrine of Theosis in Nicholas of Cusa* (Washington, D.C.: Catholic University of America Press, 2007), examines the influence of Greek philosophy on the fifteenth-century German Catholic theologian's understanding. (Whether the volume includes consideration of Eastern Orthodox teaching is not clear from the book's description.)

Christianity experienced its most pronounced division in the sixteenth century over an issue of the application of salvation, namely, the question of *justification.* While Western Christian teaching about the application of salvation cannot be reduced merely to the question of justification, that doctrine has unquestionably played a pronounced role in Western Christian understandings. In contrast, justification is not a significant question in the Eastern Orthodox approach to the application of salvation.

The contrast can be recognized on a more popular level than that of technical doctrinal terminology. Eager evangelists have confronted people with the burning question, "Are you saved?" This is a question about the application of salvation—in which the would-be evangelist is ready to assist. The question assumes a particular understanding of that application—namely, that by an instant of faith alone one can be justified by God and thus be saved. This approach certainly does not reflect the full teaching developed in Western Christianity about the application of salvation, whether in classic Protestantism or in Roman Catholicism. What the question offers is a "bare bones," minimalist fixation on justification as the quintessential concern in the application of salvation. It is, as it were, a caricature of Western Christianity's fundamental concern. A leading Orthodox spokesman answered this question by saying, "I trust that by God's mercy and grace I *am being* saved."[3] While this is not an answer the questioner would be prepared either to hear or to assimilate, it nevertheless reflects well the Orthodox understanding of the application of salvation.

Western Christianity on the Application of Salvation

In order to be better able to appreciate the distinctiveness of Eastern Orthodoxy's teaching on the application of salvation, it would be helpful to reflect on the way Western Christianity views it. We can best do this by focusing first on the fundamental question addressed by all Western Christian thought on the topic. Second, we will reflect on the way Western Christianity typically deals with the broader package of teaching on the application of salvation.

The basic question. Western Christianity is far from uniform in its teachings about the application of salvation. A wide variety of viewpoints on the issue exists among the several traditions within Western Christendom. Indeed, the various answers often clash headlong—can such dissonance be harmonized? This presentation will not argue that there is somehow a basic similarity underlying the di-

---

[3]Bishop Kallistos Ware, *How Are We Saved? The Understanding of Salvation in the Orthodox Tradition* (Minneapolis: Light & Life Publishing, 1996), p. 4.

verse answers. Instead, we will argue that all the various answers respond to the same basic question.

Western Christianity's treatment of the application of salvation has been significantly molded by the legal inheritance received from ancient Rome. As we have previously discussed, this Roman influence has shaped much of the way in which Christianity in Western Europe and North America has framed its questions, especially about humanity and its relationship to God. Indeed, within Western Christendom, the fallen human condition is understood especially in legal terms, and the accomplishment of salvation is overwhelmingly understood within this framework. Given this orientation, it is not surprising that juridical categories have predominated in Western Christian understandings of the application of salvation. Preeminent among these is the question of how one is accepted as righteous in the court of God: the term for this is *justification.*

As Christianity in Western Europe interacted with and responded to its cultural heritage, it especially emphasized the legal foci in biblical teaching on humankind as guilty sinners, on the work of Christ as a satisfaction to divine justice and on the question of how one could be accepted by God the righteous Judge. The question of justification—that is, of how, why, when and on what basis God accepts or accounts someone as righteous in his sight—consequently demanded special consideration. Divergent, even conflicting, answers came to be propounded within Western Christianity by the fourteenth and fifteenth centuries;[4] thus, the question about justification was not sprung on Western Christendom by the Protestant Reformers in the sixteenth century. During the Reformation era, this issue about the application of salvation received disparate answers from Protestants and Roman Catholics: are humans justified by *faith alone,* or by *faith plus good works*?[5]

Deep-seated divergences on this issue, preeminently, led to a division within Western Christianity, a division that has persisted to this day. It must be acknowledged that misunderstandings (as well as misrepresentations) on both sides have too often exaggerated the differences between Roman Catholics and Prot-

---

[4]See the treatment in Heiko A. Oberman, *The Harvest of Medieval Theology: Gabriel Biel and Late Medieval Nominalism* (Grand Rapids: Eerdmans, 1967), pp. 120-84; cf. also Oberman's summary conclusions on the topic at pp. 427-28.

[5]This bald contrast reflects the popular assessment of the disagreement on the question between Roman Catholicism and Protestantism. As spokespersons on both sides recognized during the sixteenth century and as scholars have demonstrated since then, the viewpoints expressed on the issue during the sixteenth century were often considerably more nuanced, both among Roman Catholic and among Protestant theologians. Even refined by such nuances, though, the divergence between the two camps boiled down to approximately this popular assessment.

estants on justification, and also that much more is involved in Western Christian understandings of the application of salvation than just the question of justification. Nevertheless, that doctrine has played the dominant role—not only because of the sixteenth-century division but also because justification especially speaks to the primary Western Christian way of conceiving of the relationship of humans to God.

The basic approach. However, the biblical teaching on the application of salvation includes other elements beyond the clearly juridical one of justification. While that one has dominated in Western Christian understandings, others have also received attention. The conflicts over justification have influenced the precise ways in which the other elements are presented, but these other elements are nonetheless recognizable. For our purposes, it is important to look at two of them, and then to consider how Western Christianity typically—again, for all its differences—sees these several elements coming together in the application of salvation.

In addition to justification, the application of salvation includes *sanctification*—the process of growing in holiness. Sanctification is not a legal decree, but a process of transformation within the person. In sanctification, a sinner receives grace from the Holy Spirit to enable him or her to turn from sin and increasingly to live a holy life, as modeled after Christ and granted because of the salvation he accomplished. *Glorification* is the ultimate step in the application of salvation; it will take place only at the end of time. In glorification, a person is utterly transformed, cleansed finally from all remnants of sin and perfected in holiness in body and soul.

Justification, sanctification and glorification are juxtaposed in St. Paul's declaration, "For those whom he foreknew he also predestined *to be conformed to the image of his Son* [i.e., *sanctified*], in order that he might be the firstborn within a large family. And those whom he predestined he also called; and those whom he called he also *justified;* and those whom he justified he also *glorified*" (Rom 8:29-30, emphasis added). This passage has contributed to a second typical development in Western Christianity's approach to the application of salvation, as follows.

Within Western Christianity, the Romans 8 passage's delineation of the elements of that application—together with the *predestination* and the *calling* it mentions, plus various related doctrinal refinements, implications and assumptions[6]—has been developed into a focus on the "steps" in the process and in what order

[6]Among these are "gospel call" and "illumination" in Lutheran designation, styled "external call" and "internal call" in Reformed terminology; regeneration and conversion (including treatments of faith and repentance); and adoption. Between (and within) the two large Protestant traditions, disagreements arose as to which element precedes or leads to another, including questions regarding the relationship between repentance and faith, justification and faith, and regeneration and faith.

they occur. That is to say, the various traditions within Western Christianity have typically argued that a particular *order* is followed in the application of salvation. Among Protestants, for example, Lutherans and Reformed differ on several issues in the *ordo salutis* ("order of salvation"). Indeed, within both these large camps, further dissension has arisen as other refinements have been added to the basic Lutheran or Reformed scheme. This Western Christian concentration on the question of the order of the application of salvation affirms that all these "steps" occur in each person to whom salvation is applied. The concern with the order of the application of salvation has been typical of Western Christian teaching in virtually all its various strands.[7]

This concentration on the *ordo salutis* was more pronounced in times past than it is now, except in very conservative theological and ecclesiastical circles. Part of the reason for this change is the long-standing recognition that a major biblical element of the application of salvation cannot be readily fit into the structure. What used to be called, in discussions of the *ordo salutis,* "the mystical union" undeniably required attention[8] but defied placement within any such order.[9] While the term itself has largely passed from contemporary doctrinal usage in favor of "union with Christ," its importance for the application of salvation is undeniable. By way of comparison, the Greek term for *justification* and its cognates appears thirty-three times in the New Testament, while the biblical basis for "union with Christ"—the phrases "in Christ," "in him" and the like—appears more than 140 times. Western Christian theologians have long acknowledged that this "union with Christ" somehow serves as an overarching category within which all the other elements of the application of salvation play their various roles. However, to this day, no Western Christian tradition has developed an approach to union with

---

[7]To be sure, within Western Christianity, Roman Catholicism and Anglicism have not shown the same proclivity for a specific *ordo salutis* as classic Protestantism has. However, Roman Catholic insistence that justification has in view the final judgment, at which the results of the process of sanctification will be taken into account, and its related assessment of conversion and faith imply a firm position on the order of the steps in the application of salvation. Also, much of evangelicalism has not officially adopted a particular stance on the *ordo salutis.* The movement is nevertheless marked by specific attitudes regarding the priority of faith to regeneration and the justification-sanctification connection, such that the above statement is warranted.

[8]While the Anglican tradition has been reticent to engage the *ordo salutis,* it has emphasized mystical union.

[9]The Presbyterian theologian John Murray argues this cogently in his *Redemption Accomplished and Applied* (Grand Rapids: Eerdmans, 1968), pp. 161-62; see also his declarations, "Union with Christ is a very inclusive subject. . . . It is not simply a phase of the application of redemption; it underlies every aspect of redemption both in its accomplishment and in its application" (p. 165), and "Union with Christ is the central truth of the whole doctrine of salvation" (p. 170).

Christ which has allowed it to be slotted somewhere into an *ordo salutis*. Significantly, this "union" emphasis is precisely what the Eastern Orthodox teaching on *theosis* is all about.

Eastern Orthodoxy on the Application of Salvation

In contrast to the Western Christian focus on the steps in the application of salvation, Eastern Orthodoxy looks at "the whole package": within Eastern Christianity, what recent Western Christian teaching intends with the phrase "union with Christ" has received the concentration. In this, the Orthodox follow out an emphasis found especially prominently in St. Paul, who teaches that all that happens to the followers of Christ in the application of salvation takes place "in him."[10] While union with Christ is at the core of Orthodoxy's teaching on the application of salvation, the designation used in Eastern Christian doctrinal parlance for this is not the "union with Christ" phrase encountered in contemporary Western Christian teaching; since Christian antiquity Orthodoxy has spoken of that application as *theosis*—"deification" or "divinization."

Deification: Eastern Orthodoxy and ancient philosophy. The term *theosis* was originally borrowed from ancient intellectual culture; the Greek word does not appear in the New Testament itself. However, this origin is not in itself an argument against the term: neither "Trinity" nor "millennium" (nor a host of other accepted doctrinal terms) appears in the biblical text. The significant question is whether what the word is used to set forth is supported by Scripture.

Since ancient pagan Greek thought among the Hellenic and the Hellenistic philosophers used the expression, this question is important. As it has done in other similar situations, so also in regard to the word *theosis*, Eastern Orthodoxy has appropriated ancient intellectual culture but filled it with a different content than it had in the ancient Hellenic and Hellenistic philosophies. This can be seen in two regards.

In the first place, *theosis* (or "deification" or "divinization"—the terms will be used interchangeably from here on) as understood and taught by Eastern Christendom does not involve a reabsorption into some immaterial ultimate being, as the concept did in the various permutations of ancient Platonism. This ancient Greek philosophical notion was intellectualistic in tendency, dualist in orienta-

[10] See the following: redemption and forgiveness are "in him" (Eph 1:7); there is no condemnation for those "in Christ Jesus" (Rom 8:1); Christians are made alive "in Christ" (1 Cor 15:22), justified "in Christ" (Gal 2:17), sanctified "in Christ Jesus" (1 Cor 1:2); and "in Christ Jesus" human beings are children of God through faith (Gal 3:26).

tion, and it implied a merging with the "Ultimate," either through the intellect or by going beyond the intellect (depending on the variety of "Platonism" espoused). In stark contrast, Orthodoxy teaches that those who are divinized remain eternally distinct from God: deification does not result in a human drop getting swallowed up in a divine ocean (as in Hinduism).

Second, and closely related to this, is the clarification that the Eastern Christian understanding of divinization does not obliterate the distinction between the Creator and the creature (as it did in the ancient Greek philosophies which used the term *theosis*). Although the goal and ultimate completion of the application of salvation is deification, even in the fullness of deification we will not lose our creaturely status. In the final or ultimate state, we do not receive and are not transformed into God's being. God's essence and our human essence remain everlastingly distinct. The difference between Creator and creature is never obliterated, according to Eastern Christian understanding, even in the final state. Theosis involves a real union with God, but never a fusion or confusion with God.

Deification: Biblical warrant. If *theosis* does not mean in Orthodoxy what it meant in the ancient Greek philosophies, what does it mean? To set the stage for dealing with that question, it would be helpful to consider some of the biblical evidence Eastern Christianity offers for its doctrine of deification. The warrant for the doctrine of *theosis* is not just its patristic heritage: Orthodoxy affirms that Scripture teaches deification.

In John 10:34-36, Christ quoted Psalm 82 during his argument with Jewish leaders. Jewish teaching had had a hard time assimilating the psalmist's reference to "gods" (Ps 82:6). In the way in which Christ used Psalm 82, he indicated that it points not only to him (as the incarnate Son of God) but also to others, whom the psalm categorizes as "gods." While what may be intended by calling these others "gods" is not clear from either passage, the reference to some human beings as "gods" is striking, and it certainly invites thoughtful reflection on what this might mean. At the least, this opens the way to considering "deification." From an Orthodox perspective, the testimony of two of the disciples of Christ offers significant help in this regard.

In writing to the early Christians, St. John reflected on their current privilege and their future hope when he taught, "Beloved, we are God's children now; what we will be has not yet been revealed. What we do know is this: when he is revealed, we will be like him, for we will see him as he is. And all who have this hope in him purify themselves, just as he is pure" (1 Jn 3:2-3). God's love has granted Christians the awesome privilege of being denominated his "children" already in this life and in an assured future. Their future status will be an enhancement of their current privilege, but that future status "has not yet been revealed." The apostle indicates what can be said about it, though, when he writes about what will happen to them: when Jesus Christ returns in the second advent, the apostle declares, "we will be *like him.*" Transformation is in store, a transformation to become like the incarnate Son of God. St. John urges that the pursuit of purity in which Christians engage in this life already moves toward this likeness and is stimulated by the assured hope of this ultimate conformity to the incarnate Son of God. However, Orthodoxy stresses that this conformity is not just an attitudinal or moral likeness or something of that order in the inner person. According to the apostle, the likeness to Christ held out as the end result of salvation will be a *visible likeness* to the Christ whom Christians will *see* on the last day.

What does this have to do, though, with deification? The words of St. Peter offer help in that regard:

> His divine power has given us everything needed for life and *godliness,* through the knowledge of him who called us by his own glory and goodness. Thus he has given us, through these things, his precious and very great promises, so that through them you may escape from the corruption that is in the world because of lust, and may *become participants of the divine nature.* (2 Pet 1:3-4, emphasis added)

The pursuit of purity of which St. John wrote is designated by St. Peter as *godliness*—which, in its most basic connotation, means being "like God" in some sense. It includes turning from the corruption brought into the world by human sin, as the "negative" side of this godliness. The way St. Peter describes the "positive" side of this likeness to God is striking: he calls it "participating in the divine nature." This is the goal of the application of salvation, according to the apostle. The Orthodox thus understand *deification* as an appropriate designation for this hope, given the way the apostle describes it. But how does this relate to what St. John presented?

The joint testimony of St. John and St. Peter is especially important, according to Eastern Orthodoxy, not because of their assumed presence while Christ argued about Psalm 82 with the Jewish leaders, but because they were (with St. James) eyewitnesses of the transfiguration of Christ. It is significant, the Orthodox urge, that St. Peter validated his teaching presented above by stating:

> We did not follow cleverly devised myths when we made known to you the power and coming of our Lord Jesus Christ, but we had been eyewitnesses of his majesty. For he received honor and glory from God the Father when that voice was conveyed to him by the Majestic Glory, saying, "This is my son, my Beloved, with whom I am

> well pleased." We ourselves heard this voice come from heaven, while we were with him on the holy mountain. (2 Pet 1:16-18)

Unquestionably, as the apostle wrote about the application of salvation, he had in mind what had transpired on the Mount of Transfiguration. Likewise, what St. John presented has clear points of connection to what transpired on Mount Tabor. It is necessary that we consider how Eastern Christianity views the transfiguration.

In the Orthodox understanding, the transfiguration is an event of fundamental importance for the church. The Transfiguration has not played a prominent role in Western Christian thought; we may give special attention to Christmas, Palm Sunday, Good Friday and Easter, but the story of what took place on Mount Tabor does not figure significantly in Western Christian teaching (or, for those denominations who follow it, the church year). However, the account of the transfiguration (Mt 17:1-8; Mk 9:2-8; Lk 9:28-35) plays a prominent role in Orthodox teaching on the understanding of salvation itself and on what happens in the application of salvation.

In all three Synoptic Gospels, Christ advised his disciples collectively, "There are some standing here who will not taste death before they see the Son of Man coming in his kingdom" (Mt 16:28; cf. Mk 9:1; Lk 9:27). In all three Synoptic Gospels, that declaration is immediately followed by the account of Christ's transfiguration, which occurred a few days later, at which only "some" of the disciples—Peter, James and John—were present. According to Orthodox teaching, the promise about *seeing the Son of Man coming in his kingdom* must, consequently, be understood as fulfilled in what transpired in the transfiguration. The phrase pointed to Christ as "the Son of Man"—the true descendant of Adam (or in the designation later used by St. Paul, "the last Adam"). The phrase further spoke of what he would accomplish in salvation—namely, "his kingdom." Finally, the phrase especially emphasized his "coming" in that kingdom, intending both the inauguration of it through what he would accomplish in salvation and also the "coming" at the final day when—in the words of one of the eyewitnesses, St. John—his subjects will "see him as he is" (1 Jn 3:2). According to Orthodoxy, then, the transfiguration is a tremendously important event: it shows who Christ is, what he will achieve in salvation, what he will be like when he appears and what his people will ultimately become.

But what was it that took place at the transfiguration? The account in the Gospel of St. Matthew states: "Six days later, Jesus took with him Peter and James and his brother John and led them up a high mountain, by themselves. And he was transfigured before them, and his face shone like the sun, and his clothes became dazzling white. Suddenly there appeared to them Moses and Elijah, talking with him" (Mt 17:1-3). According to Orthodoxy, on Mount Tabor divine glory shone through Christ's humanity. His humanity, without ceasing to be humanity, was transformed by and suffused with divine glory: Christ's humanity was *deified.* This showed forth his deity as the Son of God incarnate, in confirmation of St. Peter's confession a few days earlier (Mt 16:16). However, the glory manifested was not simply the glory he had from eternity as the Son of God; rather, as the last Adam, he had so acquired likeness to God that divine light shone forth through his humanity itself.

This was not only true for him, though; as the last Adam, he would secure it also for his people. This glorious transformation took place as Moses and Elijah discussed with Christ the "exodus" (Lk 9:31)—that is, the deliverance or salvation—which Christ would accomplish in Jerusalem. In presenting Christ speaking with the representatives of the law and of the prophets about the salvation he would accomplish, the passage makes clear that what took place with Christ was the fulfillment of the Scriptures and the salvation God had promised to humanity.

Christ's transfiguration, thus, was the manifestation of who he is, what would be achieved through the salvation he would accomplish, what he will be like when he returns for the *ultimate* "coming of his kingdom" and what his people will eventually be in the full application of salvation. What Christ is, his people will surely become. According to Eastern Christian thought, the transfiguration of Christ anticipates the suffusion of our redeemed humanity by the divine glory which the Holy Spirit has worked within us in the application of salvation. We will be *deified,* as Christ was deified in his human nature. St. Peter taught that divine glory would so work within us that genuine godliness—likeness to God—would result, a likeness that could be designated participation in the divine nature. The same idea was put more succinctly by St. John when he declared that we will see him and be like him. Orthodoxy understands this, the application of salvation, as deification.[11]

Two other passages can be considered briefly. St. Paul declares that "seeing the glory of the Lord, . . . [we] are being transformed into the same image from one degree of glory to another" (2 Cor 3:18). The affirmations regarding "seeing," "transformation" and "glory" all concur with what we have examined. As well, from an Eastern Christian perspective, it is striking that the passage considered above for the basic approach taken by Western Christianity in focusing on the

[11]Much more could be considered regarding Orthodox perspectives on the transfiguration; for a wide-ranging treatment, see John Anthony McGuckin, *The Transfiguration of Christ in Scripture and Tradition* (Queenston, Ont.: Edwin Mellen, 1986).

steps in the process of the application of salvation indicates that "those whom he [God] foreknew he also predestined to *be conformed to* the *image of his Son,* in order that he might be the firstborn within a large family" (Rom 8:29, emphasis added). The "family resemblance" to be attained on the final day will be all-pervasive.

Deification: Exposition of the doctrine. According to the Orthodox, their doctrine of *theosis* does not mean what it meant in the ancient Greek philosophies, and it has biblical warrant. What is the shape of the doctrine, then, in Eastern Orthodoxy? To answer that question, it should be observed that Eastern Christianity orients its concerns regarding the application of salvation on the process of that application, not on the particular steps in that process.[12] We must also note that Orthodoxy views the process itself from the ultimate goal of that application. That goal is the original purpose for which humankind was created.

As we have seen, humanity was created in the image of God, with the call to achieve likeness to God. Through communion with God and growing in his grace, humankind was to attain that likeness. However, human sin intervened, and humanity plunged into corruption instead of attaining the divine likeness. God promised salvation from this situation, but that salvation is not, according to Orthodoxy, an end in itself; rather, it is the means to an end. The salvation accomplished by Christ sets creation anew on its divinely intended path—communion with God for the whole of creation, but for humanity, likeness to God as well. This is all achieved through the incarnate Son of God.

The Christocentric understanding of receiving likeness to God was strikingly presented in the patristic period by St. Athanasius and affirmed, in various formulations, by other church fathers. Revered for his doctrinal faithfulness in Western and Eastern Christendom alike, Athanasius declared, "He [the Son of God] became man so that man might become god."[13] This pithy declaration has commended itself to subsequent generations in Eastern Christendom and encapsulates the Orthodox understanding to this day.

This approach builds on the apostolic description of salvation as an exchange between Christ and his followers. St. Paul taught, "For you know the generous act of our Lord Jesus Christ, that though he was rich, yet for your sakes he became poor, so that by his poverty you might become rich" (2 Cor 8:9). The "becomings"

---

[12]"According . . . to the soteriological perspective of the Orthodox Church, salvation—when viewed from the standpoint of the human subject that receives it—is not a single event in that person's past but an ongoing process" (Ware, *How Are We Saved?* p. 6).

[13]St. Athanasius *On the Incarnation of the Word* 54.3; see also St. Irenaeus's affirmation, "Because of his transcendent love, our Lord Jesus Christ became what we are, that he might bring us to be what he is" (*Against Heresies* 5.preface).

of Christ and of Christians move in opposite directions, with the poor/rich metaphor summarizing salvation accomplished and applied. Even more graphically, the apostle affirms, "For our sake he [God the Father] made him [Jesus Christ] to be sin who knew no sin, so that in him we might *become* the *righteousness of God*" (2 Cor 5:21, emphasis added). According to Orthodoxy, this is not an exaggerated metaphor but a straightforward declaration: through salvation in Christ, Christians do not just "receive" righteousness via imputation and sanctification—they actually *become* the *very righteousness of God.* God is righteous; Christians become *like God.*

This perspective depends, further, on Eastern Christianity's understanding of the significance of the incarnation. As part of the accomplishment of salvation, the Son of God took on himself a complete human nature. The way Orthodoxy appropriates that for the application of salvation is thought-provoking: "Our Lord saves us by becoming what we are, by sharing totally in our humanity, *thereby enabling us to share in what he is.* Thus through a reciprocal exchange of gifts he takes our humanity and communicates to us his divine life, reestablishing that communion between Creator and creation which sin has destroyed."[14] The incarnation is the foundation for likeness to God; deification is the assured result of salvation.

As the Son of God, the Logos was unquestionably *like* God; indeed, he is God. In his incarnation, however, the Logos did not simply bring that divine likeness to the humanity he assumed. As the last Adam, he fulfilled the first Adam's created purpose. The incarnate Son of God lived in utter faithfulness to God, always walking in his ways: all his decisions and actions, all the manifestations of his will and energy, were performed in submission to and conformity with God's will. The incarnate Logos, as human, thus acquired likeness to God. As the last Adam, he accomplished this not only for himself but for all those who are "in him." In the recapitulation achieved by the last Adam, he assured the fulfillment of humanity's ultimate calling, including likeness to God: "He takes into himself what is ours and in exchange he gives us what is His own, so that we become by grace what God is by nature, being made sons [and daughters] in the Son."[15] In the application of salvation, humans increasingly receive that likeness in the process known among the Orthodox as deification.

In Christ, deification is secured and assured. As a process, though, it is not finished in an instant, nor even by the end of a Christian's life: *theosis* depends on grace, but it involves a lifelong struggle. On the one hand, divinization involves

---

[14]Ware, *How Are We Saved?* pp. 52-53 (emphasis added).
[15]Ibid., p. 57.

turning from sin and its attendant corruption, not as a one-time phenomenon, but as an ongoing process of increasing alertness to sin in both self and surroundings, an alertness that issues into repentance. On the other hand, deification involves trusting God for grace and mercy in Christ, communion with God, and serving him faithfully in all of life. Death came as consequence of sin; life comes in communion with God. In its ultimate state, the *eternal life* promised in the gospel (Jn 3:16) triumphs over the last remnants of sin. In the present state, that eternal life is in struggle with sin. Divinization involves, then, a change from the present state of corruption in this world to one of incorruption. The struggle may be long and arduous, but divine grace supports and encourages. As Christ triumphed over death in his resurrection, so all those "in him" will ultimately triumph over death.

Theosis means so relying on divine grace that we live in God and he in us. Orthodoxy affirms the indwelling of the triune Godhead within Christians in an intensely realistic fashion: in the divine energies, God himself—Father, Son and Holy Spirit (Jn 14:16-17, 23)—dwells and works within humans, enabling them to become increasingly like him. This indwelling occupies the entire person, body and soul. As God created humans to participate in both realms, and as he made them his image-bearers in both body and soul, so he intended that his likeness pervade both the immaterial and the material components of human beings. Scripture declares that "God is light" (1 Jn 1:5) and speaks of the work of grace within Christians as the diffusing of light within them.[16] This divine light will suffuse not only our souls in holiness but also our bodies; they will be transformed and permeated by divine light, as Christ's humanity was in the transfiguration. St. Paul indicates that the resurrection bodies which Christians will receive are different from and yet in continuity with the bodies that they have known.[17] Theosis includes the entire person, body and soul together. Deification will only attain its fullness on the final day, at the resurrection.

Because of this, deification cannot be thoroughly understood or adequately described. The fullness of what humanity was to become in God's creative intention, and what it will become in the completed application of salvation, belong to the ultimate state—into which we have only dim insights. In comparing the situation of Christians during this age and what will come in the final one, St. Paul declared:

[16]"For it is the God who said, 'Let light shine out of darkness,' who has shone in our hearts to give the light of the knowledge of the glory of God in the face of Jesus Christ" (2 Cor 4:6).

[17]Writing about the resurrection from the dead, the apostle declared, "What is sown is perishable, what is raised is imperishable. It is sown in dishonor, it is raised in glory. It is sown in weakness, it is raised in power. It is sown a physical body, it is raised a spiritual body" (1 Cor 15:42-44).

> We know only in part, and we prophesy only in part; but when the complete comes, the partial will come to an end. When I was a child, I spoke like a child, I thought like a child, I reasoned like a child; when I became an adult, I put an end to childish ways. For now we see in a mirror, dimly, but then we shall see face to face. Now I know only in part; then I will know fully, even as I have been fully known. (1 Cor 13:9-12)

Even the apostle indicated that he could not intellectually apprehend the ultimate status into which Christians will be ushered. The child-adult comparison indicates both the continuity and the unfathomable difference between current privilege and future situation. Unquestionably, though, what will be exceeds by far what can be fully experienced and comprehended in the present. To similar effect, St. John asserted, "we are God's children now; what we will be has not yet been revealed" (1 Jn 3:2). Although his use of "children" does not carry the contrast to "adulthood," he affirms the same attitude as St. Paul: the fullness of the application of salvation is beyond our comprehension in the present age.

From an Orthodox perspective, this should come as no surprise. The complete realization of likeness to him must lie beyond our intellectual grasp in the present: not only are we merely creatures who have not yet ventured into the final state, but in the present life we are also still enmeshed in sin and corruption. Divinization increasingly delivers us from the latter and ushers us toward the former, but the goal remains beyond our intellectual apprehension.

However, according to Orthodoxy, this does not mean that we cannot speak truly about deification. It is just that our words must fall short and that we consequently live in the midst of a great mystery, the mystery of *theosis*. However, this mystery is not a foreboding one, murky with threatening doom; it is the mystery of God working within his image-bearers to enable them to become what they cannot begin to comprehend but what he has intended for them since the beginning of time—to be like him.

Deification defies comprehension. It arises from divine love toward human beings, transforms them by grace, and makes them all that God originally intended. Orthodoxy's affirmation of deification reaches back to the purposes of creation and forward to the final goal at the end of time. The ultimate attainment—likeness to God—shapes Eastern Christianity's treatment of the entire process of the application of salvation, bathing it in a numinous radiance that beggars explanation without frustrating study. Given all this, one can appreciate the declaration, "The idea of Theosis, of the Deification of humanity, is at the heart of Christian faith and theology and yet its meditation can only be pursued to a certain point before words fail."[18]

Although deification is beyond explanation, it is experienced in the present by all those "in Christ." Challenging as a concept, arduous as a struggle, *theosis* is the path on which every Christian walks. According to Orthodoxy, comprehension is not only not possible; it is not needed. What is needed is to live by grace, through a faith that entrusts oneself fully to divine love in Christ. With that, the Orthodox perspective on deification allows one to say with humble confidence, "I trust that by God's mercy and grace I am being saved."

Deification: The work of the Holy Spirit. Deification is the work of the third person of the Trinity, the Holy Spirit.[19] He was poured out on the Day of Pentecost and now works with and within the followers of Christ to effect their divinization. He does so through the sacraments, through the church and through "synergy."

Baptism and the Eucharist serve as means of deification. Through baptism, Eastern Christianity teaches, humans are initially united to Christ. This builds on St. Paul's vigorous declaration: "Do you not know that all of us who have been baptized into Christ Jesus were baptized into his death? Therefore we have been buried with him by baptism into death, so that, just as Christ was raised from the dead by the glory of the Father, so we too might walk in newness of life" (Rom 6:3-4). The apostle's powerful assertion leaves little space for a merely symbolic understanding of baptism, such as has become common in much of evangelicalism in Western Christianity. But while other varieties of Western Christianity affirm a more robust view of baptism uniting recipients with Christ, the concomitant understandings of baptism interpret the connection to the recipients in terms of cleansing from sin. While that makes its appropriate connection to Western Christian perspectives on the relationship of humans to God, it is not the apostle's focus here; he points to a transition from death to life via baptism. This is congruent with Orthodox emphases on the human condition: as sinners, we are caught up in death, but salvation given in Christ restores humans to life with God. Life in Christ is communicated to us in baptism. In the words of St. Paul, baptism is "the water of rebirth and renewal by the Holy Spirit" (Tit 3:5).

Further, in baptism God adopts the recipient as his son or daughter and makes the baptized one his heir (Gal 4:5; 3:29). This was celebrated by the Greek church

---

[18]Bishop Seraphim Sigrist, *Theology of Wonder* (Torrance, Calif.: Oakwood Publications, 1999), p. 88.

[19]"The Son has become like us by the incarnation; we become like Him by deification, by partaking of the divinity in the Holy Spirit. . . . The redeeming work of the Son is related to our nature. The deifying work of the Holy Spirit concerns our persons" (Lossky, *In the Image and Likeness of God,* p. 109).

fathers: St. John of Damascus declared, "Through him [Christ] we were made children of God, by being adopted through baptism,"[20] and St. Cyril of Jerusalem urged his hearers, "Do not imagine that you are being given something insignificant [in baptism]: you, a pitiable creature, receive the family name of God."[21] Moreover, in baptism we are cleansed from sin and "clothed with Christ" (Gal 3:27). The one baptized is called to "walk in newness of life" (Rom 6:4), seeking to be found spotless (Jude 24) before God. The Greek church fathers stress the wonder of God's gifts in baptism, which apply salvation to us: "What is given you in baptism is great: ransom for captives; forgiveness of sins; death of sin; spiritual rebirth; a shining garment; a holy, inviolable seal; a chariot to heaven; the delights of paradise; a welcome into the kingdom; the gift of adoption."[22] The Orthodox tradition continues to emphasize all this.

Some Western Christians, especially those in the "free church" and evangelical traditions, would wince at these affirmations and would probably reject them as "sacramentalism." However, the apostle certainly has more in mind than the notion that baptism is merely a symbol of something else. Indeed, according to St. Paul, God works in a special and mysterious way in the sacraments, honoring Christ's institution of them. These Western Christians would want to emphasize the necessity of faith, of a personal embrace of what is proclaimed in the sacraments; Eastern Orthodoxy (and the rest of Western Christendom too) would agree.[23] But Orthodoxy emphasizes that the priority belongs with God, who unites us to Christ in baptism and grants us all the benefits of his salvation: in baptism, our deification commences.

Our deification is furthered through the Eucharist. Christ himself declared, "unless you eat the flesh of the Son of Man and drink his blood, you have no life

---

[20] *The Orthodox Faith* 4.8.

[21] *The Catechetical Lectures*, Introductory Lecture.6.

[22] Cyril of Jerusalem *The Catechetical Lectures*, Introductory Lecture.16. Thus the exuberant declaration of Clement of Alexandria: "When we are baptized, we are enlightened; enlightened, we become adopted children; adopted as children, we are made complete; and becoming complete, we are made divine. It is written, *I have said, 'You are gods and all of you the sons of the most High'* [Ps 82:6]. This ceremony is often called 'free gift,' 'enlightenment,' 'perfection,' and 'cleansing'—'cleansing,' because by it we are completely purified of our sins; 'free gift,' because through it the punishments due to our sins are remitted; 'enlightenment,' since by it we behold the wonderful, holy light of salvation (that is, it enables us to see God clearly); finally, we call it 'perfection,' since we need nothing else—for what else could anyone need who possesses the knowledge of God?" (*Christ the Educator* 1.26).

[23] Thus the declaration by an Orthodox bishop, "The Spirit is always and only personal. . . . So valid and right though the administration of the sacrament is, it awaits to be awakened into conscious and personal experience. If the experience of the Holy Spirit is really personal, then it must be unique in each person" (Sigrist, *Theology of Wonder*, pp. 56-57); see also Lossky, *The Mystical Theology of the Eastern Church*, p. 166.

in you. Those who eat my flesh and drink my blood have eternal life, and I will raise them up on the last day; for my flesh is true food and my blood is true drink. Those who eat my flesh and drink my blood abide in me, and I in them" (Jn 6:53-56). By the time St. John wrote these words, the church had long since learned to view the Lord's Supper as the partaking of the body and blood of Christ. Moreover, St. Paul's rhetorical questions in 1 Corinthians 10:16—"The cup of blessing that we bless, is it not a sharing in the blood of Christ? The bread that we break, is it not a sharing in the body of Christ?"—clearly demand a positive answer: his argument depends on the affirmation that Christians participate in the body and blood of Christ in the Eucharist.

In the early second century, St. Ignatius of Antioch expressed this confidence elegantly when he declared, "We break one bread, which is the medicine of immortality, the antidote we take in order not to die but to live forever in Jesus Christ."[24] This eternal life belongs to no one but God himself. The purpose of the incarnation and the whole economy of salvation was for human beings to share in that divine life: "When God revealed himself, he united himself with our mortal nature in order to deify humanity through this close relation with deity. Since this is so, through his flesh, constituted by bread and wine, he implants himself in all believers."[25] In the Eucharist, divine life is thus communicated to us: "If the flesh of the Savior became life-giving, since it was united with that which is life by nature—i.e., the Word that is from God—when we taste of it we receive that life within ourselves, since we too are united with the flesh of the Savior."[26] This is our privilege when we receive the Eucharist: "Bread, produced from the earth, when it receives the invocation of God is no longer common bread, but the Eucharist. It consists of two realities, earthly and heavenly. So also, when our bodies receive the Eucharist, they are no longer corruptible, since they have the hope of the resurrection to eternity."[27]

Again, for many in the evangelical traditions, this will sound like sacramentalism—exaggerating the effects of ecclesiastical ordinances. However, in Orthodoxy, the dominical and apostolic declarations are taken with consummate real-

---

[24] *Letter to the Ephesians* 20.2.

[25] St. Gregory of Nyssa *Catechetical Oration* 37.

[26] St. Cyril of Alexandria *Commentary on John* 6.53; see his further declaration, "We come to the mystical gifts and are sanctified, becoming partakers of the holy flesh and the honorable blood of Christ, the Savior of us all. We do not receive it as ordinary flesh, . . . but as genuinely life-giving and the Word's own flesh. Since, by his nature as God he was life, when he became one with his own flesh, he made it life-giving" (St. Cyril of Alexandria *The Third Letter to Nestorius*).

[27] St. Irenaeus of Lyons *Against Heresies* 4.18.5.

ism. In this regard, Eastern Christianity follows the instruction of St. Cyril of Jerusalem: "Do not think of the elements as merely bread and wine. According to the Lord's declaration, they are Christ's body and blood. Although sense suggests the opposite, let faith hold you firm. Instead of judging the matter by taste, let faith give you an unshakeable confidence that you have been privileged to receive the body and blood of Christ."[28] For the Orthodox, this can only be believed, not explained. That is true, though, not only of the Eucharist but of all God's ways toward humanity. As St. John of Damascus points out, "All the things of God are above the natural order and beyond speech and understanding."[29]

While virtually all the strands of Western Christianity have tried to answer the question as to *how* the communal elements are or become the body and blood of Christ, Eastern Christianity has not done so.[30] In this, Orthodoxy stands steadfast in the approach of the Greek church fathers: "And now you ask how the bread becomes the body of Christ and the wine and water the blood of Christ. I tell you that the Holy Spirit comes down and works these things which are beyond description and understanding."[31] Orthodoxy simply affirms that in the Eucharist we receive the body and blood of Christ—a perspective in keeping with St. Paul's words and those of Christ himself.

Beyond this, the Holy Spirit uses the church in the process of deification. This is not only because the church is the place where baptism and the Eucharist are received. The role of the church in our divinization is more than just that of "institutional channel" for the sacraments. To be sure, the significance of that channel should never be underestimated: in baptism and the Eucharist granted in the church, human beings, although wrapped up in death in themselves, experience the intersection of the temporal and the eternal realms. Already now, in this brief life, human beings participate in the eternal life which belongs only to God. In

---

[28]*Mystagogical Lectures* 4.6; see his further asseveration: "'O taste and see that the Lord is good' [Ps 34:8]. Do not entrust the judgment to your bodily palate, but to steadfast faith: in tasting you taste, not bread and wine, but the body and blood of Christ" (5.20).

[29]*The Orthodox Faith* 4.11.

[30]To be sure, in the pressures of the seventeenth century and subsequently to respond effectively to Protestant and especially Roman Catholic challenges, some Orthodox appropriated elements of Roman teaching, giving them an Orthodox turn; however, those modifications were not accepted by all the Orthodox and have been repudiated by the leading figures of Orthodox teaching and practice.

[31]St. John of Damascus *The Orthodox Faith* 4.13; note also his further statement: "The bread and wine are transformed into the body and blood of God. If you ask how this is done, let it suffice for you to hear that it is done through the Holy Spirit, just as it was through the Holy Spirit that the Lord himself took on flesh for himself from the blessed mother of God. More than this we do not know: the word of God is true and effective and omnipotent, but the manner in which this is done cannot be searched out" (4.13).

this, received only in the church, they are made "like God"—deified.

Theosis is not individualistic, though: it is granted in and for the church as a whole. According to Orthodoxy, humanity was not created to be distinct individuals unrelated to each other. Deification as it is worked out in the church takes place in the individual but is not individualistic. Long ago, St. John Chrysostom made the point sharply when he urged, "Individual righteousness is not enough for salvation."[32] For Orthodoxy, deification is communal.[33] An Orthodox bishop has presented this clearly: "The conviction [is] deeply rooted in the Orthodox conscience that we are not saved in isolation but in union with our fellow humans from every generation. 'We are members of one another' (Eph 4:25): salvation is not solitary but social."[34]

In deification, the whole is more than the sum of its parts. Apostolic teaching indicates the inescapable interconnectedness of the members of the church as "the body of Christ" (Rom 12:1-10; 1 Cor 12). According to Orthodox teaching, human beings only become what God intended them to be—"like God," deified—in the intimacy of the church. The living and loving communion of the triune Godhead is lived out within humanity in the church, the body of Christ. In the church that loving communion finds expression in this broken world. The church thus serves not only as a signpost of the coming fulfillment of divine purposes with and for the whole creation but as a manifestation of that fulfillment "ahead of time," as it were—already in this age, yet to become fully whole in the eschaton.

As the church meets to worship God, we enter into his presence and experience communion with him. We were created to seek this communion and be drawn by it to his likeness, so worship furthers our divinization. As we engage in this worship, we also meet with other Christians, both past[35] and present. We join with them in finding our fulfillment in serving and loving God. Drawn to him, we are drawn to them; serving and loving him, we learn to serve and love these brothers and sisters in Christ, who are also made in his image and growing in his likeness. In the worship offered in church, thus, we find the opportunity and call to live a life of loving service to others and to receive the service of others. The church summons us to become now what God intended in creation long ago and has assured in the fullness of his plan for the creation.

In the meanwhile, in the church we have a special opportunity to live out our

---

[32] *Homilies on Ephesians,* Sermon 21 (on Eph 6:1-4).
[33] See the treatment below, chap. 10, pp. 169-72.
[34] Ware, *How Are We Saved?* p. 26.
[35] See the treatment of this below, chap. 10, pp. 174-76.

calling to love God and our neighbor. For Orthodoxy, "We cannot be saved in any other way than through the neighbor."[36] In the hurly-burly of life with others in the church, where real people rub each other the wrong way, we experience the difficulty and privilege of the divine mercy that transforms us to become like God. St. Maximus Confessor expressed this winsomely when he wrote, "We find the forgiveness of our trespasses in forgiving our brothers and sisters: the mercy of God is hidden in mercifulness toward our neighbor."[37] In thus learning to love our neighbors as ourselves we live up to our *logos*. As we do so, we respond faithfully to the greatest of God's commandments—and deification entails living by God's commandments.

A distinctive element in the Orthodox understanding of how the Holy Spirit works deification within us is the doctrine of "synergy"—"working together." This working together is the collaboration of God's grace and a person's will. While Western Christianity has argued about the alternatives of "monergism" and "synergism"—that is, the question of whether salvation is accomplished only by God or by God and human beings cooperating—this issue did not become a tension within Orthodoxy. Eastern Christendom has not focused on the issues of guilt, debt, questions of merit and so on, that flowed from the juridical approach of the Christian West and made the monergism/synergism issue a matter of concern.[38] Orthodoxy insists on synergy, but Orthodox teaching approaches the question of divine grace and human will working together from quite a different perspective.

In the Eastern Christian understanding of synergy, God's grace and human response work together without the questions of rivalry that have bedeviled the Western Christian disagreement about monergism and synergism. As we have seen, Eastern Christianity emphasizes that human beings always have the freedom to choose, in their personal (gnomic) wills, whether to walk with God or turn from him. In regard to synergy, this means that each person must respond, freely and consciously, to divine grace. In so personally deciding to go in God's way, one is thus working with, not against, the Holy Spirit. This does not mean that the respective contributions are of equal weight. A leading Orthodox spokesman has stressed that "what God does is incomparably more important than what we humans do; yet our voluntary participation in God's saving action is altogether indis-

---

[36]Pseudo-Macarius *The Spiritual Homilies* 37.3.

[37]*The Ascetic Life* 42.

[38]The Orthodox theologian Vladimir Lossky forthrightly states, "The notion of merit is foreign to the Eastern tradition" (*The Mystical Theology of the Eastern Church*, p. 197).

pensable."[39] In deification, we yield to the promptings of the Holy Spirit and walk in the ways of the Lord. Divine grace and human will work together: this was what was to be true in Adam, was actually true in Christ, and must be true in all those who are being deified.

CONCLUDING OBSERVATIONS

The divergence between the perspectives of Western Christianity and Eastern Orthodoxy is probably nowhere as dramatic as it is in the treatments of the application of salvation. The approaches are significantly different, and the emphases do not readily coincide. While both speak about the same wonder of salvation, they come at it in such different ways that it might at first appear that the two have little to say to each other. However, when we recall that the divergence is in understanding what St. Jude poignantly calls "the salvation we share" (Jude 3), we may step back from this hasty assessment. While several suggestions might be made, five will suffice for our considerations.

In the first place, if we can admit that both sides have significant biblical warrant for their viewpoints—as they do—then we cannot jump to the conclusion that Western Christianity and Eastern Orthodoxy have nothing to say to each other. To be sure, the two Christendoms have approached and dealt with the biblical data in profoundly different ways. Rather than dismiss the other, however, each should be willing to consider the alternative perspectives in the endeavor better to understand and appreciate the fullness of biblical teaching about the application of salvation. As we saw with regard to the apostolic witness about the accomplishment of salvation, so too in the biblical presentation regarding its application: what is presented (and promised) is beyond enclosure in a single approach. If nothing else, that recognition will engender some openness toward brothers and sisters in Christ who speak dramatically differently about "the salvation we share."

Second, it needs to be stated that Western Christianity has paid closer attention to the precise ways in which the apostles spoke of the particular "moments" of the application of salvation than the Eastern Christian tradition has. It is striking that the various declarations in Scripture regarding justification, adoption and sanctification, for example, find little resonance in Orthodoxy's treatment of the

---

[39]Ware, *How Are We Saved?* p. 34; cf. his further declaration, "Instead of thinking in terms of shares, equally or unequally distributed, we should consider that the work of our salvation is *totally and entirely* an act of divine grace, and yet in that act of divine grace we humans remain *totally and entirely* free" (p. 40).

application of salvation.[40] Unquestionably, these could be incorporated within the presentation of *theosis,* but that has not been done within Eastern Christianity. To do so would not be to depart either from commitment to the doctrine of deification or from tradition, but would be to listen even more attentively to the apostolic witness regarding the application of salvation.

Third, Orthodoxy's presentation of deification has protected the glorious mystery of salvation in ways that the analytic, step-defining approach of Western Christianity does not. From first to last in the consideration of deification, one is aware of not being able intellectually to grasp the wonder of salvation, in which we become by divine grace all we were intended to be from the dawn of human history. The consideration that the application of salvation will only be complete at the end of time, when we will receive resurrected bodies immeasurably improved over the ones we have known and we will enter into a new creation in which no corruption or sin is present—so utterly beyond our imaginations, even at their most sanctified—surely ought to be enough to cause hesitation in speaking too confidently about our grasp of the application of salvation.

That consideration leads, in the fourth place, to a comparison of the two approaches of Western Christianity and Eastern Orthodoxy in a particular regard. Orthodoxy treats the application of salvation as a process, viewing it from its ultimate completion; Western Christianity has focused on the respective steps. Of those steps in any *ordo salutis,* the last is always *glorification*—which is the ultimate completion of the application of salvation, to be received only at the resurrection on the final day. Western Christianity, typically, has done little with this final "step" in the application of salvation, but Orthodoxy has laid its heaviest emphasis on it. It would be simplistic to suggest that Western Christianity could just splice Orthodox teaching about deification onto Western Christian approaches. However, it may not be too much to suggest that Western Christianity could listen to its brothers and sisters in Orthodoxy as they speak about deification and learn again to appreciate the unfathomable wonder of what is in store for us.

Finally, it should be stressed that Western Christians could learn from Eastern Christians to appreciate the significance of the transfiguration of Christ in a much

[40]Some of these find expression in the Orthodox liturgical tradition: e.g., the liturgy for baptism promises the one receiving baptism "justification." In addition, regeneration, justification and sanctification are mentioned several times in the rich Lenten liturgical materials (see Mother Mary and Archimandrite Kallistos Ware, eds., *The Lenten Triodion* [South Canaan, Penn.: St Tikhon's Seminary, 2002 (reprint of 1978 edition)], passim). Even so, although the liturgical tradition has significantly shaped Orthodox teaching in most regards, that is not evident in their doctrinal teaching about the distinct elements in the application of salvation.

richer way than has hitherto been the Western Christian practice. Unquestionably, Orthodoxy's treatment of the transfiguration shows a greater attentiveness to the biblical text of that passage and a richer assessment of its significance than Western Christianity has mustered. With that, we might also learn to look with new appreciation on the significance of what St. John and St. Peter, the eyewitnesses of that event, had to say about the application of salvation. As we do that, our insights into what is promised in the fullness of the application of salvation will undoubtedly be enriched and deepened.

9

What Is Grace?

THE CHRISTIAN FAITH IS ALL ABOUT GRACE. While other religions of the world have their moments in which a sort of ultimate or transcendent benignity may reach all the way to mere creatures, in Christianity grace is the story from first to last. The God of Christianity is straightforwardly referred to in apostolic witness as "the God of all grace" (1 Pet 5:10), and the Christian message as "the good news of God's grace" (Acts 20:24). According to the Christian faith, we live by grace and are saved by grace, our future comes by grace, and our hope rests on grace. Nothing in the message of Christianity makes sense apart from God's grace.

Both Western Christianity and Eastern Orthodoxy teach that grace is absolutely necessary in order to be and live as a Christian: all the steps in the various versions of the *ordo salutis* in Western Christianity, the overarching conception of union with Christ, and deification as taught in Orthodoxy are by grace. In both Western and Eastern Christianity divine grace receives constant, repeated emphasis. Whatever differences there are between one and another tradition within Christendom regarding the role of human beings in receiving grace, all Christian traditions stress that it is grace that takes the initiative in salvation, from beginning to end. Even with this commonality, however, there is an interesting difference between Western Christianity and Eastern Orthodoxy in talking about grace—specifically, in a question asked about grace and, with that, the startling answer that arises.

Western Christianity on Grace

We in the Christian West agree regarding the necessity of grace, but we have also argued and split from each other over questions about grace. Many of our Western Christian divisions have arisen over opposing assessments of what can and must be said about grace. Examples include the conflict between Protestants and Roman Catholics over precisely how, when and why we are *justified by grace* and the division within Protestantism between the Reformed and the followers of Arminius over the way in which saving grace is appropriated in salvation.[1] The differences that thus arose, however, were not arguments as to whether grace was necessary (despite what vigorous protagonists in the respective arguments alleged), but as to its relationship to human will and work.

An overlooked question. Within Western Christianity, we have debated questions about grace in numerous controversies. We have examined in considerable detail biblical minutiae regarding grace. Given this extensive and intensive attention to questions regarding grace, it may be surprising to discover that a significant question about it has hardly been addressed in Western Christianity and certainly does not figure in Western Christian understandings of grace. With all our concentration on grace, we have considered carefully *what grace does,* how it operates upon us, the effects it has on believers and so forth. But we have not often directed our attention to the question of *what grace is.* This is true both for the rarified heights of academic theology in the Christian West and for the less elaborated understandings of Western Christian laypeople.

One might respond that the common emphasis in Western Christendom so stresses grace that every Christian recognizes he could not even be a Christian, much less live a Christian life, without grace—and, of course, that response would be true as far as it goes. Does a Christian need to ask what something is which she cannot possibly be (or consider being) without? If grace is, as the apostolic witness clearly affirms, the "ground of being," as it were, for a Christian, is it necessary to ask what grace *is?* One can certainly live as a Christian without asking that particular question; indeed, it would appear that Western Christians have been doing so for centuries. Even so, Eastern Christianity has asked the question—and once one hears the question, it is unforgettable and inescapable.

Perhaps someone might object that Western Christianity *has,* in fact, dealt with that question. One of the common Western Christian ways of describing "grace" is to say it *is* "unmerited favor." That short phrase affirms an important truth, indeed: it declares what grace is *with regard to the recipient.* However, only a little reflection is sufficient to indicate that the description of grace as "un-

---

[1]The controversy over the views of Arminius and his followers resulted in the calling of the Synod of Dordrecht, 1618-1619, at which the Canons of the Synod of Dordt were promulgated, denouncing various Arminian tenets and affirming a strict monergism in grace (often referred to as "the five points of Calvinism"); the Roman Catholic Church experienced a similar tension with Jansenism in the seventeenth and early eighteenth centuries, but in that controversy the strict monergist approach was repudiated.

merited favor," valuable as it may be, does not tell us what grace itself *is.* Similarly, Christians in the English-speaking world have sometimes used an acrostic to describe grace: in that acrostic, "grace" is "*G*od's *R*iches *A*t *C*hrist's *E*xpense." Clever a teaching device as that is, however, it describes how divine grace comes to humankind and suggests what it brings, but it does not set forth what grace *is.*

Grace in the history of Western Christian thought. One can search the history of Western Christian doctrinal teaching and find virtually no consideration of the question of what grace is—a question long ago posed and answered in Orthodoxy. As a way of appreciating what the Eastern Christian question offers for our reflections on grace, it would be helpful to survey the path traversed by the Western Christian treatment of grace over the centuries.

During antiquity in the Christian West, the question about what grace is did not arise. Even St. Augustine, for all his emphasis on grace and his elaboration of numerous facets of how grace affects Christian life, did not address the question. His profound mind raised a host of questions regarding divine grace and human will, about divine sovereignty and human responsibility, and the answers he articulated have continued to stimulate discussion about that complex of questions in the history of Western Christian thought. However, St. Augustine himself did not pay any special attention to the question of what grace is.

The medieval scholastic theologians did bring up the question but did not pursue it; their focus in treating grace remained on what happens as it takes hold of a human being. We can see this in the treatments offered by two key theologians, St. Bonaventure and St. Thomas Aquinas. St. Bonaventure affirmed that "grace is a gift bestowed and infused directly by God, . . . a gift by which the soul is perfected and transformed, . . . a gift that cleanses, enlightens, and perfects the soul; that vivifies, reforms, and strengthens it; that lifts it up, makes it like to God, and unites it with Him, thus rendering it acceptable to Him." According to St. Bonaventure, this grace is not "God . . . in His immutable essence," but "an *influence* that emanates from Him. . . . This grace is granted directly by God acting as the Source of grace."[2] St. Thomas presented the same basic orientation. He affirmed that divine grace works within human beings to produce a "habitual gift" (Latin, *habitus*) within them, a "created" grace that enables them to respond to di-

[2]Citations are from St. Bonaventure's *Breviloquium,* as found in *The Works of Bonaventure,* trans. José de Vinck, vol. 2 (Paterson, N.J.: St. Anthony Guild Press, 1963), pp. 181-83 (emphasis added). The *Breviloquium* has rightly been praised as one of St. Bonaventure's greatest works; it offers a condensation of the much more massive treatment of doctrine found in his *Commentaries on the Four Books of Sentences.*

vine precepts and live unto God.[3] The two great medieval theologians both proceeded to extended treatments on grace, but neither explored the question of what grace itself is, other than to call it an "influence" from God that profoundly transforms human recipients. Medieval theologians subsequently turned their attention somewhat to that question, though. As a reflex of the teaching about "created" grace *(gratia creata),* they posited an "uncreated" grace *(gratia increata)* which is the source of "created" grace. This *uncreated* grace can only be the one uncreated, God. Thus, according to these medieval theologians, God somehow communicates himself to human beings: this self-communication of God is the foundation of all the grace infused into human beings in salvation.[4]

These medieval scholastic emphases have been continued within Roman Catholicism. The basic pattern has persisted, but with an interesting modification during the later twentieth century. Some Roman Catholic theologians have asserted, in contrast to St. Bonaventure's perspective, that in *uncreated* grace God communicates *his own nature* to human beings.[5] This orientation approaches the question posed by Orthodoxy, but the answer offered is one Eastern Christianity could not endorse.[6]

Protestant theologians have not directed their attention to the question we are considering. The sixteenth-century Reformers urged that salvation is entirely *sola gratia* ("by grace alone"), as against what had become by then a common understanding within Western Christendom that salvation is an amalgam of grace and human accomplishment. Thus, they considered extensively the significance of grace for salvation and as manifestation of divine love, but the Reformers did not plunge into the question of what grace itself is. This was true of Martin Luther, Ulrich Zwingli, Martin Bucer and John Calvin. Of all the major sixteenth-century Protestant Reformers, only Philipp Melanchthon came near to addressing the question. In his 1521 *Loci communes*—the first attempt to set forth the Reformation message in a systematic form—he assayed a definition of grace: "Grace is nothing else, if it is to be most accurately defined, than God's goodwill toward us, or the will of God which has mercy on us. Therefore the word 'grace' does not mean some quality in us, but rather the very will of God, or the goodwill of God

---

[3]St. Thomas Aquinas, *The Summa Theologica,* part 2 (first part), number 3, questions 90-114 (London: Burns, Oates & Washbourne, 1927), pp. 349-50.

[4]R. Kearsley, "Grace," in *New Dictionary of Theology,* ed., Sinclair B. Ferguson, David F. Wright and J. I. Packer (Downers Grove, Ill.: InterVarsity Press, 1988), p. 280.

[5]Karl Rahner has set this forth in his article "Grace" in Karl Rahner and Herbert Vorgrimler, *Theological Dictionary,* trans. Richard Strachan (New York: Herder & Herder, 1965), p. 194; Rahner offers a fuller treatment in *Sacramentum Mundi: An Encyclopedia of Theology,* 6 vols. (New York: Herder & Herder, 1968-1970), 2:418.

[6]See the treatment below, pp. 163-64 and n. 18.

toward us. . . . To sum it all up, grace is nothing but the forgiveness or remission of sins."[7] He thus opposed what the medieval scholastic theologians had affirmed about grace as a *habitus* within human beings, but his definition went no further than to assert that grace is divine benevolence to humanity; he did not engage the question of what grace is.

The situation changed somewhat with the Reformers' successors during the period of Protestant scholasticism.[8] Among them, grace was presented, as in St. Bonaventure, as a divine "influence" on us and, with St. Thomas, as a "habitual gift" by which we respond appropriately to divine overtures.[9] Some of them also taught about "uncreated grace," but they went no further than to urge that it is the power of God that causes "created" grace; apart from this, however, little relevant to our question was presented.[10]

This pattern has persisted in subsequent Protestant treatments to the present day. Many theologians have given grace extensive study, but they have not broached the question we are investigating.[11] A standard treatment of systematic theology in the Reformed tradition is in this mold: the volume deals only with what grace effects, not what it is.[12] Treatments on a more popular level have followed the same path: during the late 1990s, a bestselling book on grace included no consideration whatsoever of the question of what grace is.[13]

---

[7]Philipp Melanchthon, *Loci communes theologici,* in *Melanchthon and Bucer,* ed., Wilhelm Pauck (Philadelphia: Westminster Press, 1959), pp. 87-88.

[8]The best theological source books for Lutheran and for Reformed theology during the Protestant scholastic period are, respectively, Heinrich Schmid, *The Doctrinal Theology of the Evangelical Lutheran Church,* trans. Charles A. Hay and Henry E. Jacobs, 3rd rev. ed. (Minneapolis: Augsburg, 1961); and Heinrich Heppe, *Reformed Dogmatics: Set Out and Illustrated from the Sources,* trans. G. T. Thomson, rev. ed. (Grand Rapids: Baker, 1978). It is striking that neither volume includes any treatment of the question we are considering.

[9]See the discussion of grace as a *habitus* in Schmid, *Doctrinal Theology of the Evangelical Lutheran Church,* pp. 674-75; see also the treatment in Richard A. Muller, *Dictionary of Latin and Greek Theological Terms: Drawn Principally from Protestant Scholastic Theology* (Grand Rapids: Baker, 1989), p. 134.

[10]Muller, *Dictionary of Latin and Greek Theological Terms,* p. 134; cf., though, the interesting affirmation by Johann Heidegger, "God's grace is His virtue and perfection, by which He *bestows and communicates Himself* becomingly on and to the creature beyond all merit belonging to it" (Heppe, *Reformed Dogmatics,* p. 96, emphasis added). However, Heidegger's provocative adumbrations on grace as God communicating himself to human beings did not attract either much discussion or any significant following in Reformed theological circles.

[11]Even Karl Barth, for all his vigorous reexamination and reformulation of Protestant theology, and with all the emphasis he placed on grace as divine act, did not go on to ask what grace is.

[12]Reference is to the presentation in Louis Berkhof, *Systematic Theology* (Grand Rapids: Eerdmans, 1968), p. 427.

[13]Reference is to the volume by Philip Yancey, *What's So Amazing About Grace?* (Grand Rapids: Zondervan, 1997).

Within Western Christianity, theologians have given no particular, deliberate or sustained attention to the question of what grace is: one can check in virtually any volume on doctrines in general or on grace in particular, and still not find the question even raised, much less discussed. This is not brought forward as an indictment of Western Christian teaching: the apostolic testimony regarding grace falls on what grace brings to the undeserving and how it affects us, from the beginning of our lives in Christ, throughout them and on into eternity. Thus, one cannot assert that Western Christian teaching has defaulted on the biblical witness regarding grace, since that teaching has dealt with the main questions. However, recognizing that should not preclude considering whether there is something more that could be asked about grace—something which might enrich Western Christian understandings about grace. Such a question has been raised in Orthodoxy.

EASTERN ORTHODOXY ON WHAT GRACE IS

Perhaps a good way to get into the question of what grace is would be to ask some related questions. Certainly in grace God influences us, but is grace merely a divine influence? And what do we even mean by "a divine influence"? How do we understand its relationship to God? It is *from* God, of course—but how is it from him? Is grace something that "oozes out" of God toward us? Is grace a sort of immaterial or spiritual "stuff" that God imparts to us? And how does he "impart" it? Is it something that comes to us at arm's length from God, something he pours out on us, as it were, from a spiritual pitcher? Further, when we speak of "divine grace," in what sense is that grace divine?

Once one begins to ask questions such as these—and many more could be generated—it becomes evident that, even with all the emphasis on grace in the history of Christendom, both East and West, and for all our published and preached treatments of it, grace remains in many ways mysterious. From an Orthodox perspective, this should not be a surprise. After all, grace is God's activity, and divine activity must always remain beyond human comprehension. Even so, Orthodoxy has made bold to enter into the question of what grace is; the result of its reflections is a stimulating and striking insight into grace.

When Christians speak of God's grace toward us, we do not intend merely to utter a symbolic affirmation meaning that God is in some sense tender toward creatures. For Christians, *grace* is a word for God's work within us. We also believe, as Scripture tells us, that God dwells within us. Christ promised this on the night before he was betrayed: he assured his disciples, and through them the church of all time, that the triune God would indwell them.[14] In the Eastern Christian understanding, these are tied together intimately: a leading Orthodox theologian indicated the interrelationship when he wrote, "Through the coming of the Holy Spirit the Trinity dwells within us and deifies us."[15] It is through the Holy Spirit that grace—which deifies us, in the Eastern Christian understanding of the application of salvation—comes to us. As God dwells within us and graciously works within us, though, what is that deifying grace?

A speculative question? Before proceeding further to consider this question as asked and answered within Eastern Christianity, it would be well to anticipate and respond to an objection (or at least a question) that may occur to some readers. By this point in our treatment, it will have become unmistakably clear that Eastern Orthodoxy has long had considerable hesitation about the capabilities of human intellection to deal adequately with God and his activities. Closely related is the Eastern Christian suspicion of merely human philosophies and their problematics as ways of apprehending the mysteries of God. The question about what grace is sounds like the sort of speculation Eastern Christianity has traditionally eschewed in its approach to doctrine. The question may well arise, consequently, how it is that Orthodoxy not only came to ask but to consider a question that seems, on the face of it, so obviously philosophical—a question, moreover, not even directly raised by the apostolic witness in Scripture itself. Given these Orthodox orientations, how is it that the question of what grace is has even been given such widespread consideration?

This is a fair question—one to which there is a ready answer. The question about what grace is did not arise out of philosophical speculations; it arose out of a basic worldview consideration for Eastern Orthodoxy. As a way of recognizing both the relationship of God to his creation and also the chasm between them, and in order to deal with affirmations that might transgress those bounds, Eastern Christianity learned to make a basic distinction. St. Gregory of Nyssa put it simply but memorably when he observed, "All existence is divided into what is created and what is uncreated."[16] All that is must either be God—the only uncreated—or

---

[14]Jesus declared, "Those who love me will keep my word, and my Father will love them, *and we will come to them and make our home with them*" (Jn 14:23, emphasis added); he had already promised, "And I will ask the Father, and he will give you another Advocate, to be with you forever. This is the Spirit of truth. . . . [H]e abides with you, and he will be in you" (Jn 14:16-17). Thus, he declared that all three persons of the Trinity would indwell believers.

[15]Vladimir Lossky, *The Mystical Theology of the Eastern Church* (Crestwood, N.Y.: St. Vladimir's Seminary Press, 1976), p. 171. In Western Christianity, we most commonly think of the Holy Spirit indwelling Christians; we have given less attention to the biblical declarations in John 14 that the Father and the Son also dwell in the hearts of Christians.

[16]St. Gregory of Nyssa *Catechetical Oration* 39; he makes the same point in his *Against Eunomius* 8.5.

else something which came into being because of God's creative activity. With this, Eastern Christians have been able to structure basic thought in such ways as not to transgress the Creator-creation distinction. Since much of ancient intellectual culture regularly violated that distinction, the created-uncreated contrast came repeatedly into play; it is hardly surprising that it was used not only in regard to the assumptions of ancient philosophy but also with regard to the emphases of apostolic teaching. Given the focus on grace in the Scriptures, the question came to be asked whether grace is created or uncreated—the question of *what grace is.* The question thus arose not out of philosophical speculation but out of basic considerations of faithful Christian teaching.

Created or uncreated? Is grace, then, *created* or *uncreated?* If it was *created,* then it did not exist in eternity and came as part of creation. While one might quickly respond that grace must have been created, inasmuch as it reaches out to the creation and especially to humanity, that assumption fixes upon what grace does vis-à-vis humanity and the rest of creation, without determining whether grace "came into being," as it were, with the rest of creation. Only a little reflection will reveal, though, that this is not a possible option. Grace is God's activity toward his creation, indeed, but should we therefore assume that grace was created too? Is it not obvious that grace, as presented in Scripture, is God acting toward his image-bearers in love and mercy? Did God "begin" to "become" gracious at humanity's creation or at the fall of our first parents? If so, then that "beginning" or "becoming" would have constituted a change in God. However, the biblical witness indicates that with God "there is no variation or shadow due to change" (Jas 1:17). God's love, mercy and grace are not created or merely time-originated responses to creation: they are *in* God, they are true of him as God.

We can appreciate that the love of God is eternal: the three persons of the Trinity exist in the communion of intratrinitarian love. However, love for creation—and for humanity—is of another sort than intratrinitarian love. Such love for creation did not *begin to be* with the creative activity of God; rather, divine love received avenue for expression in the creation. If, as the Scriptures teach, "God is love" (1 Jn 4:8), then the love for creation did not mean a change in or for God. With creation, divine love found another outlet, one attuned to the created, not the uncreated.

We cannot assert, though, that grace is involved in the relationship of the three persons of the Trinity with each other, for they dwell in perfect love and harmony from eternity; there is no *need* or *place* for grace in the intratrinitarian communion. Yet grace could not have been only a possibility within God in eternity "past," for that would entail a change in God with the "development" or "emergence" of divine grace. God did not change, though, with creation. In creation, God brought into existence beings that depend entirely on him for their well-being and continued existence from moment to moment, throughout the whole of their existence. The tenderness of God expressed in intratrinitarian love thus found an outlet in the needy beings he brought into existence; that tenderness to such beings, and to nature as a whole, is his grace. God gently sustains and maintains all he has brought into existence; this is his grace toward all creation. In granting and sustaining eternal life in salvation in Christ, grace comes to its richest expression. As in the case with divine love toward creation, grace did not *begin* to be with creation. Rather, it found an outlet for expression in creation.

What this is leading us to—as it led Orthodoxy long ago—is the recognition that grace is *uncreated.* If it is uncreated, then it is God; but what can that mean? In our common Western Christian ways of speaking, this affirmation sounds strange indeed. What do the Orthodox mean by it?

The divine energies and grace. In endeavoring to understand this, it is necessary to keep in mind the Orthodox distinction between the divine essence and the divine energies. The Orthodox doctrine of grace is founded on the distinction between the essence and the energies of God. Indeed, that distinction was adopted within Orthodoxy as a way of defending the reality of grace.[17] According to Eastern Christianity, God is and always will remain inaccessible and incomprehensible to his creatures in his essence. The divine nature is, in virtue of divine transcendence, utterly beyond created natures. Further, the divine nature remains, from eternity, ever the same; even with the advent of creation, the divine nature is unchanged. The Christian faith also teaches that God has brought creation into existence and that he continues to work within it—including the work of salvation for fallen humanity. In all this, it is God himself who is working with the creation he brought into and sustains in being. Eastern Christianity teaches that God does this not through his *essence* but through his *energies.*[18]

According to Orthodoxy, the divine energies are eternal. They are not part of creation, and they were not brought into being at the time of creation. The divine energies reside within God; better put, the divine energies *are* God. The energies are God acting outside the divine essence. In the divine essence, the persons of the

---

[17]Vladimir Lossky, *In the Image and Likeness of God,* ed. John H. Erickson and Thomas E. Bird (Crestwood, N.Y.: St. Vladimir's Seminary Press, 1985), pp. 59, 68.

[18]The essence/energies distinction, insisted upon within Orthodoxy, would prohibit an Eastern Christian from endorsing the assessment by Karl Rahner above, for which the reference is given in n. 5, that *uncreated grace* is God's *nature* communicated to human beings.

Trinity dwell in eternal communion; in the divine energies, God deals with all he has made. God brought the universe into existence through the divine energies, and through them he continues to sustain it. The divine energies are God dealing with the creation. All God's involvement with creation—in providence, protection *and salvation*—is through his energies, which are God.

Thus, God is never at a distance from his creation, and he never deals with it at arm's length. When he acts upon or with his creation, he is not merely exerting some "influence" on it: he is dealing intimately with it, through his energies—which are God himself. This is true for all God's dealings with his creation—and certainly and especially in salvation. Thus, the grace in which we are deified is not some immaterial or spiritual influence exerted upon us from afar, or something poured out upon or into us at arm's length. Grace is God himself working within us, effecting our deification within us (or, to use Western Christian terminology, leading us through the steps of the *ordo salutis* and thus uniting us to Christ). In the Orthodox understanding, "Grace . . . refers to divine energies *insofar as they are given to us and accomplish the work of our deification*. . . . Grace is . . . more than a relation of God to man; far from being an action or an effect produced by God in the soul, it is God Himself, communicating Himself and entering into ineffable union with man."[19]

As a leading Orthodox spokesman has put it, "By the energies of God is meant not some created gift that God bestows on humankind but God Himself in action. The energies, then, are not an intermediary between God and the world, but they are God Himself entering into direct, unmediated contact with us."[20] Since the divine energies are none other than God himself acting toward the creation he has made, we can, must and are privileged to say that grace is God himself, working directly within us. An outstanding Orthodox theologian has put it graphically:

> Grace is uncreated and by its nature divine. It is the energy or procession of the one nature: the divinity in so far as it is ineffably distinct from the essence and communicates itself to created beings, deifying them. . . . [It is not] an effect produced in the soul by the divine will acting externally upon the person. . . . It is the divine life which is opened up within us in the Holy Spirit.[21]

Thus, grace is not an "influence" or an "effect" which God works within us; grace is God himself, working within us.

---

[19]Lossky, *In the Image and Likeness of God*, p. 59 (emphasis added).
[20]Bishop Kallistos (Timothy) Ware, *How Are We Saved? The Understanding of Salvation in the Orthodox Tradition* (Minneapolis: Light and Life Publishing, 1996), p. 58.
[21]Lossky, *Mystical Theology of the Eastern Church*, p. 172.

Concluding Observations

This understanding of grace is a startling thought for Western Christians to consider: that grace of which we so frequently speak is nothing less or other than God himself. The grace for which we praise God is not merely an influence that God mercifully imparts to or pours out upon us. The divine grace we receive and that works within us *is God.*

Western Christianity has emphasized, in keeping with biblical teaching, that grace deals intimately with us, drawing us to God and uniting us to Christ, working the full effects of salvation within us. Grace transforms us, in keeping with God's purposes for us in creation and salvation. Grace brings us into fellowship with God. Even so, the instinctive sense of Western Christianity unreflectively views grace as an influence God exerts on us—a wonderful and transforming influence which he somehow imparts to us. The Eastern Orthodox presentation of what grace is immeasurably deepens and enriches that awareness of the intimacy of grace. Grace is nothing less than God himself, at work within us. All that grace does within and to us is done not at arm's length or merely through influences, but directly by God.

This orientation offers rich and profound insights into and humbling and comforting perspectives on apostolic teaching. An example from St. Paul's teaching can suggest the wide potential offered by the Orthodox perspective on what grace is: the apostle urged, "Work out your own salvation with fear and trembling; for *it is God who is at work in you*" (Phil 2:12, emphasis added). Our various Western Christian appropriations of this passage affirm the apostle's teaching about perseverance, faithfulness and service, but we pass over the last words cited with only a vague (but important!) sense that this all comes from God. An Orthodox perspective on this verse would affirm the importance of perseverance, faithfulness and service, but it would conclude with an awe-inspiring recognition that all is *by grace,* by the divine energies—that it all comes because, indeed, *it is God at work within us.*

Unquestionably, the Orthodox understanding of what grace is offers a way for Western Christians to deepen and enrich their understanding of grace. This challenging Eastern Christian conception of grace shows that the grace which we in Western Christianity emphasize as so essential to the Christian life is even more wonder-inducing than we have hitherto sensed. The Orthodox understanding of what grace is should challenge, enable and encourage us much more deeply to appreciate in humble awe what grace is. Grace is God, working within us.

10

GOING TO CHURCH

IN BOTH WESTERN CHRISTIANITY AND EASTERN ORTHODOXY, the church figures prominently in the lives of the faithful: they are involved in the life of a congregation[1] and participate in the worship it offers to God. In Western Christianity, a phrase commonly used to cover all this participation is "going to church"; what is intended with that phrase summarizes the relationship of a believer to a church in Eastern Christianity as well. However, by this point in our considerations, it will hardly be surprising to encounter the claim again that Orthodoxy has a view of the church that is distinctive from what we find in Western Christianity. The Eastern Christian view has developed along paths other than those taken in the Christian West.

Ecclesiology figures prominently in Eastern Christian thought and practice: as a leading Orthodox spokesman has said, "The doctrine of the Church . . . is the hidden determining force of the thought and religious life of Orthodoxy."[2] Orthodox ecclesiology is multifaceted and wide-ranging; we cannot begin to discuss all its components, plus their implications for church-state relationships, ecumenical involvements and so forth here.[3] Instead, we will focus on two elements of the

---

[1]Treating ecclesiology requires distinguishing among the meanings of the word *church*—local congregation, denomination and universal church. Traditionally the word has been capitalized to refer to the universal Church, composed of all Christians in all times, and written lower case (church) to refer to a local congregation, parish or other geographical or temporal subset of the universal church. However, current publishing conventions now only capitalize the word in proper names of a congregation or denomination, or when "the Church" clearly refers to the Orthodox Church or the Roman Catholic Church. This book follows the current practice, but the reader should still be aware of the distinctions between the various meanings. Although even with the older convention the usage is sometimes ambiguous, the reader should usually be able to understand from the context how *church* is being used.

[2]Vladimir Lossky, *The Mystical Theology of the Eastern Church* (Crestwood, N.Y.: St. Vladimir's Seminary Press, 1976), pp. 111-12.

[3]For a good introductory treatment of Eastern Orthodox understandings of the doctrine of the church, see Bishop Kallistos (Timothy) Ware, *The Orthodox Church,* 2nd ed. (New York: Penguin, 1993), pp. 239-63.

Eastern Christian understanding of the church that have the promise of speaking to ecclesiological questions in Western Christianity: the relationship of a Christian to a church and what is going on as a congregation gathers in worship. In order to appreciate what Orthodoxy offers for these considerations, it will be helpful to reflect on the contemporary situation of Western Christian views on ecclesiology.

Background: Western Christianity and Church

If most Western Christians were asked about "church," they would probably respond by talking about their functioning local congregation; some might speak about their denomination, and a few might converse about the ecumenical body of the church. Whatever the orientation or particular denomination, in Western Christianity we deal with the church in terms of its contemporary function; we are not particularly prone to reflection about the church except to ask whether it is *doing* what it ought to be doing. We have a distinctively *practical*, down-to-earth approach to church. In its own way, this orientation is another manifestation of the ancient Roman heritage in the Christian West, one that has become increasingly common in Western Christianity since the mid-twentieth century.

In the Christian West, it is more common to *be* "church" than to *think about* church; that is, in Western Christianity we are more likely to do (or at least talk about) whatever it is we believe the church is supposed to do than we are to reflect searchingly about what the church is. Of course, this is not universally true within Western Christianity, and it has not always been the case. Anyone even remotely familiar with the history of Roman Catholicism will recognize that it has given extensive space to questions of ecclesiology, both in traditional scholastic teaching and in the documents of the Second Vatican Council. Even so, contemporary Roman Catholicism seems more aware of the present situation (and perceived failures, whether from a conservative leadership or from a radicalized laity) than steeped in the Roman Catholic ecclesiological heritage. As for Protestantism, some denominations have given special attention to ecclesiological questions;[4] however, even among such Protestant denominations, the concern to continue to ask theoretical questions about "church" has been relegated to the sidelines or to an old guard. The preponderance of concern in contemporary Western Christianity is focused on what the church should be doing, rather than what it is.

[4]For example, in the Dutch Reformed tradition, vigorous debates have periodically arisen over whether a denominational name should be singular or plural (i.e., "church" or "churches"). These debates have arisen from concerns regarding ecclesiological integrity and ecclesiastical government; they have often enough led or contributed to further ecclesiastical divisions.

In many ways, this is a welcome development: the fractiousness of Western Christendom has long been aided and abetted by triumphalistic assessments of one's own church—and where ecclesiologies had been carefully developed, they invariably played prominent roles in the triumphalistic hubris. One of the best ways of turning from such divisiveness that has been developed within Western Christianity is to concentrate on what the church is to do. As a result of this focus, the commonality among Western Christian churches has become much more apparent than it ever could have through the other approach. In intriguing ways, the discovery of these commonalities has challenged ecclesiology to catch up. What this will mean for the articulation of ecclesiologies remains to be seen; that it must be reckoned with is obvious. At the least, increasing awareness of what the church *does* will increasingly shape teaching about what the church *is*.

As it does so, Western Christians will doubtlessly discover more of what the Scriptures teach about the church. We in the Christian West should not assume that the ecclesiologies articulated in our various denominational pasts have exhausted the lode of the biblical witness regarding the church. To be sure, significant veins of Scripture were mined for indications of what the church is, both by divine gift and in human actualization. However, we will discover that Scripture has considerably more to teach us than we have often been able to hear. In that regard, a distinctive emphasis of Eastern Christian ecclesiology derives directly from scriptural teaching which has, to date, not particularly influenced Western Christian thought on the topic—an Orthodox understanding of what the church *does* that tells us what the church *is*.

Another issue with which contemporary Western Christian understandings of the church have had to deal is the phenomenon of people claiming to be Christian but sustaining no relationship to any particular congregation. The individualism thus assumed as legitimate (or at least not entirely objectionable) by these people has its roots in Western European and North American developments: spawned by Enlightenment emphases, encouraged by the breakdown of older forms of political and social relationship in the American and French revolutions, and given virtually free reign in the aftermath of immigration to an uncharted New World where one had to forge his or her own way, individualism operates as a foregone conclusion for many people in Western Europe and North America. The individual *is*, and anything beyond the individual is only a *becoming* drawn from the free association of discrete individuals. However sociologically and psychologically naive this assumption may be, it nevertheless reigns supreme in the unreflective self-consciousness of Western humanity. Regarding questions of faith and church, this orientation implies that when such an individual gives himself or herself to faith in Christ, he or she becomes fully a Christian. Any church-relatedness beyond that, however, is a matter of one's own individual preference—after all, it is the option of the individual.

This individualism can be defended from many viewpoints—culturally, politically and even with reference to experience with a church (i.e., experiences in which a church has profoundly disappointed, hurt or failed someone). In its own way, this orientation manifests our ancient Roman heritage again, with its focus on the practical: individualism is the most down-to-earth, simple to understand of all approaches to social organization—and one, furthermore, that draws strength from the pride that dogs fallen humans' steps. Individualism unmistakably pervades the Western world (especially in North America). How should the church deal with it—not in general, but as that individualism shapes views of "being Christian" that make being part of any particular congregation a matter of free individual choice? Is "being a member" (to use the most common description for that connectedness) only an option on the spiritual purchase of faith (like air-conditioning or automatic transmission in a car)? Can one make the purchase without it? These are questions that have not been asked often enough in the past few generations. It is increasingly obvious to many reflective Western Christians that this issue of "individualistic Christianity" needs to be addressed. In this regard, we may find help from our Orthodox brothers and sisters: Orthodoxy offers a distinctive approach to this issue that deserves careful consideration.

Eastern Orthodoxy on the Individual and the Church

In Eastern Orthodoxy one does not find the individualism which marks not only so much of Western culture but also so much of contemporary Western Christian ecclesiastical practice. To be sure, the cultures in which the Orthodox churches have existed have not passed through the crucible of the Enlightenment, the immediate effects of the French and American revolutions or the experience of the New World. Thus, they have not been exposed to what has put so much pressure on and has undeniably shaped and influenced the culture in which Western Christianity has developed—and, consequently, shaped and influenced Western Christianity itself.

However, it is questionable whether even such tectonic shifts as those noted above would have changed the Eastern Christian perspective: all the way back to its earliest beginnings, Orthodoxy has stressed that one is a Christian only in concert with other Christians. According to Orthodoxy, one's Christianity finds itself in and is nourished by communion with other Christians: it not only does not exist on its own, it could not. Eastern Christianity is definitely a churchly Christianity, not an individualistic one.[5]

For Orthodoxy, to consider someone a Christian apart from his or her regular involvement with and fellowship in a church is not conceivable. As we previously saw, every Christian needs the church: deification is inconceivable (and impossible) without being part of the church.[6] Yet as much as the Orthodox believe in a universal church, Eastern Christians do not take refuge in that universality to the neglect of the local. One cannot be involved in the universal church without being involved in a local one; deification can only take place in the hurly-burly of living with and for others in the immediate community of a church. Only within a church can one find a community—for all its flaws and the peculiarities of particular members—which is grounded in that divine love that is to shape our relationships with others in human love. In a church one has the calling and opportunity to live out the interconnectedness within God's love which was the divine purpose for humanity in Adam and is now the divine purpose in Christ the last Adam. This is not a negotiable option for especially interested Christians: it is basic to being a Christian. As an Orthodox bishop has stated, "Salvation is *social* and *communal,* not isolated and individualistic."[7] Furthermore, only within a church can one receive the sacraments which are essential to deification. To think one can dispense with them in favor of one's spiritual independence is hubris of amazing proportions, from an Orthodox perspective. To claim not to need these "means of grace" is to protest one's self-sufficiency, not merely over against a church but over against God himself, who gave the sacraments to deify us. To partake of them without being part of the church in which they are given would be a sort of spiritual theft—taking something to which you have no claim. From Orthodox perspectives, "individualistic Christianity" is an oxymoron.

But is this the full story for Eastern Christianity? What about the place of monasticism? Was not monasticism itself, in its beginnings with the hermits, quintessentially individualistic? Did not many go out to live by themselves, apart from

---

[5]Bishop Kallistos (Timothy) Ware writes, "Salvation involves the Church. It is ecclesial. We are not to set bounds to God's saving power, and it may be that in His mercy He will grant salvation to many people who in this present life have never been visibly members of any church community. But, so far as we on our side are concerned, the appointed means to salvation is always in and through the community of the Church" (*How Are We Saved? The Understanding of Salvation in the Orthodox Tradition* [Minneapolis: Light & Life Publishing, 1996], p. 68).

[6]See above, chap. 8.

[7]Ware, *How Are We Saved?* p. 68.

regular involvement with any church? Does not Orthodoxy still endorse monasticism? How does this fit in with the rejection of an "individualistic Christianity"?

Even in antiquity, with the development of monasticism, hermits were not understood as individuals separated or cut off from the church. They were the valiant ones who sought out that solitude in which they could encounter their own weakness and the power of evil and overcome them by grace. After training in this struggle, they were expected to make themselves available to the generality of the church, functioning within it both as members and as spiritual guides. This is hardly individualism: this is training to live for and with others in God's service.

However, this pattern did not always work. Some of these monks never considered themselves proficient enough in spiritual insight to offer themselves as counselors to society and church, and so they remained in the wilderness. Others found the wilderness, with its interaction with other fellow strugglers in the spiritual disciplines, as their spiritual home, and so they did not return to society and church either. In these cases, communities of hermits (called *lavras* in Eastern Christianity) developed as a way of providing a distinctive form of church in which even these solitaries lived in Christian community, received the sacraments and were nurtured by other Christians.

To be sure, Eastern Christianity has always recognized the place of hermits as a legitimate one—a place in which a person might live in heroic solitude and seek to draw ever nearer to God. However, at least two of the strictures regarding hermits show that contemporary individualistic Christianity cannot claim support from the Orthodox allowance of hermits. In the first place, hermits not only eschewed involvement with a local congregation; they also had to forego every kind of contact with other humans. Not only church but society was forfeit to the hermit; contemporary individualistic Christianity is hardly prepared to do that. Second, while allowing for the continued possibility of an eremitic existence, Orthodoxy has stringently warned about (even against) it: such an existence is only for the spiritually most accomplished and self-denying of Christians, not for the generality of them—and even such Christian athletes face grave dangers in adopting the lifestyle of a hermit. Few of those who espouse individualistic Christianity in the present day could pass muster on either of these requirements.

This does not mean that the Orthodox recognize no room for God's grace to operate outside normal churchly structures. Eastern Christian ecclesiology admits that God can and may well include among those he saves people who have no connection to a church. However, Orthodoxy urges that such possibilities lie in the mystery of God's wide love and must not be treated as an assumed rule: what God *may* do should not become the outer perimeter of what humans *should* do. To sunder all ties to the church—or never to develop them at all—and to claim to be Christian is an act of arrogance and a defiance of God's appointed structures for our salvation. That is hardly the course of wisdom; nor is it the mark of that humility in which genuine spirituality manifests itself. Orthodoxy's recognition of the wideness of God's merciful love offers no comfort to willful individualism that wants to be recognized as Christian.

However, Orthodoxy recognizes the complexity of human existence in a fallen world and the struggles that anyone—including those who are Christian—encounters in this life. Eastern Christianity is quite willing to recognize that, for a period of time and for a variety of reasons or excuses, a Christian might cut off his relationship with a church—if not in a formal sense, then in the actual sense. Young persons passing through the turbulence of their teen years, adults struggling with the complications of marriage break-up or ill health, people caught up in the increasing busyness of contemporary life, those who have suffered real or imagined hurts from others in a church—all these, and others, might well back away from church for a time. They might only gradually return to it or do so only by fits and starts. In this reluctance or neglect, such people are cutting themselves off from the very source that could offer them strength. Even so, Orthodoxy approaches such struggles with a gentle wisdom that encourages rather than demands. Eastern Christianity has no room for individualistic Christianity, but it does make room for the struggles of individual Christians.

While the Christian West has encountered much individualistic Christianity, from Eastern Orthodox bases the phenomenon is inconceivable. Individuals may struggle with their relationship to a church, but individualistic Christianity is a contradiction in terms. Christ died for his church. He gives his salvation to his people, not just to discrete persons—and he gives it to them in concert with and interaction with the others of the church. In church we not only have the opportunity and calling to live in love as God originally intended; and we not only have the privilege of receiving the sacraments, in which we receive grace. In church we collectively *do* something that we could not possibly do otherwise, and in doing it, we *are* something that we could not otherwise be. This takes us to the second of our considerations of what Orthodox ecclesiology offers to contemporary Western Christianity.

EASTERN ORTHODOXY ON THE CHURCH AT WORSHIP

Eastern Orthodoxy offers a distinctive and stimulating perspective on how what the church *does* shows what the church *is.* According to Orthodoxy, the church's most characteristic activity is worship—or, as worship is more commonly described in Eastern Christianity, *liturgy. Liturgy* comes from the Greek term *leitourgia,* used in the Greek version of the Old Testament (the Septuagint) for the service of God by his people in general or, more specifically, for that service rendered in and around the temple by the priests and Levites. It was soon appropriated by the ancient church to describe its public worship. "Liturgy" thus describes what the people of God do—namely, worship him. The term has come to denote also the particular structures of words and forms in which the people of God offer their worship to God. The importance of worship to Orthodox understandings of the church can hardly be overstated. This importance can be appreciated by remembering that in Eastern Christian understanding *orthodox* means "right praise; proper worship." In liturgy, a church becomes something significantly more than it is sociologically as a gathering of individuals.[8] The church, of course, does other things than whatever takes place in stated services of worship; these things the church does also show what the church is. However, according to Orthodoxy, the church's preeminent *doing* is worship.

Consequently, for Eastern Christianity, worship shows especially clearly what the church is. This is borne out by a biblical text that has played little if any role in Western Christian understandings of either ecclesiology or worship. Western Christianity most often uses this particular text as an indicator of the special privilege enjoyed by Christians in the present age. The text certainly speaks to that, but Orthodoxy understands it to mean far more: for Eastern Christianity, this text describes what happens as a church engages in worship or liturgy. The text is Hebrews 12:18-24:

> You have not come to something that can be touched, a blazing fire, and darkness, and gloom, and a tempest, and the sound of a trumpet, and a voice whose words made the hearers beg that not another word be spoken to them. (For they could not endure the order that was given, "If even an animal touches the mountain, it shall be stoned to death." Indeed, so terrifying was the sight that Moses said, "I tremble with fear.") But you have come to Mount Zion and to the city of the living God, the heavenly Jerusalem, and to innumerable angels in festal gathering, and to the assembly of the firstborn who are enrolled in heaven, and to God the judge of all, and to the spirits of the righteous made perfect, and to Jesus, the mediator of a new covenant, and to the sprinkled blood that speaks a better word than the blood of Abel.

---

[8]See the treatment in Alexander Schmemann, *For the Life of the World: Sacraments and Orthodoxy* (Crestwood, N.Y.: St. Vladimir's Seminary Press, 1973), p. 25.

Clearly, the author contrasts the situation of ancient Israel at the foot of Mount Sinai with that of the Christian church. Far greater privilege is extended to the church, to be sure, than the ancient Israelites knew. As the Orthodox interpret this passage, though, it describes what the situation is for the church *at worship*. In the passage, the thought is of God's people being in his presence—precisely what the church celebrates as its great privilege when it worships God.

For Eastern Christianity, Hebrews 12:18-24 shows what the church does and, in so doing, shows what the church is. Orthodoxy understands this passage to teach that whenever a congregation engages in worship, that congregation is not "alone" in the presence of God, but is included with the whole church. This inclusive sense does not limit itself, though, to an awareness that the congregation is somehow upheld in or encouraged by the thought that others of its denomination are also engaged in worship (or will be within a few hours one way or the other, depending on the geographical expanse of the denomination across time zones). Nor is the inclusiveness bounded by the broader sense of the ecumenical body of the church worshiping throughout the contemporary world. Rather, as a congregation meets to worship God, it comes into God's presence—where the multitudes of angels unceasingly praise God, in concert with the fullness of the church of all times and places, the faithful Christians of past ages who have departed this life and live in God's presence. According to the Orthodox understanding of this passage, any congregation—no matter how humble its building, how sophisticated its people or how gifted its leaders—partakes of this privilege as it worships God. In this its quintessential *doing*, a church discovers what it *is*. It is part of, joined to and in harmony with the entirety of the worshipers of God of all times and places—not just in ideal or thought, but in actuality.[9]

There is no question that this is a breath-taking perspective on worship. For that reason, it also gives a new appreciation of what the church is. In many ways, Eastern Christianity calls Christians to an awareness of their connection with the church of all times and places—through its devotion to tradition, its confession of the Nicene Creed, its recollection of the saints and martyrs. Eastern Christianity can do all this because that is what the church *is*—the present embodiment of the church of all times and places, at multitudes of particular times and places. Each church—whatever its time and place—enters God's presence as it worships him, joining in the worship offered by the total number of the faithful departed. Thus, whenever a congregation engages in worship, it does so in concert with the saints

---

[9]See the presentation by Ware, *The Orthodox Church*, p. 265.

of all ages, the martyrs and all those—whether famous in the history of the church or known only to God—who have died in Christ. These departed ones are not dead witnesses from the past, but living worshipers in God's presence; they are our brothers and sisters in the faith, devoted to God (as the worshiping congregation is) and concerned for the well-being of his church (both in heaven and on earth).

This sense is reinforced by an Orthodox church building itself. Inside the sanctuary, one finds numerous icons (religious artwork of a distinctive style, type and with a distinctive purpose).[10] The icons—of Christ, the angels and the saints—are not mere decorations for bare walls. Rather, these representations of the Savior, the angelic hosts and the great leaders of the church (both men and women, clergy and laypeople, theologians and martyrs) serve to remind the congregation that all these, and all the rest of the faithful departed, are *there* with the congregation as it worships—or rather, that the congregation is *there, with them all in God's presence.* If these icons are rightly appropriated by the congregation, "The faithful feel that the walls of the church open out upon eternity."[11]

To Eastern Christians, the saints of the ages are not merely historical examples of what Christians could and should be; rather, they are our brothers and sisters in Christ today, siblings whom we meet as often as we join them in worshiping God. From this perspective, it is hardly surprising that Orthodox readily refer to and read the works of those who have long since died. After all, the works of other Christians—whether flourishing in the third, the fourteenth or the nineteenth century—are the writings of brothers and sisters with whom we commune as often as we meet with the triune God. This helps explain, as well, why Orthodox pray to the saints. Eastern Christians do not view the saints as mediatorial intercessors in the medieval Western Christian sense, whom believers seek out for help because it is too frightening to come into the presence of a holy God. As we have seen, Orthodox do not construe their relationship to God in the kind of legal understanding that contributed to that medieval Western Christian practice. In Orthodoxy, the saints are our brothers and sisters in Christ, alive now in God's presence; to pray to them is not, from an Orthodox perspective, qualitatively different from asking another contemporary brother or sister in Christ to pray for us. Neither excludes or neglects prayer to God; both just seek the loving Christian support of others to uphold us in our needs.[12]

---

[10]See the discussion of icons in chap. 11.

[11]Ware, *The Orthodox Church,* p. 271.

[12]It is not assumed that this brief discussion of the Eastern Orthodox understanding of praying to the saints will be enough to convince some Western Christian readers of the legitimacy of the practice. However, it should indicate that there are other reasons for engaging in the practice and understanding it than many Western Christians have hitherto encountered.

Quite apart from questions about praying to saints, however, the Orthodox understanding of the church at worship offers a stimulating insight into what the church is. A church is not just a collectivity of individuals gathered for some form of religious observance; it is a point of contact with the church of all times and places. It is a place where one encounters the entire church as often as one joins with a congregation in worship. Admittedly, this Orthodox viewpoint stretches our understanding of time and place to the snapping point. From an Eastern Christian perspective, though, one understands what the church *is* from what it *does*—and what it is and does is awe-inspiring. This perspective has much to offer Western Christian considerations of ecclesiology.

Concluding Observations

Neither of these Eastern Orthodox perspectives on the church offers easy answers for questions we in Western Christianity have on the subject. The fact that the Orthodox repudiate the idea of an individualistic Christianity will almost certainly not be significant enough to convince those in the Christian West who try to practice it—but it might jolt them to discover how long ago, how consistently and how vigorously this large branch of Christianity denies the possibility of an individualistic Christianity. And if these defenders of "lone ranger" Christianity consider why Eastern Christians insist on being part of a church, it should give them much to consider—probably more than they have heard in some of our Western Christian attempts to address the issue. Finally, if these would-be solitary Christians ponder the advice to and expectations of the genuine solitaries of the Eastern Christian tradition (the hermits), those allegedly individualistic Western Christians would find much that would dissuade them from their course and convince them of their folly and/or hubris. If any of these take place, we in the Christian West will have been richly rewarded for considering this element of the Orthodox understanding of the church.

For all Western Christians, the Orthodox approach to what takes place in worship is challenging and awe-inducing. To realize that whenever we meet in worship in our local congregation, we meet with the totality of the redeemed; to become aware that this totality is not just composed of all those who in that day or week worship God in the entire world, but that this totality includes all those in the history of the world who have gone before us into God's presence; and to think that all these are lifting their voices in praise to God with us, as our elder brothers and sisters concerned with and for us and devoted to God's glory and the good of his people—this opens up awe-inspiring, humbling, exciting vistas on what it means to worship God. Truly, what the church *does* tells us what the church *is*. This point is not only a stunning contribution to our contemporary Western Christian struggles to reorient the discussion of ecclesiology; it is a view of the church that will speak to Christians long after contemporary struggles have ceased. What the church *does* in worship shows us what the church *is*. "Going to church" never looked so good.

11

ICONS

AS WE TURN TO CONSIDER THE ICONS THAT ARE a distinctive element of Eastern Orthodoxy, we enter the question of religious art, a question on which Western Christians have significant differences among themselves: Roman Catholicism has long endorsed and encouraged religious artwork, but much of Protestantism has rejected it. Two things can be noted about this divergence, as over against Orthodoxy's iconography. On the one hand, the arguments presented within Roman Catholicism in defense of religious art have historically not offered as vigorous or thoroughgoing a defense as has been marshaled by Orthodoxy. On the other hand, among Protestants, a fairly wide diversity of practice can be found with regard to the acceptability of religious art. In both cases, it can be instructive to consider the arguments offered in favor of icons by Orthodoxy: Roman Catholic readers will find additional supports for their own defense of religious imagery, but Protestants will encounter much to ponder. Since the contrast between Protestant sensibilities and Orthodox practice is so sharp, the following presentation will focus on that contrast.

An unsuspecting Protestant who walked into an Orthodox church would be visually assaulted by the plethora of religious imagery within it. Few Protestant churches display any kind of religious imagery beyond basic symbols such as a cross, a fish, or a picture of bread and a cup. Such churches are, to use technical terms, "aniconic." Some other Protestant churches have explicitly condemned religious imagery;[1] this stance of forthright rejection of religious imagery is styled "iconoclastic." In either case, Protestantism has traditionally been opposed to artistic representations used for corporate worship or personal devotional purposes. A certain inconsistency in this regard, nevertheless, frequently manifests itself within Protes-

[1]The repudiation of religious imagery is straightforward and unmistakable in the Heidelberg and both the Westminster Catechisms; these are confessional standards, respectively, of Reformed and of Presbyterian churches.

tant circles in the widespread use of pictures in children's Sunday school literature and in children's story Bibles, as well as in the pictures of the head of Christ (the one by Salomon being only the best known), of Christ praying in the garden of Gethsemane or of him standing and knocking at a door (representing what is said in Rev 3:20) found in some churches and in the homes of many Protestants.

In sharp contrast, an Orthodox church is filled with religious imagery: icons cover the walls and ceiling, and they fill the screen (the "iconostasis") at the front of the sanctuary. The Orthodox faithful use them in worship, both private and corporate. Icons play a prominent role in Orthodox devotion, theology and liturgy. Indeed, a special service during the church year is annually devoted to the celebration of the restoration of icons (the "Sunday of Orthodoxy," celebrated on the first Sunday of Lent). This endorsement and use of religious imagery did not arise from careless toleration and eventual approval of incautious practices, but from rigorous doctrinal and exegetical argument brought forward during an intense struggle within Eastern Christianity during the eighth and ninth centuries. That struggle, known as the Iconoclastic Controversy, ended with the reaffirmation in 843 of the legitimacy of religious imagery for Christianity, as it had been declared at the Seventh Ecumenical Council (Nicea II, 787). The history of that controversy is usually unknown territory for Western Christians, and this treatment cannot begin to map that terrain.[2] In this chapter we will consider the arguments adduced by the defenders of icons that led to that affirmation of legitimacy, and then consider the instruction offered within Orthodoxy about how icons should and should not be used.[3] Before proceeding to either of these, however, it would be helpful to consider the background to and nature of the original Protestant reaction to religious imagery, for that reaction continues to shape contemporary Protestant instincts about and reactions to religious imagery.

[2]Treatments of the history of the Iconoclastic Controversy can be found in Jaroslav Pelikan, *The Spirit of Eastern Christendom* (Chicago: University of Chicago Press, 1974), pp. 91-145; also, his *Imago Dei: The Byzantine Apologia for Icons* (Princeton, N.J.: Princeton University Press, 1990); Ambrosios Giakalis, *Images of the Divine: The Theology of Icons at the Seventh Ecumenical Council* (Leiden: E. J. Brill, 1994); and Kenneth Parry, *Depicting the Word: Byzantine Iconophile Thought of the Eighth and Ninth Centuries* (Leiden: E. J. Brill, 1996).

[3]Treatises dealing with the issue by two of the leading defenders of icons are available in English translation: St. John of Damascus, *On the Divine Images: Three Apologies Against Those Who Attack the Divine Images,* trans. David Anderson (Crestwood, N.Y.: St. Vladimir's Seminary Press, 1980); and St. Theodore the Studite, *On the Holy Icons,* trans. Catharine P. Roth (Crestwood, N.Y.: St. Vladimir's Seminary Press, 1981). In addition, an English translation of the relevant portions of the acts of the Seventh Ecumenical Council (Nicea II, 787), at which the legitimacy of icons was declared, is available in Daniel J. Sahas, *Icon and Logos: Sources in Eighth-Century Iconoclasm* (Toronto: University of Toronto Press, 1986).

RELIGIOUS IMAGERY AND THE CHRISTIAN WEST

During the Reformation of the sixteenth century, many Protestant leaders brought vigorous objections against the statues and pictures that filled the churches of Western Europe. In defense of that religious imagery, Roman Catholic spokesmen urged that such statues and pictures served as "books for the illiterate." That defense was, significantly, the only argument for religious imagery that had been articulated during the whole of the Middle Ages in the Christian West.

Long before, at the end of the sixth century, Pope Gregory the Great first offered this justification for pictures in churches. In the chaos in which the church in Western Europe then found itself, he defended religious imagery out of pastoral concern: the illiterate—then the vast majority of those in the Christian West—had a desperate need for something to remind them of the stories of the Scriptures and the work of Christ. Over the course of ensuing centuries, pictures and statues multiplied in the churches of Western Christendom, but no further or more profound defenses for them were developed along the way. During the medieval period, a number of leaders within Western Christianity expressed reservations about how people were actually responding to that imagery, at times accusing it of lapsing into idolatry. However, warnings about such abuse did not lead to either the reexamination of the issue or the articulation of other defenses.[4]

Subsequently, with little evidence that abuse had lessened, the sixteenth-century Protestant Reformation turned a critical eye on the religious imagery that had become so abundant within church buildings.[5] Rather than seeing this imagery as a pastoral help, the Protestant leaders denounced it as an idolatrous abuse. In rejoinder to Gregory's hoary dictum, the Protestants argued that people could now read the Bible and should be hearing it faithfully preached.[6] Since Gregory's defense was the only one these original Protestant leaders encountered, it is hardly surprising that they, and their Protestant descendants after them, have assumed that this was an adequate and sufficient answer to the question of religious imagery.

---

[4]For a consideration of medieval teaching on and concerns about religious imagery in Western Christianity, see Helmut Feld, *Der Ikonoklasmus des Westens* (Leiden: E. J. Brill, 1990), pp. 11-118.

[5]The amount of religious imagery to be found in church edifices by the sixteenth century can be gauged by considering that the iconoclastic outbreak in Basel on February 9, 1529, resulted in 35 wagon-loads of the debris of religious imagery being carted away from the cathedral.

[6]The treatments of the second commandment in the Heidelberg and the Westminster Catechisms, which condemn religious imagery, include pointed declarations against the problems associated with and the defense offered for that imagery during the medieval period: cf. the Heidelberg Catechism, Questions 95-98; the Westminster Shorter Catechism, Questions 49-52; and the Westminster Larger Catechism, Questions 107-10.

Religious Imagery and the Christian East

During the eighth and ninth centuries, Eastern Christianity wrestled with the question of religious imagery: the Iconoclastic Controversy resulted in the Christian East endorsing icons. While in the Christian West the argument for religious imagery was limited to help for those who could not read, in the Christian East that argument played a relatively insignificant role. The defenders of icons adduced much more profound and compelling arguments, and these more powerful arguments were the ones that finally carried the day in the resolution of the controversy.

The objections of the opponents of icons (the "iconoclasts") will probably sound familiar to many Protestants, whose objections to religious imagery emphasize many of the same concerns. The iconoclasts denounced religious imagery as a violation of the second commandment (Ex 20:4-5), pointed out that Moses had forbidden Israel to make any image of God since they "saw no form [of God]" at Mount Sinai (Deut 4:12, 15), and stressed that God had told Moses that no one can see him (Ex 33:20). Since God is invisible, it would be impossible to make any representation of him. Making representations of anything in creation would be to follow the error of Israel's neighbors, who used these idols to worship mere creatures rather than the Creator. But God had privileged Israel beyond the nations, for he had given himself, the true God, to them. Consequently, Israel must not follow the practices of the surrounding nations, but follow the Lord's commandments and worship him alone (Deut 4:15-19; cf. Deut 6:4, 13-15). Since nothing in all creation is like God, no likeness of him is possible (Jer 10:1-11), and worshipping creatures rather than the Creator invites divine wrath (Rom 1:18-23). Because of all these biblical warnings, the iconoclasts urged, religious imagery is not legitimate in Christianity.

Significantly, the defenders of icons (known as "iconophiles" or "iconodules") took no issue with the iconoclast arguments just noted. With the iconoclasts, the iconophiles urged that the true God is invisible, that he is Spirit and thus has no body, and that he cannot be pictured. They urged as well that offering worship to any created thing itself or to any image of a created thing is forbidden to Christians. Further, the iconodules thoroughly agreed that the second commandment still applies to God's people in the present day, so one dare not violate it. However, from the iconophile perspective, having and using icons was not a violation but the fulfillment of that commandment; having and using icons arose from what God had done for his people to save them, rather than from the rebellion of sinners against divine precepts. These assertions needed clarification then—and explanation for Western Christian readers today.

Scriptural considerations. The iconophiles argued that their opponents' treatment had overlooked a considerable portion of scriptural evidence which related directly to the question at issue. Part of that evidence was a fuller consideration of what the Old Testament had to say about God's attitude toward religious art.

The iconodules laid a basic foundation for their perspective in their appeal to part of God's instructions to Moses regarding the building of the tabernacle:

> The LORD spoke to Moses: See, I have called by name Bezalel son of Uri son of Hur, of the tribe of Judah: and I have filled him with divine spirit, with ability, intelligence, and knowledge in every kind of craft, to devise artistic designs, to work in gold, silver, and bronze, in cutting stones for setting, and in carving wood, in every kind of craft. Moreover, I have appointed with him Oholiab son of Ahisamach, of the tribe of Dan; and I have given skill to all the skillful, so that they may make all that I have commanded you: the tent of meeting, and the ark of the covenant, and the mercy seat that is on it, and all the furnishings of the tent, the table and its utensils, and the pure lampstand with all its utensils, and the altar of incense, and the altar of burnt offering with all its utensils, and the basin with its stand, and the finely worked vestments, the holy vestments for the priest Aaron and the vestments of his sons, for their service as priests, and the anointing oil and the fragrant incense for the holy place. They shall do just as I have commanded you. (Ex 31:1-11)

From this passage, the iconodules pointed out that the God who had forbidden carved images did not do so as one opposed to skillful and artistic work itself. On the contrary, he wanted such workmanship within his tabernacle, the place where he would meet with his people. To assure that result, God had sovereignly intervened to fill Bezalel with the Spirit of God, and Oholiab and others with the requisite skill to enable them all to accomplish God's plans for the tabernacle. Among the various works Bezalel was to produce for the tabernacle were some that would be carved. This clearly indicated to the iconophiles that the second commandment did not intend an absolute prohibition of skillful and artistic work in general or carved workmanship in particular.

From this point, the iconophiles moved on to consider the divine instructions regarding the ark of the covenant. In the directions for that most special element of the tabernacle furniture, God gave explicit instruction about its cover, the mercy seat:

> Then you shall make a mercy seat of pure gold; two cubits and a half shall be its length, and a cubit and a half its width. You shall make two cherubim of gold; you shall make them of hammered work, at the two ends of the mercy seat. Make one cherub at the one end, and one cherub at the other; of one piece with the mercy seat you shall make the cherubim at its two ends. The cherubim shall spread out their

> wings above, overshadowing the mercy seat with their wings. They shall face one to another; the faces of the cherubim shall be turned toward the mercy seat. You shall put the mercy seat on the top of the ark; and in the ark you shall put the covenant that I shall give you. There I will meet with you, and from above the mercy seat, from between the two cherubim that are on the ark of the covenant, I will deliver to you all my commands for the Israelites. (Ex 25:17-22)

In this passage, the iconophiles noted that among the things Bezalel and Oholiab were spiritually enabled to produce were two cherubim. Significantly and undeniably these would be *carved images*. These cherubim were to be made at God's command and to be part of the mercy seat, which God himself would take as his throne (Ps 80:1), and from which he would speak to his people. The iconodules emphasized that these were not images of God, but of angels: no images could be made of God. Even so, he commanded images to be made for his tabernacle and for his mercy seat. Evidently God was not absolutely opposed to carved images of mere creatures, even in the holiest confines of his place of worship.

The iconodules pointed out that this divine perspective was also evident in the successor to the tabernacle, the temple built by Solomon. When David's son built that temple, he did so under God's blessing (1 Kings 5:3-5; 2 Sam 7:12-13) and with divinely granted wisdom (1 Kings 3:5-14). As he had the temple erected, Solomon modified various particulars of the tabernacle. Presumably, he did this with the wisdom God had given him and with divine blessing, for no rebuke from God challenged these changes. Some of the information about those modifications was relevant, in the iconophiles' estimation, to the question at hand:

> In the inner sanctuary he made two cherubim of olivewood, each ten cubits high. Five cubits was the length of one wing of the cherub, and five cubits the length of the other wing of the cherub; it was ten cubits from the tip of one wing to the tip of the other. The other cherub also measured ten cubits; both cherubim had the same measure and the same form. The height of one cherub was ten cubits, and so was that of the other cherub. He put the cherubim in the innermost part of the house; the wings of the cherubim were spread out so that a wing of one was touching the one wall, and a wing of the other cherub was touching the other wall; their other wings toward the center of the house were touching wing to wing. He also overlaid the cherubim with gold.
>
> He carved the walls of the house all round about with carved engravings of cherubim, palm trees, and open flowers, in the inner and outer rooms. (1 Kings 6:23-29)

Under divine blessing and wisdom, Solomon's additions included two cherubim, each standing fifteen feet high. Much larger than the cherubim of the mercy seat, the wingspans of Solomon's colossal cherubim spread across the inner sanctuary (1 Kings 6:27); they could hardly be considered an insignificant addition. Moreover, Solomon had the walls of the temple filled with carved imagery; these images were not abstract symbols, but carvings of creatures—cherubim, palm trees and flowers. To none of this is there a divine objection. Evidently God was not opposed to such artistic representations being multiplied in his house of worship.

To the possible objection some might draw that these Solomonic modifications were enthused changes God merely tolerated, the iconophiles appealed to the vision God vouchsafed to Ezekiel of the ultimate temple (Ezek 40–43). This purified temple, to which the glory of God would return with delight and which would never be defiled again (Ezek 43:4-7), was one totally in keeping with God's desires. Significantly, it fairly abounds with religious imagery. The palm tree decorations added by Solomon now are found virtually everywhere (Ezek 40:16, 22, 26, 31, 34, 37), and carvings of cherubim and palm trees appear in abundance:

> And on all the walls around in the inner room and the nave there was a pattern. It was formed of cherubim and palm trees, a palm tree between cherub and cherub. Each cherub had two faces: a human face turned toward the palm tree on the one side, and the face of a young lion turned toward the palm tree on the other side. They were carved on the whole temple all around; from the floor to the area above the door, cherubim and palm trees were carved on the wall. (Ezek 41:17-20)

The final temple, purified by God himself, would include an exponential increase in religious imagery beyond what Solomon had begun: from the floor to the top of the doors, the walls were filled with carved imagery of creatures in the house where God would be faithfully worshiped.

From their consideration of these elements of the biblical witness, the iconophiles drew three conclusions. In the first place, God is not opposed to all artistic skill used in the making of carvings, gold overlay and other related endeavors; indeed, such abilities are his gifts. Second, he is not definitively opposed to such representations, even in the place where he is to be worshiped: by his permission and command, such work is found in the tabernacle, in its successor temple built by Solomon and in the final temple pictured by God himself. Finally, God does not limit such artistic representations to abstract symbols; rather, he includes likenesses of creatures he had made (cherubim, trees and flowers). Quite obviously, an understanding of the second commandment which prohibited all such representations—such as the iconoclasts held—exceeded God's intent. This led the iconophiles to ask what, precisely, it was that God prohibited in the second commandment.

As the iconophiles understood it, the second commandment forbade making images of created things—they could not be made of the invisible God, after all—with the purpose of worshiping them (either the images themselves or the created things represented in them). The point of the prohibition of idols was that no created thing was to be worshiped or adored in the place of the Creator: only God is to be worshiped. The second commandment did not forbid religious imagery in toto. The Scriptural evidence about the tabernacle and the temples made such an idea untenable.

These insights regarding the intent of the second commandment were not all that could be said about God's purpose with that commandment. The Ten Commandments had not been given as a code of religious laws without a context: God gave them to his people in the historical outworking of his promised salvation. For the iconodules, this had significance for the question at issue.

Hermeneutical considerations. Turning to that history meant that the iconodules had to deal with the hermeneutical question of the relationship between the Old and the New Testaments and, more specifically, the significance of the coming of Christ for the understanding of the second commandment. With the church back to the time of the apostles, the iconophiles saw the Old Testament as focusing toward and fulfilled in the person and work of the incarnate Son of God. Because of who he is and what he has done, the situation of the church in the period after his ascension is different from what it had been for the people of God before the incarnation. The New Testament witness stresses that point repeatedly, in various ways relevant to the question of religious imagery.

According to St. Paul, Christians are "not under law but under grace" (Rom 6:14). To a similar effect, he argues, "Now before faith came, we were imprisoned and guarded under the law until faith would be revealed. Therefore the law was our disciplinarian until Christ came, so that we might be justified by faith. But now that faith has come, we are no longer subject to a disciplinarian" (Gal 3:23-25). Furthermore, the Old Testament law "has only a shadow of the good things to come, and not the true form of these realities" (Heb 10:1). These apostolic affirmations indicate that a significant change has taken place in God's pattern of dealing with humanity. With the coming of Christ, the relationship of the people of God to their Lord has been significantly transformed from what it had been under the law. This change involves a distancing from the law, not in the sense that Christians can now dispense with it, but in the sense that it is only a "shadow" cast by the coming reality—that is, Christ. With his incarnation, the reality has come, and the people of God must respond to that reality.

The difference in situation is graphically described with the contrast of *law* and *grace*. This does not mean that there was no grace in the Old Testament or no requirements for the church in the present. Rather, the apostolic affirmation points to the difference in where the emphasis is placed in God's dealings with his people in the two periods. What could only be indicated by shadows previously has now come in its reality, and grace now abounds, with the coming of Christ. The law, in its fullness and its specific particulars, was a shadow cast by the coming Christ. The law was meant, according to the iconophile understanding, to lead the people of God to look forward to the coming one casting the shadow, to prepare them for him.

Much more was involved in this contrast than was expressed in these arguments, of course. But the iconophiles recognized that these apostolic declarations had significant implications for understanding the law and the church's present relationship to it. At the least, they required a christological focus for understanding the law in general and the second commandment in particular. What this meant for the second commandment, in the iconodule view, was that the prohibitions regarding religious imagery were meant to lead humanity, in its religious childishness, away from the crude worship of the idol itself, or of the created thing represented in the idol, to the adoration of the Creator alone. And the law did this, so as to drive human beings to the true God and prepare them for the coming of *that* God *in the flesh*. Given that, the iconophiles asked, what does it mean that Christians are "not under law, but under grace," that they are "no longer subject to the disciplinarian"? Raising the question thus involved further exploration of the New Testament teaching about the significance of the coming of Christ.

The opening affirmation of the letter to the Hebrews addressed that question pointedly when it stated: "Long ago God spoke to our ancestors in many and various ways by the prophets, but in these last days he has spoken to us by a Son, whom he appointed heir of all things, through whom he also created the worlds. He is the reflection of God's glory and the exact imprint of God's very being" (Heb 1:1-3). In these words, the author contrasts the many ways in which God had revealed himself to his people in prior ages (i.e., the periods of the law and the prophets) with the dramatically new and final fashion—"by a Son." With this change, the former ways have now been superseded and replaced. As the author would later urge, those must be relegated to the category of "shadow" by contrast to the incarnate Son, the reality (Heb 10:1). In this incarnate Son, a decisive and eternal change has taken place: he is "*the reflection* of God's glory and *the exact imprint* of God's very being" (Heb 1:3). As the iconodules read this passage, it had something profound to indicate about the possibilities of religious imagery.

The opening chapter of the Gospel of John added to this insight by declaring, "And the Word became flesh and lived among us, and we have seen his glory, the glory as of a father's only son, full of grace and truth. . . . The law indeed was given through Moses; grace and truth came through Jesus Christ. No one has ever seen God. It is God the only Son, who is close to the Father's heart, who has made him known" (Jn 1:14, 17-18). The contrast already encountered between Old and New Testament privileges finds profound expression in the contrast between "the law . . . given through Moses" and the "grace and truth [which] came through Jesus Christ." In the revelation through the Son, the "truth" pointed to by the Old Testament law's shadows has come. To the iconophiles, it was significant that this contrast appears in the apostle's inspired reflection on the incarnation, and does so along with a consideration of the impossibility of seeing God. As St. John presents it, the frequent Old Testament affirmation—"No one has ever seen God"—was overcome by God himself when "the Word became flesh." The incarnation of the Son has made the Father known in *truth* and grace. Significantly, that "truth" was not, in the apostle's presentation, a series of ideas for the intellect, but the manifestation of the Son of God *in the flesh*.

For the iconodules, these considerations were essential to dealing responsibly with the question at issue between them and their opponents. According to the iconodules, God has culminated his dealings with humanity by sending his Son in the flesh. Weaning humans away from the childishness of pagan idolatry's worship of created things, God had finally made a full disclosure of himself. He had done so not in any further shadowy ways such as he had used in previous ages, but in full reality. In the second commandment, God had forbidden his people to worship images and had called them to worship him alone, but he had forbidden them to try to make any kind of image of him, *because he intended to send his own!* As the iconophiles read the specifics and the flow of Scripture, God himself had fulfilled the second commandment with the coming of Christ. In so doing, he had radically transformed the way his people must obey it. From the iconophiles' perspective, Christianity must respond to *this* God, as he has made himself known—God in the flesh.

While the declaration that the coming of Christ had transformed the way in which the second commandment should be obeyed may have struck the iconoclasts as strange, the iconodules could point out that this was the pattern within the entire church in regard to another of the ten commandments. Although the fourth commandment had stipulated the hallowing of the seventh day of the week as a day of rest and devotion to God, the church hallowed the first day of the week. The justification for that modification was that Christ had risen from the dead on the first day of the week; it had since come to be known as "the Lord's Day" (Rev 1:10). From the church's perspective, the commandment was still in force, but the form of its fulfillment had been altered by the coming and work of Christ. From the iconodule perspective, the same christological focus needed to be given to the second commandment. It was still in force, but the God who had forbidden making images had now sent his own image, in his incarnate Son, who had made the invisible Father known. Indeed, according to St. Paul, Christ is "the *image* of the *invisible God*" (Col 1:15); in that phrase, the Greek word translated "image" is *eikōn (icon)*. In view of all this, to make icons of the incarnate Son was not a violation of the second commandment but a recognition of God's fulfillment of it—and, consequently, an obedient response to the commandment.

Christological considerations. The christological focus of the issue had been at the heart of the controversy from the beginning. The iconoclasts had urged that one must not attempt to picture the incarnate Christ, but the iconophiles jumped on that prohibition and declared that it dropped their iconoclastic opponents into a heretical labyrinth. As the iconophiles argued the case, if Christ cannot be portrayed by painting, then he must not have had a genuine human nature. However, to affirm that would be to fall into the ancient heresy of Docetism—which said that Christ only appeared to be human but actually was not. Another alternative argument would be that Christ could not be portrayed because, in the incarnation, the human nature had been so overwhelmed by union with the divine nature that the human nature had been radically changed. However, to urge that would be to argue for the heresy of Eutychianism—which taught that Christ's human nature was, by its union with the divine nature of the Son of God, no longer really the same as that of mere human beings. These universally condemned heresies barred the christologically faithful from opposing religious imagery of Christ. Along with the church since the time of the apostles, the iconodules insisted that the incarnate Son of God had a genuine human nature.

But if an icon of Christ were made, who (or what) was being portrayed? The iconophiles affirmed, with the iconoclasts (and the Scriptural emphasis), that the divine nature itself cannot be portrayed. Did that mean that the icon would only portray the human nature? That must not be, for separating the human and the divine natures into self-subsistent wholes was the condemned heresy of Nestorianism. Such a separation also could not be since human nature can only be encountered in persons. But the iconodules reminded their opponents what the universal church had come to embrace in its struggles with the christological heresies—namely, that in the incarnation the Son of God took to himself a human nature. That is, the second person of the Trinity so took on human nature in the womb of the Virgin Mary that it became his own nature. That human nature finds its personal center not in a separate human person—an idea which would, again, be Nestorianism—but in the person of the divine Son, who made that human nature his own in the incarnation.

What this meant was that, in the days of Christ's sojourn on earth, the eyes of believers saw God in the flesh as they looked upon him. Those believers could remember him and could have drawn pictures of him. For subsequent believers, instructed by the words of those who had seen him (1 Jn 1:1-3), the one of whom they heard was also the one who, because of the incarnation, could be portrayed in pictures. In making such icons of Christ, the iconophiles argued, believers were not making icons of the invisible God, but of the God who became visible in the flesh, of the one who is *as incarnate* the icon of the invisible God—the one who is the only way to the Father (Jn 14:6). As the iconophile spokesmen urged, the only way to deny the validity and legitimacy of making such icons of Christ was to deny the genuine incarnation of the Son of God.

With the arguments summarized above, the iconodules were victorious in the Iconoclastic Controversy. That does not yet tell the whole of the relevant story, however: the iconodules also dealt with the obvious and important question of how one ought and ought not to respond to such religious imagery. If such imagery is legitimate, how may it be used?

Proper use of religious imagery. In dealing with this concern, the iconophiles brought up several related points. For one thing, having icons of Christ inescapably invited using them in exercises of piety. Whereas the iconoclasts urged that such practice would constitute idolatry, since the icons would be treated as if they were God, the iconophiles urged that the icons were obviously not God, but representations of God in the flesh. They were not and could not be of the same essence as the one pictured—a point true of any picture at all. In using an icon in devotion, one could legitimately accord it honor, because of the one portrayed in it, but this did not constitute idolatry. All such honor was directed to the one portrayed in the icon, and not to the painted materials themselves.

In making this distinction, the iconodules were not simply trying to shore up a weak position; rather, they were recognizing a common human phenomenon. Whether (in the example offered by the iconodules during the controversy itself) in the way one responds to the picture of the emperor, or in the way a young man might treat the picture of his girlfriend back home, people distinguish between the picture itself and the one portrayed, and yet they do not hesitate to treat those pictures with special honor, as having a unique connection to the ones pictured in them. So would and must it be with icons of Christ, according to the iconodules.

Related to this consideration, the iconophiles went on to urge that there was an undeniable difference between the response one offers to a picture and that offered to the one pictured. One should offer an icon *douleia*—respect or reverence. That was a lower form of response than the *latreia*—worship—one owed to God. While the two are undeniably related, worship is specific to God alone, as the second commandment requires; respect might be shown to any of a number of created things, including pictures.

The iconodules warned that one dare not give *latreia* to anything other than God, including an icon of God in the flesh. However, to deny the legitimacy of lesser forms of reverence was, the iconodules argued, to fail to acknowledge the way God had set up human society. The iconophiles appealed to numerous biblical examples, including Old Testament patriarchs, civil leaders and prophets who bowed before various figures, and to several forms of deference shown to others than God in the biblical record. As well, they pointed to several forms of respectful or deferential treatment accorded leaders or special places in their own day. To make that appeal current in Western European and North American society, the use of titles of respect for position or achievements—such as Doctor, Your Honor, Professor or Reverend—indicates that respect can be shown which, while on a continuum with worship, does not get confused in the minds or practices of those offering it with the worship that is offered to God alone.

Thus, according to the iconophiles, Christians might legitimately have icons of Christ as God in the flesh, and they might use them appropriately in exercises of piety. That some people, in ignorance or folly, might abuse icons did not invalidate their proper use. And, for the iconophiles, their proper use was a believing and obedient response to God's ultimate form of communication, his incarnate Son.

CONCLUDING OBSERVATIONS

A Western Christian, especially from an aniconic or iconoclastic Protestant background, has much to consider in the arguments offered in defense of icons in Eastern Orthodoxy. Sixteenth- and seventeenth-century Protestants did not know the arguments developed during the course of the Iconoclastic Controversy. The early Protestant rejection of the argument for religious imagery may have dealt adequately with the justification adduced in the early Middle Ages by Gregory the Great and repeated in the intervening centuries in the Christian West, but those Protestant responses do not begin to deal with the scripturally, exegetically and christologically more sophisticated defenses propounded by the iconophiles during that controversy. Indeed, down to the present day, no Protestant church has dealt with the arguments offered in defense of icons within Eastern Orthodoxy.

Apart from the question of the legitimacy of religious imagery, Western Christians might have several other questions. For one thing, the Iconoclastic Controversy has, potentially, much to say about a Christian aesthetics. Within Roman Catholicism, this question has been dealt with extensively, but Protestant Christianity has much work to do in developing such an aesthetics. It should be noted, however, that from an Orthodox perspective the defense of icons was not primarily or even significantly involved with the specific question of a Christian aesthetics. Even so, perspectives on such an aesthetics have been developed within Orthodoxy. Furthermore, a Western Christian might well be intrigued, if not perplexed, by the traditional style of iconographic portrayal; it certainly does not stress the naturalism or realism that Western aesthetic tastes often expect. This style has particular reasons inherent in the Orthodox understanding of what and who is being portrayed and the way in which that portrayal should be made. Moreover, there are a host of related matters—about perspective, the question of subject/object in the viewing and the use of color—which bring up issues foreign to Western Christian perspectives. On all of these, information is available elsewhere.[7]

Apart from these concerns for possible further investigation, Western Christians can recognize the presence and prevalence of icons in Eastern Orthodox churches as an obvious and visually striking difference from Western Christianity. It is hoped that the presentation in this chapter will enable them to do so without reflexively opposing the Orthodox practice. At the least, Western Christians should acknowledge that icons have deep historical, exegetical and christological roots in Orthodoxy. Roman Catholics may well find their own endorsement of religious imagery strengthened by the Eastern Christian arguments. Protestants, on

---

[7]Eastern Orthodox treatments of these questions can be found in Paul Evdokimov, *The Art of the Icon: A Theology of Beauty*, trans. Steven Bigham (Redondo Beach, Calif.: Oakwood Publications, 1990); and Leonid Ouspensky and Vladimir Lossky, *The Meaning of Icons* (Crestwood, N.Y.: St. Vladimir's Seminary Press, 1983).

the other hand, may well find it awkward to consider religious imagery more positively than has been common among them for centuries. Even so, any Western Christian should find it challenging to consider how our brothers and sisters in Christ in Eastern Orthodoxy have wrestled with the question of religious imagery. Surely in this, too, we can learn from them.

12

TRADITION AND SCRIPTURE

IT MAY SEEM SURPRISING THAT WE ONLY TURN TO CONSIDER tradition and Scripture near the end of our treatment of Eastern Orthodoxy's distinctives. In the Christian West, the question of religious authority—within which the relationship of Scripture and tradition plays a prominent role—typically receives treatment much earlier in studies of doctrine. Indeed, religious authority is usually among the introductory issues dealt with in Western Christian volumes on doctrine, as part of what is designated "prolegomena" in technical theological parlance. This is not the pattern in Orthodox studies of doctrine.[1]

The difference in location already reflects notable differences between Western and Eastern Christendom. On the one hand, it is another evidence of the contrasting approach to and expectations of the study of doctrine in Western Christianity and Eastern Orthodoxy. On the other, it reflects a significant difference in the history of the two segments of Christendom. We need to consider both of

---

[1]A nuanced treatment of prolegomena can be found in Peter Bouteneff, *Sweeter Than Honey: Orthodox Thinking on Dogma and Truth* (Crestwood, N.Y.: St. Vladimir's Seminary Press, 2006). In addition, some works written to present Orthodoxy to Western Christian readers deal with the question of religious authority in a prolegomenal manner: after an overview of the history of Orthodoxy, Bishop Kallistos (Timothy) Ware treats the question in this fashion in his *The Orthodox Church*, 2nd ed. (New York: Penguin, 1993), pp. 195-207; similarly, Sergius Bulgakov deals with it in the second chapter of his *The Orthodox Church*, trans. Lydia Kesich (Crestwood, N.Y.: St. Vladimir's Seminary Press, 1988), pp. 9-35. However, while Vladimir Lossky's work, *Orthodox Theology: An Introduction* (Crestwood, N.Y.: St. Vladimir's Seminary Press, 1978), offers a treatment of his subject according to the basic approach of Western Christian systematic theologies, he has no such introductory chapter on religious authority; indeed, the volume does not even address the question. In treatments of doctrine written to present Orthodoxy primarily to Orthodox readers, one rarely finds distinct treatments of the question of religious authority, and virtually never any such as prolegomenon. See the presentation in Vladimir Lossky, *The Mystical Theology of the Eastern Church* (Crestwood, N.Y.: St. Vladimir's Seminary Press, 1976); also, Bishop Kallistos (Timothy) Ware, *The Orthodox Way*, rev. ed. (Crestwood, N.Y.: St. Vladimir's Seminary Press, 1995). This is also true of the classic presentation of Eastern Orthodoxy by St. John of Damascus, *The Orthodox Faith*, available in *Saint John of Damascus: Writings*, trans. Frederic H. Chase Jr. (Washington, D.C.: Catholic University of America Press, 1958), pp. 165-406.

these before we proceed to examine Orthodoxy's understanding of the relationship between tradition and Scripture.

PRELIMINARY CONSIDERATION: TERMS OF REFERENCE

Prior to embarking on that investigation, however, it is necessary to make some preliminary remarks about the two terms *Scripture* and *tradition*. The first is scarcely problematic: *Scripture* in Christian circles refers to the canonical books of the Bible. While there is some disagreement among Roman Catholics, Protestants and Eastern Orthodox over the exact extent of the canon,[2] that particular issue rarely occasions misunderstanding.

The same cannot be said, however, of *tradition*. As used in discussions among Christians, the term carries numerous connotations, which can lead to considerable confusion and miscommunication. Tradition is both a process and a package. As a process, tradition is the handing down of something from one generation to another; as a package, tradition refers to what is handed down. These two connotations are, obviously, intimately interrelated; separating them in thought is easier than in discussion. Usually, context will make clear whether the process or the package is intended. A further complication is that the "package" of tradition includes everything from the foundational message of the Christian faith through what has become common understanding to a host of particulars about all sorts of issues in life, worship and practice. All these have been handed down from prior generations. However, only the most triumphalistic exclusivists within any Christian tradition would insist on the absolute importance of everything included in the tradition of his or her particular segment of Christianity.[3]

---

[2]There is consensus regarding the canonicity of the books of the Hebrew Old Testament and the New Testament. The disagreement concerns the books known among Protestants as Apocrypha, but usually referred to among Roman Catholics as Deuterocanonical; Protestants do not accept these books as canonical, but Roman Catholics do. Orthodoxy has never officially adopted a list of the canon. However, the Orthodox have commonly treated the Septuagint (a Greek translation of the Old Testament produced before the time of Christ and used by both the apostles and the ancient church) as their version of the Old Testament, and the Septuagint includes the Deuterocanonical books. Even so, between Roman Catholicism and Orthodoxy there is some difference about certain of these "additional" books. Indeed, even among the Orthodox themselves, different views are held. Roman Catholicism accepts Tobit, Judith, Additions to Esther, Wisdom of Solomon, Ecclesiasticus (also known as Sirach), Baruch, Letter of Jeremiah, Additions to Daniel, and 1 and 2 Maccabees; within Orthodoxy, in addition to these, 1 Esdras, Prayer of Manasseh, Psalm 151, and 3 Maccabees are accepted; in the Slavonic versions (used among the Slavic peoples of Orthodoxy), 2 Esdras is also accepted as canonical.

[3]Orthodoxy recognizes the danger here: Ware urges, "Orthodox, while reverencing this inheritance from the past, are also well aware that not everything received from the past is of equal value," but he goes on to admit, "In Byzantine and post-Byzantine times, Orthodox have often been far too uncritical in their attitude to the past, and the result has been stagnation" (*The Orthodox Church*, p. 197).

This treatment is not the place to try to unravel the Gordian knot of the term *tradition*. It will be used below to refer to both process and package. As regards the package component, focus will be kept on the basic message of Christianity, how its fullness has unfolded under the Spirit's guidance of the church, and (to a lesser extent) the practices of worship which carry the understanding of the message forward from one generation to the next.

Divergence in Treating Tradition and Scripture

In turning now to consider the divergence between Eastern and Western Christendom in their respective treatments of tradition and Scripture, it is important to recall in the first place something we have repeatedly noted: that Western Christianity manifests a far greater confidence in the capacity of human thought to deal with divine revelation than does Eastern Christianity and, consequently, that Western Christianity places considerably greater stress on rationality than Eastern Orthodoxy does. It is not surprising, therefore, that questions of religious authority are treated in the introductory chapters of systematic theologies written in Western Christendom; one must lay the foundation carefully if one is properly to erect the structure of Christian thought after all. By contrast, in Orthodoxy greater emphasis is placed on mystical knowledge—on intimate communion with God. In this approach, the basic question is about relating to God, not about an appropriately orderly approach to thinking about him.

An analogy from Scripture may help to clarify why the Eastern Christian approach does not lead to a preliminary consideration of religious authority. The particular analogy has abundant biblical warrant in both the Old and the New Testaments: it is the relationship between a wife (the church) and a husband (God). In such a relationship, the fundamental issue is the relationship itself, not the structures of authority which sustain it. Something is desperately defective in a marital relationship if the fundamental consideration for it is one of authority, no matter how important that consideration may otherwise be. Correlatively, within Orthodoxy, with its emphasis that knowing God is more fellowship with him than mastery of data about him, questions of religious authority are recognized as important but are not dealt with as foundational. Rather, such questions come up along the way, as it were, as the intimacy of knowing God leads to discourse about life before him.

In the second place, the two segments of Christendom have passed through significantly different experiences with regard to the question of religious authority, and these historical divergences go a long way toward explaining the dissimilar approaches to the relationship of Scripture and tradition. Both Eastern and Western Christianity grew out of the ancient church, which embraced the Old Testament as God's inspired revelation of the coming Christ and which prized the apostolic proclamation of Christ. Since the apostles had been eyewitnesses of Christ and had been appointed by him to spread the message about Christ to the ends of the earth, it was early recognized that the apostles' witness to Christ needed to be treasured and passed on to subsequent generations. A determination to remain faithful to the apostolic message marked the church from antiquity onward into what we in the Christian West call the Middle Ages. The apostolic faith was challenged by various heresies which would have undermined parts of it,[4] but the early church was punctilious about passing on the teaching and practice of that faith unimpaired.

Among other things, this led in due course to the demarcation of the canon of the New Testament. The faith was handed on from generation to generation, but the faith as thus construed included not only specific teachings (the Scriptures and the Nicene-Constantinopolitan Creed embraced by the whole church, plus the doctrinal declarations of ecumenical councils) but also the practices of worship and approach to life in which the church responded to God. This packaging of the faith was not problematic, since all within the church embraced it.

As with other elements of the Christian faith, the question of religious authority did not become an issue until a divergence on it developed within the church. It never became a point of controversy in the Christian East, but it did in Western Christianity during the late Middle Ages. By that time, the scholastic theologians' viewpoints on doctrine had become extremely diverse. In order to deal with the scholastic dissonance, the process of sifting out the questions of religious authority began. However, by the fourteenth and fifteenth centuries, religious authority in the Christian West had become a largely undifferentiated mass of what Christians practiced, believed and thought. It included the Scriptures, the Nicene-Constantinopolitan Creed, the decisions of ecumenical councils, the teachings of the church fathers, decrees enacted by the popes, and the numerous

---

[4]This can be seen in the cases of Gnosticism, Marcion, Arius and Apollinaris (to name no others). Gnosticism rejected the goodness of the material creation and consequently denied the genuine incarnation of the Son of God, thus undercutting the significance of his death and resurrection. Marcion repudiated both the Jewish heritage of the church and the Old Testament. Consistent with this, he rejected all the apostolic writings which spoke to or showed appreciation for that background, or which did not explicitly set Christianity in opposition to Jewish practices. In so doing, he denied the history of redemption as God had worked it out through Abraham's descendants down to Jesus Christ. Arius denied the full deity of Jesus Christ, and Apollinaris his full humanity. The ancient church recognized that either position renders impossible the accomplishment of salvation as proclaimed by the apostles.

practices that had become customary (in worship, penitence, fasting and so on). Among these, it was generally recognized that Scripture led in some undefined way, but the issue had not been addressed purposefully within Western Christendom. The question of religious authority was not decided during the fourteenth or the fifteenth centuries.

During the sixteenth century, the Protestant Reformation brought the issue to the fore. As a way of sorting out what the Protestant Reformers came to view as faithful teaching and practice from the rest of what had come to be accepted and practiced, they asserted *sola scriptura.*[5] By this they meant that Scripture alone was unquestioned as religious authority. While they did not repudiate all other claimants to religious authority, they urged that Scripture stood above them all, as the one by which all the rest must be evaluated and qualified. With this measuring rod, the Protestant Reformers ended up rejecting certain teachings and many practices that had come to be accepted within medieval Western Christendom. In response, Roman Catholic theologians urged that tradition also must be embraced; this was a main argument in their defense of many of those teachings and practices rejected by the Protestants. In due course, this Roman Catholic argument was endorsed by the Council of Trent, which affirmed that the faith is received through two sources, Scripture and tradition.[6] The contrast in approach was thus starkly set forth: Protestants urged Scripture alone, to the detriment of tradition; Roman Catholicism urged Scripture plus tradition.

Since the sixteenth century, this contrast has usually been taken as an adequate assessment of the respective views within the two large parts of Western Christianity. However, in recent times, that contrast has been criticized as overdrawn. On the one hand, it has been urged that, rather than viewing Scripture and tradition as two parallel sources, the Roman Catholic perspective sees religious authority as inhering in Scripture as practiced and handed down through the history of the church.[7] On the other hand, it has been argued that the Protestant Reformers'

---

[5]This is true for the "magisterial" Reformers (Lutherans and Reformed); the Anabaptist and Spiritualist reform movements accepted somewhat different perspectives on the question. The magisterial Reformers' perspective became accepted, in due course, as the classic Protestant response to the question.

[6]The fourth session of the Council of Trent decreed, "This [the Christian] truth and discipline are contained in the written books [of the Scriptures] and the unwritten traditions. . . . [This council] receives and venerates, with an equal affection of piety and reverence, all the books of both the Old and the New Testaments—since God is the author of both—as well as the said traditions, both those relating to faith and to morals" (*The Canons and Decrees of the Council of Trent,* Session 4: "Decree Concerning the Canonical Scriptures" [April 8, 1546]).

[7]See George Tavard, *Holy Writ or Holy Church: The Crisis of the Protestant Reformation* (New York: Harper & Brothers, 1959), pp. 195-209, 244-47.

actual perspective on religious authority did not repudiate all other ostensible religious authorities in favor of the judgments of individuals based on their reading of Scripture. Rather, the Protestant Reformers accepted other religious authorities (as, for example, the creeds or a consensus of faithful teaching from the church fathers down through the centuries) as genuine religious authorities superior to the judgments of private individuals but nevertheless subordinate to Scripture. In other words, Scripture was "alone" in the sense of being the only unquestioned religious norm, and not that it was the only religious authority.[8]

Rapprochement on the question has taken place not only among scholars of the Reformation era; it has taken place among Roman Catholic and Protestant scholars of the New Testament as well. As Western Christian scholarship has examined the process leading up to the production of the works of the New Testament, it has come to be accepted on both sides that the Gospels were shaped in their final forms by the teaching that had gone on within the church. "Redaction criticism" has shown that variant presentations within the Synoptic Gospels (Matthew, Mark and Luke) reflect the ways the apostles (and others) had articulated the Christian message within the church, and that the churches' various situations had molded the resultant writings somewhat. Thus, the spoken message, handed on and proclaimed and practiced within the church, influenced and in its own way led to the written message as ultimately found in the New Testament writings. This understanding of what transpired in the first-century church sees Scripture and church as intimately wrapped up together; Scripture and tradition have been brought together as friends, rather than being contrasted as rivals or enemies. With all this, the old contrasts of "Scripture alone" and "Scripture plus tradition" have been exposed as inadequate to the treatment of religious authority. Contemporary Western Christian scholarship (on both the Reformation and the New Testament eras) is in some considerable ferment and upheaval, with more nuanced views on the relationship of Scripture and tradition being suggested, views which deal more responsibly with the relevant data.

In stark contrast, Orthodoxy has never experienced a controversy over religious authority such as Western Christianity knew in the sixteenth century. The question about the relationship between Scripture and tradition that attracted so much attention in the Christian West in the late Middle Ages and the Reformation era never agitated the Christian East. Eastern Christianity has a distinctive approach

---

[8]This summarizes some of the findings in my doctoral dissertation, "*Sola Scriptura* and Church History: The Views of Melanchthon and Bucer on Religious Authority in 1539" (University of Waterloo, Waterloo, Ont., 1982).

to religious authority, but that approach is not structured around the particular issues that have come to be taken as foundational concerns in Western Christendom. With regard to tradition and Scripture, Orthodoxy has continued the pattern of the ancient church, in which Scripture and tradition work together to preserve, shape and transmit the apostolic message. It is time we considered how Eastern Christianity sees that collaboration.

Scripture as Part of Tradition

Orthodoxy emphasizes the closest possible coherence between tradition and Scripture. Indeed, according to Eastern Christian understanding, Scripture itself is part of tradition. It is the first part, the leading part, the preeminent part, but it is unquestionably part of and not separate from tradition.

Eastern Christians urge that this should be recognized simply from the historical situation of the early church. Obviously, the New Testament Scriptures were written at some point subsequent to the beginning of the apostolic proclamation of Christ. By the time the Gospels and the apostles' letters began to be penned, the apostolic message had been preached and passed on already for several years.[9] Thus, a tradition of Christian proclamation had developed prior to the first New Testament writings, a tradition in which that apostolic message was preached and passed on over the years subsequent to the initial proclamation.

The apostles themselves continued to preach the Christian message, and others joined with them in the proclamation (e.g., Barnabas and Timothy). These others were not free to change that apostolic message; they were expected to preserve it carefully and transmit it faithfully.[10] They passed on the apostolic message they had heard and received.

Doing this, though, was engaging in the work of tradition. Thus, these others proclaimed the tradition received by the church from the apostles. Within the churches founded prior to the writing of the New Testament Scriptures, the faithful adhered to what the apostles or others had handed on to them: they were faithful to the apostolic tradition. That faithful adherence did not change with the be-

---

[9]New Testament scholarship argues that the earliest possible date for a New Testament book would be c. 45 A.D. (the Gospel of Mark), although that early date is questioned. Apart from this possibility, the earliest books in the New Testament to be penned were St. Paul's letters to the Thessalonians, which scholars agree were written in the early 50s A.D. Thus, at least fifteen and perhaps more than twenty years passed between the beginning of the apostolic preaching and the first Christian writings that were received as part of the New Testament.

[10]See St. Paul's injunction to Timothy, "what you have heard from me through many witnesses entrust to faithful people who will be able to teach others as well" (2 Tim 2:2).

ginning of the writing of Gospels and apostolic letters; the church continued to hold on to the tradition received from the apostles.

In the period while the Gospels and the apostolic letters were being written, the church continued to embrace, protect, preserve and hand on the apostolic tradition. It can scarcely be surprising that it did so: if that apostolic tradition presented the message of divine grace to undeserving humanity, then that message in all its richness must be passed on without corruption or confusion. With this, it would hardly be surprising, either, that the practices surrounding the proclamation itself would be transmitted inviolate, as part of the tradition—practices such as the celebration of baptism and of the Eucharist, the structure of a worship service (with readings from Old Testament Scripture, singing of psalms and hymns, presenting of alms or other gifts, prayers, etc.), and other practices that had became common in the church's life in and proclamation of the Christian message. Being faithful as the church meant living according to the apostolic tradition in proclamation and practice, with or without apostles themselves or apostolic writings.

Thus, the church existed prior to the writing of the New Testament Scriptures; the church continued during the period in which the various works eventually accepted into the New Testament were being written; the church lived on through the subsequent interval during which those works were copied and disseminated among the churches; the church continued during the extended interim in which decisions were made regarding the New Testament canon (well into the fifth century); and the church lasted during the following period until the completed biblical canon became available throughout the whole church. During this entire span of time, churches lived without the full corpus of what was eventually accepted as the New Testament. They could do so, and could continue within the apostles' teachings, because they held to the apostolic tradition.[11]

The writings that came to be embraced within the church as the New Testament presented what the apostles had taught—which means that the New Testament presented the apostolic tradition. Further, it is clear that the Scriptures themselves have been copied, printed and handed on down through the centuries of church history. In this sense, too, Scripture is part of tradition within the

[11]This was recognized as an actuality already in the late second century by St. Irenaeus of Lyons, who asked a hypothetical question and responded to it by reference to the experience of the church among the illiterate nations: "How would it be if the apostles themselves had not left us writings? Would it not then be necessary to follow the tradition which they handed down to those to whom they committed the Churches? In fact, this is what has taken place among the many nations of those barbarians who believe in Christ, on whose hearts salvation has been written by the Spirit without paper or ink, and who carefully preserve the ancient tradition [from the apostles]" (*Against Heresies* 3.4.1-2).

church. According to Orthodoxy, it is necessary to view the Scriptures themselves as part of Christian tradition: "In reality there is only one source [of the Christian faith], since Scripture exists *within* Tradition."[12]

To Western Christian ears, this may sound strange indeed, accustomed as we are to stressing the primacy of Scripture (whatever we may go on to say about tradition). But we must remember that Eastern Christianity does not think in terms of a contrast between Scripture and tradition or of any sort of rivalry or division of authority between them, as has long been common in Western Christian thought. In the Orthodox understanding, there is neither contrast nor rivalry between tradition and Scripture; according to Eastern Christianity, Scripture and tradition do not need to be reconciled because they are friends.

Scripture Interpreted by Tradition

The affirmation that Scripture exists within tradition is not meant to diminish Scripture in favor of tradition. Orthodoxy maintains that, while Scripture is part of tradition, it holds the preeminent place within that tradition.[13] In the perspective of Eastern Christianity, tradition is not independent of Scripture and presents nothing at odds with it. Indeed, the rest of tradition serves the understanding of Scripture.

Directed by tradition. For Eastern Christianity, tradition includes how the church, back to the time of the apostles, has viewed the Old Testament—namely, as preparing the way for the coming of the Savior. It further includes the Christocentric understanding of salvation as proclaimed in the New Testament. Thus, tradition focuses on the salvation God has brought to humanity in the person and work of Jesus Christ.

Beyond that broad sweep, tradition includes how to interpret particular passages that have been in dispute in various doctrinal controversies in the church's history, interpretations that the church collectively has recognized as essential to maintaining what the apostles proclaimed and to avoiding heresy. In this regard, the monuments of those controversies are especially important: the Nicene-Constantinopolitan Creed holds a special place as the only creed embraced by the entire church; the doctrinal decrees of the ecumenical councils guide in thought

---

[12]Ware, *The Orthodox Church*, p. 197.

[13]See the affirmation by Sergius Bulgakov: "The inclusion of Holy Scripture in tradition by no means compromises its originality and its value as the Word of God; the Word of God is above all other sources of faith, especially of all tradition in all its forms. . . . Tradition cannot be in disagreement with Scripture. . . . Tradition always supports itself by Scripture; it is an interpretation of Scripture" (Bulgakov, *The Orthodox Church*, p. 18).

and interpretation; and the written works of the church fathers show how to approach Scripture and doctrine.

The above elements of tradition obviously serve the interpretation of Scripture directly. Tradition also includes the context in which the Scriptures are read, believed and practiced: the church's worship serves as the living framework for understanding Scripture. The particulars of worship are not specified in detail in Scripture; they have been handed down through the ages and themselves constitute part of the church's tradition. In the fourth century, St. Basil the Great mentioned several of these, pointing out that they had been passed down from the church's beginning to his day through the channels of tradition.[14] All these, plus others unmentioned by the Cappadocian father, have been maintained within Orthodoxy; they embody the proclamation of the apostolic message as the church has practiced it through the ages. They, too, are part of that tradition which serves the interpretation and understanding of the apostolic message. The church interprets Scripture by way of tradition.

The role of the church. According to Eastern Christianity, God has given his Scriptures to the church and has empowered it alone to interpret them. Scripture does not come to each new generation of the church, though, as a blank slate on which that believing generation inscribes its own understanding. Rather, tradition carries Scripture to each succeeding generation so that next generation can hear the message always proclaimed and embraced within the church and can itself embrace and proclaim it, in whatever circumstances or milieu the church finds herself. To understand Scripture rightly, one must abide within the church's tradition. Devising "one's own interpretation" (2 Pet 1:20) is the mark not of exegetical genius but of proud rebellion. In holding steadfastly to its tradition, the church serves as the faithful guide to understanding the Scriptures. According to Orthodoxy, it is necessary, if one wants to understand the Scriptures rightly, to understand them with the church down through the ages.

This approach to the interpretation of Scripture ties in, obviously, with the Eastern Christian understanding of being a member of the church discussed above. According to Orthodoxy, we are not rugged individualists, independently opening the Bible to discover truth. Rather, with the church of all ages, with whom we meet whenever we worship, we understand Scripture and stand together

---

[14]St. Basil the Great *On The Holy Spirit* 27.66. His list included making the sign of the cross over those who profess faith in Christ, turning to the east in prayer, the words of consecration for bread and wine in the Eucharist and other elements of that liturgy, blessing the water used in baptism, renunciation of the devil and his angels, triple immersion, blessing the oil for chrism (and chrism itself). These are all still practiced within Eastern Orthodoxy.

in the truth. The church is never free to add to or change the apostolic message. Building on the heritage of the apostolic faith, the church is required to be—and, according to the Eastern Christian understanding, has been—faithful to the apostolic tradition.

So, Orthodoxy emphasizes strongly that tradition is necessary to the right understanding and practice of Scripture. Tradition serves the church's continuity in and faithfulness to the apostolic proclamation enshrined in Scripture. As the inspired record of the apostolic witness to Christ, the New Testament Scriptures lead the rest of tradition, a tradition which exists to support and enable the proper understanding and practice of the apostolic message. According to Orthodoxy, Scripture and tradition are not in competition; they cohere within the church because of the Holy Spirit.

The guidance of the Holy Spirit. Eastern Christianity emphasizes that the same Spirit who inspired the first apostolic proclamation has continually indwelled the church since the Day of Pentecost, long before the first apostolic writings. In keeping with Christ's promise, the Spirit has guided the church, keeping it in the truth (Jn 16:13)—before, during and subsequent to the writing of Scripture. Thus, the Spirit who guides the church and keeps it faithful to the apostolic heritage superintends tradition; it is not the product of human ingenuity or ecclesiastical bureaucratism, but the living and dynamic presence of the Spirit within the church.

For Orthodoxy, tradition is not something frozen or mechanical. The Holy Spirit does not work that way. The Nicene-Constantinopolitan Creed declares that the Holy Spirit is "the Lord and Giver of life"; his presence within the church assures that tradition remains dynamic and flexible, rather than static and rigid.[15] Tradition is indeed kept by the church, but tradition lives within the church through the power of the Holy Spirit. Tradition allows the faithful of the past to speak to the contemporary church and, through it, to the world in every generation.

While Orthodoxy has as much trouble measuring up to this as any other Christian communion, Orthodoxy nevertheless recognizes that faithfulness to tradition is something other than a barren repetition of the past. Proclaiming the Christian

---

[15]Thus Ware's declaration, "Orthodoxy can never rest satisfied with a barren 'theology of repetition,' which, parrot-like, repeats accepted formulae without striving to understand what lies behind them. Loyalty to Tradition, properly understood, is not something mechanical, a passive and automatic process of transmitting the accepted wisdom of an era in the distant past. An Orthodox thinker must see Tradition *from within,* he must enter into its inner spirit. . . . [Tradition] is the life of the Holy Spirit in the Church. The Orthodox conception of Tradition is not static but dynamic" (*The Orthodox Church,* p. 198).

message relevantly requires interacting with and responding relevantly to the contemporary situations in which the church finds herself. As a leading Romanian Orthodox theologian has put it, "Tradition keeps [the] dynamism of the Scripture contemporary without changing it. . . . At the same time as it preserves the authentic dynamism of Scripture, tradition, in its quality as true interpreter of Scripture, brings that dynamism to bear upon real life."[16] This means that, for Eastern Orthodoxy, tradition exists to make the message of Scripture effective in the church and contemporary to the milieus in which the church exists. Scripture is fleshed out, as it were, in tradition.

CONCLUDING OBSERVATIONS

It is obvious that, while tradition and Scripture have figured prominently in both Western Christianity and Eastern Orthodoxy, they have had very different histories in the two segments of Christendom. Those who have wrestled with either the historical vicissitudes that shaped the experience within Western Christianity or the outcomes of the opposing views may conclude that Orthodoxy has been exceedingly fortunate not to have endured the challenges and conflicts over religious authority that have marked much of the last half-millennium in the Christian West, since conflicts over the respective place and significance of Scripture and of tradition have often led to more heat than light. Others might opine that Orthodoxy's sanguine acceptance of the coherence of tradition and Scripture only shows that the question has not been joined within the Christian East. We do not know whether a controversy will arise which will force Eastern Orthodoxy to greater specificity on the relationship of tradition and Scripture. However, it is worth recognizing that the question was far more likely to arise within Western Christianity than within Eastern Orthodoxy, given the differences in approach to doctrine in the first place.

For some within Western Christianity, all talk about tradition is suspicious. They supposedly live by the guidance of Scripture alone, under the direct influence of the Holy Spirit. There is an undeniable naiveté about this approach, though. Tradition is inescapable in any human society, ecclesiastical or otherwise. Whether we call it custom or habit or whatever, tradition marks human existence. Everyone operates in this world by tradition, to one degree or another. At its barest, one can recognize tradition if one has a predictable bedtime or mealtime or

[16]Dumitru Staniloae, *The Experience of God—Orthodox Dogmatic Theology: Revelation and Knowledge of the Triune God,* trans. Ioan Ionita and Robert Barringer (Brookline, Mass.: Holy Cross Orthodox Press, 1994), 1:45.

some morning routines. While many churches within Western Christendom claim not to follow tradition, as soon as one tries to change the order of the morning worship service, one will find out just how firmly committed to tradition even such a church is.

In some evangelical circles, it is often claimed that the Holy Spirit directly leads discrete individuals. Upon reflection, this is more than a little curious. The promise in John 16:13 was made to the disciples collectively, not individually. That promise assures the followers of Christ that the Holy Spirit will indeed guide them, but nothing in the text offers any indication that this guidance will be discrete and individualistic. Indeed, Scripture itself warns against "one's own interpretation" (2 Pet 1:20). The connection between church, Holy Spirit and guidance in the truth is assured in the passage; it is a recipe for what the church in both Western and Eastern Christendom has long called tradition.

In the present day, when a certain rapprochement on the relationship of Scripture and tradition seems to be emerging within scholarly circles in Western Christianity, the Orthodox approach offers much to consider. The close coherence of tradition and Scripture in the Eastern Christian understanding reflects a lost heritage in Western Christian thought. Perhaps in our struggles we in the Christian West are on the way to reappropriating that heritage. If so, Orthodoxy offers us help in finding our way.

13

PRAYER

PRAYER IS AT THE HEART OF THE CHRISTIAN LIFE. Both individually and corporately Christians engage in prayer. The communion with God restored through salvation involves communicating with as well as living unto him. These are both included in what Christians refer to as prayer.

Every Christian tradition emphasizes prayer, and similar patterns have developed in Western and Eastern Christianity for promoting and facilitating prayer. Not all churches embrace every practice, although some of their adherents may venture into them on their own out of interest or a desire to enhance their own spirituality. Also, some distinctive practices have come to mark one or another church tradition's approach to prayer.

Here we will note some of the approaches and emphases common to Eastern Orthodoxy and Western Christianity, recognizing that not every variety of the latter readily engages in all of them. Then we will turn to consider a distinctive practice of prayer within Eastern Christianity.

PRAYER, EAST AND WEST

In both Western and Eastern Christianity, the faithful are called to prayer. The intention is always to help them communicate readily and freely with God. For some in the evangelical world, the only encouraged style of prayer is spontaneous—the verbal opening up of a believer to God in unscripted words. Spontaneous prayer is not unique to this segment of Christianity; every church tradition encourages and seeks to enable its adherents to open up readily and freely to God in heartfelt prayer. However, to attain this, most other Christian traditions also encourage the use of patterns of prayer.

Some of these patterns are found in collections of prayers composed over the centuries and commended by long use. Handbooks offer written prayers that Christians can read as the utterance of their own heart to God. By frequent use, these prayers can become so ingrained that a Christian prays them without referring to the printed form. Both Western Christianity and Eastern Orthodoxy offer such aids.[1]

The printed liturgies used in many Christian traditions also offer instruction on prayer. Indeed, in many Christian circles, services of worship are simply called "prayer." The understanding is that the church's entrance before God, praise of him, prayer to him, listening to a homily and celebration of the sacraments are all acts of prayer. In both Western Christianity and Eastern Orthodoxy, churches teach their people how to pray through the printed liturgies used from week to week (with whatever variations). The liturgies thus inform and shape the prayer offered by the faithful outside the times of stated worship. Books presenting Orthodox liturgies offer such aid to Orthodox faithful (and to Western Christians who seek to explore Orthodox patterns of prayer).[2]

In both Western Christianity and Eastern Orthodoxy, the life a Christian leads is sometimes referred to as prayer, since the whole of life is to be lived for God, in communion with him. As Christians live unto God, they seek both forgiveness for their sins and change of life, growth in faithfulness and deeper commitment, openness to God and encounter with him. Both Western and Eastern Christianity thus see prayer as wide as all of life.[3]

But for Western and Eastern Christians alike, prayer constitutes a challenge. It calls for a life devoted to God in the midst of a society and culture that calls us away from him. Prayer summons us to a conflict within ourselves as we seek to turn from sin and live unto God. But sometimes specific biblical injunctions to pray confront us with additional challenges. One of these is the apostolic injunction to engage in unceasing prayer.

---

[1]*The Book of Common Prayer* of the Church of England offers such prayers, in addition to the liturgical patterns it presents. Within Orthodoxy, *A Manual of Eastern Orthodox Prayers* (Crestwood, N.Y.: St. Vladimir's Seminary Press, 1999) offers a collection of prayers that has long been used within Orthodox circles.

[2]Many editions of the divine liturgies of St. John Chrysostom (used almost every Sunday in Orthodox churches) and of St. Basil the Great (used a dozen times per year) are available. Beyond these, two volumes offer the services used during Lent and on other special periods of the church year: *The Lenten Triodion*, trans. Mother Mary and Kallistos Ware (South Canaan, Penn.: St. Tikhon's Seminary Press, 2002), and *The Festal Menaion*, trans. Mother Mary and Kallistos Ware (South Canaan, Penn.: St. Tikhon's Seminary Press, 1998).

[3]For example, the Heidelberg Catechism (a confession embraced by many Reformed churches) urges, "Prayer is the most important part of the thankfulness God requires of us" (Question 116); in this catechism, gratitude is the rubric for understanding the entirety of a believer's response to his salvation. A winsome Orthodox presentation of life as prayer is found in Bishop Kallistos Ware, *The Orthodox Way*, rev. ed. (Crestwood, N.Y.: St. Vladimir's Seminary Press, 1995), pp. 105-32.

UNCEASING PRAYER

"Pray without ceasing" (1 Thess 5:17), urged St. Paul. What did he mean by that? Clearly, he wanted Christians to engage in prayer. But what can he have meant by the injunction to do so *without ceasing?*

In some of Western Christendom, St. Paul's admonition has been interpreted to mean that Christians should continually be in an attitude of prayer, or that they should be open to or "alert to" God at all times, as one would be in prayer. Unquestionably, such encouragements are in keeping with biblical instructions about piety. As expositions of the apostle's exhortation, however, they all leave much to be desired. Prayer is not less than an attitude, but it is surely more than an attitude. In prayer, we must be open and alert to God, of course, but prayer is more than that. Prayer involves us actively, not just passively or potentially.

In much of the rest of Western Christianity, another way of dealing with this Pauline directive has been followed. In this approach, the apostle's command has been apportioned to special groups within the church—specifically to monks and nuns, who give many hours of the day to prayer. The rest of the church is responsible to utilize their own particular gifts and opportunities to serve God, counting on the monks and nuns to carry out this apostolic instruction as their contribution to the collective fulfillment within the church of the divine precepts. Again, there can hardly be any question that Scripture recognizes differing gifts within the church and calls on those who have received those diverse abilities to use them, urging that, when the whole church does so, then the whole church is blessed.[4] However, valid as that understanding is, it falls short of what the apostle actually requires. He does not urge *some* Christians to engage in unceasing prayer; he urges *all* Christians to do so.

A common rejoinder to the suggestion that the apostle meant that every Christian should engage in unceasing prayer is to point to its impracticability (and even its danger). Were all Christians to engage in such prayer, then communication with others would be interrupted and we could hardly be focused enough to do responsibly what Scripture elsewhere commands us to do. Further, were all Christians to practice unceasing prayer, we would end up being distracted in activities that require our complete attention—activities as disparate but important as shaving, cooking on a gas stove or driving a car. Unquestionably, Scripture enjoins loving and undistracted attention to others, as well as the sort of alertness that protects against endangering or injuring ourselves or others. So, given these

---

[4]Rom 12:3-13; Eph 4:1-16; and the extended treatment in 1 Cor 12:4–14:40.

objections, it has seemed to many that St. Paul's directive can only be understood in one of the ways suggested above.

Orthodoxy has recognized the sorts of concerns and possibilities just noted. Even so, from early in the history of Eastern Christendom and down through the centuries to the present, Eastern Christians have understood the apostle's injunction straightforwardly, as one addressed to every Christian. Orthodoxy has urged that each Christian can and should engage in unceasing prayer. Moreover, Eastern Christianity has developed a way of doing so—with what is called "the Jesus Prayer." This little prayer is a sparkling gem of spirituality, one that richly repays attention to it. Furthermore, it allows one to do precisely what St. Paul commands: to "pray without ceasing."

The Jesus Prayer

Over the centuries, the Jesus Prayer has undergone slight modifications, but the basic structure has remained unchanged—and its practice has only been refined, not changed. As used most commonly today, the Jesus Prayer is as follows:

> "Lord Jesus Christ, Son of God, have mercy on me, a sinner."

What, though, does this little prayer have to do with *unceasing* prayer? Within Eastern Orthodoxy, many have so practiced this prayer that they pray it "without ceasing." Before we consider how they can do that, we need to examine the content of the prayer; it is because of the content that countless Eastern Christians have wanted to pray this prayer unceasingly.

Content of the Jesus Prayer

From antiquity, Eastern Christians have recognized that the Jesus Prayer offers a concise summary of the gospel—indeed, of the whole Christian message. The first phrase calls out to the Savior, asking in the second for the mercy he came to bestow. This cry is appropriate for all Christians—at the beginning of the Christian life and throughout the whole of their existence, no matter what their attainments in piety. As one Orthodox spokesman has put it, "The Jesus Prayer is a prayer of marvelous versatility. It is a prayer for beginners, but equally a prayer that leads to the deepest mysteries of the contemplative life."[5] The Orthodox insist that it would be impossible to outgrow this prayer or to need anything not included by its petition. Everything in the Christian life comes via divine mercy, from initial conversion through every moment that remains in this life—forgiveness of sins, provision of bodily ne-

[5]Bishop Kallistos (Timothy) Ware, *The Orthodox Church,* 2nd ed. (New York: Penguin, 1993), p. 305.

cessities, wisdom for decisions, divine presence throughout the day, protection or whatever one requires for body or soul. As Eastern Orthodox have often stressed, there is nothing one might need in any aspect of life that does not come by divine mercy. Thus, the Jesus Prayer covers the whole of life in a few words.[6]

Indeed, the prayer is simple; it is at the same time profound. It is at once christocentric and trinitarian. Obviously, the Jesus Prayer is Christ-centered: it is addressed to "Jesus Christ, Son of God." It calls out to him as the incarnate one who has triumphed over sin, death and the devil, and it recognizes his glory now as the ascended "Lord" over all. Even so, the prayer is trinitarian: Jesus Christ is addressed as "*Son* of God," recognizing God the Father. Further, since Scripture teaches that it is only by the Holy Spirit that one can confess Jesus as Lord,[7] the prayer embraces God the Spirit. Thus, this spare prayer acknowledges all three persons of the Trinity. There is yet more depth within the Jesus Prayer, though.

This acknowledgment of the triune God and of the glory of the resurrected and ascended Savior has, as its opposite pole, the recognition of our sinfulness: "have mercy on me, a sinner." Humanity became sinful in Adam's transgression, a transgression which ushered our first parents and their descendants into a state of mortality which entices us to sin, sin in which the whole of humanity has been enmeshed and entrapped. Sinners have no claim on God, since they are rebels against him. Even so, in this second part of the Jesus Prayer, we cry out to God in humble but confident hope.

The reason we can do so is that these two extremes—the trinitarian and christological glory, on the one hand, and human sinfulness, on the other—are tied together by the one to whom we call out. He is "Jesus"—the one who saves from sin.[8] He saved us from sin as the "Christ"—the one *anointed* by God to be the Savior. Jesus Christ is not only human, as the son of Mary, though; he is the "Son of God," sent by God the Father to become Savior. As the incarnate Son of God, Jesus Christ fulfilled the primeval promises of God to his image-bearers that he would send a Savior, but also that he would provide for human needs.[9] This all comes

---

[6]"A Monk of the Eastern Church" (Lev Gillet) has declared, "What we may say with soberness and truth on behalf of the 'Jesus Prayer' is that it helps to simplify and unify our spiritual life" (*The Jesus Prayer*, rev. ed. [Crestwood, N.Y.: St. Vladimir's Seminary Press, 1987], p. 96).

[7]See St. Paul's declaration, "No one can say 'Jesus is Lord' except by the Holy Spirit" (1 Cor 12:3).

[8]Speaking of the son whom Mary would bear, the angel declared to Joseph, "you are to name him Jesus, *for he will save his people from their sins*" (Mt 1:21, emphasis added).

[9]In his response to Adam and Eve after their sin against him, God promised that the offspring of the woman would crush the head of the serpent (Gen 3:15) and that through human effort, as blessed by God, people would have food (Gen 3:17); thus, ultimate salvation and provision of daily needs were both promised by God in his mercy.

not by human right or accomplishment but only by "mercy" freely given and richly poured out on the undeserving, to one who recognizes that he or she is "a sinner."

Yet there is still more packed into this brief prayer. The one to whom the prayer is raised is the transcendent one, the "Lord" who is the "Son of God." But he is addressed by the human name given to him, "Jesus": he is one of us, genuinely human as he also is genuinely divine. The prayer thus includes confession that he is the incarnate Son of God,[10] the one promised to our first parents (Gen 3:15). This prayer thus implicitly acknowledges the whole history of redemption, culminating in the incarnation, life, suffering, death and resurrection of Jesus Christ, through whom alone we find mercy: "The Jesus Prayer, then, indicates both man's problem and God's solution. Jesus is the Saviour, the anointed king, the one who has mercy."[11]

It may appear, to this point, that the Jesus Prayer remains, for all its unquestioned excellences, too individualistic: it asks for "mercy *on me,* a sinner." The Orthodox have recognized this danger, though, and in practice the prayer is often modified so that the concluding request is "have mercy on us sinners." In this way, one can pray for society or nation, family or church. With this slight alteration, one moves readily to the widest possible venues for divine mercy. Thus, the Jesus Prayer serves not only one's personal need for mercy but that of all others, near and far.

In the Jesus Prayer we acknowledge the Triune God and the whole history of his redemptive involvement with humanity; we confess our sin and declare our faith in the Savior; and we express our reliance on him for the mercy we always and desperately need. We do all this, in English, in twelve words. Marvelously concise, the Jesus Prayer offers a sparkling abbreviation of the entire Christian message in the form of a prayer—a prayer which one could, indeed, "pray without ceasing" without ever exhausting its meaning or encountering any need not covered by the prayer.

PRACTICE OF THE JESUS PRAYER

How, though, does the Jesus Prayer relate to Eastern Orthodoxy's understanding of unceasing prayer? For centuries, Orthodox faithful have used the Jesus Prayer in a manner that allowed it to become a prayer without ceasing. This practice recognizes the sterling quality of this sparkling summary of the Christian message as a prayer worthy of being prayed continually, but appreciation of the value of the

---

[10]Bishop Kallistos (Timothy) Ware, *The Orthodox Way,* rev. ed. (Crestwood, N.Y.: St. Vladimir's Seminary Press, 1995), pp. 68-70.

[11]Ibid., p. 69.

Jesus Prayer is something other than unceasing prayer. How is the Jesus Prayer used within Eastern Christianity to achieve unceasing prayer?

Repetition is foundational to this practice. A spiritual classic from nineteenth-century Russian Orthodoxy, *The Way of a Pilgrim,*[12] is devoted to the Jesus Prayer and its unceasing use. As the book begins, the pilgrim receives counsel from an experienced monk, who advises the pilgrim to pray the Jesus Prayer 3000 times a day. In a few days, the pilgrim has managed to do that, but when he lets his monastic counselor know this, the monk tells him now to pray the Jesus Prayer 6000 times per day. Considerable concentration and focused use of time over a few more days enable the pilgrim to achieve this. When he advises the monk that he has reached this goal, the monk then tells him to pray the Jesus Prayer 12,000 times per day. The pilgrim struggles with this but eventually manages to do so. This process has taken somewhat over two weeks, and when the pilgrim advises the monk that he has learned to pray the Jesus Prayer 12,000 times a day, the monk counsels him, "Now you may recite the Prayer as many times as you wish; call on the name of Jesus all your waking moments, without counting, and humbly resign yourself to God's will expecting help from Him."[13]

Repetition of the Jesus Prayer did not itself amount to unceasing prayer. The monk's counsel shows that repetition was not the purpose itself; rather, the repetition was the means of so practicing and becoming used to the prayer that it became "second nature" to the pilgrim. Once it had, then the pilgrim was in a position to utilize the prayer at all times and in all places. During this process, the pilgrim had discovered that the initial struggle to manage multiplied repetitions of the prayer on a daily basis had given way to an openness to God and an alertness to him such that the pilgrim came to dwell within the Jesus Prayer—sometimes praying it consciously but at other times praying it somewhere below the level of his consciousness. The rest of the book shows that the pilgrim from then on could focus on the Jesus Prayer, giving himself wholly in attention to it, or he could engage in interaction with others and other necessary tasks in life, aware that deep within him he was praying the Jesus Prayer: "I got so accustomed to the prayer of the heart [the Jesus Prayer, now deep within him] that I practiced it without ceasing and finally I felt that the Prayer of itself, without any effort on my part, began to function both in my mind and heart; it was active both day and night without

---

[12]Available in English translation in *The Way of a Pilgrim and The Pilgrim Continues His Way,* trans. Helen Bacovcin (New York: Image Books, 1978); this volume has a valuable appendix, which offers instructions on unceasing prayer from numerous Orthodox practitioners of the Jesus Prayer from earlier centuries (pp. 176-94).

[13]Ibid., pp. 20-22, 23.

the slightest interruption, regardless of what I was doing."[14] The pilgrim had thus become able to "pray without ceasing."

While such preliminary repetitions are necessary, they themselves do not constitute the unceasing prayer which is the goal of Orthodoxy. If the prayer is to capture one's heart, the praying of the prayer must go beyond repetitions in a way that gets enmeshed with who and what we are; that is, it has to become instinctive to us, something we practice without conscious decision. As a means to that end, the Orthodox have learned to advise that one pray the first portion of the prayer ("Lord Jesus Christ, Son of God") as one inhales, then praying the second half ("have mercy on me, a sinner") as one exhales. The intention with this is twofold: in the first place, this enables one to appropriate the prayer in a rhythmical and natural fashion, in keeping with our psychosomatic wholeness. And secondly, through this practice the prayer becomes—eventually, through repetition—as natural to us as breathing. The goal is that, in having joined the prayer with the act of breathing, and practicing this in multiplied thousands of repetitions, we will get to the point where the Jesus Prayer will come from deep within us as surely and certainly as we breathe. As an Orthodox theologian explains, "The Jesus Prayer . . . begins as a series of specific *acts* of prayer, but its eventual aim is to establish in the one who prays a *state* of prayer that is unceasing, which continues uninterrupted even in the midst of other activities."[15]

In this way, according to Orthodoxy, it is possible to live up to the apostolic injunction to "pray without ceasing." Eastern Christianity does not claim that the only way to do this is with the Jesus Prayer; some other form of prayer could certainly be used. But within Orthodoxy, the Jesus Prayer is one that has often been used. With the practices that have developed for using it, Christians are able to engage in the unceasing prayer to which St. Paul called them.

Before wrapping up our considerations of the practice of the Jesus Prayer within Eastern Orthodoxy, it would be good to respond to an objection that Western Christian sensibilities might raise. Some Western Christians would be suspicious of praying in this fashion, adjudging that it runs afoul of the Lord's warning, "When you are praying, do not heap up empty phrases" (Mt 6:7)—especially if those Christians recall that the King James Version translated the last words as "vain repetitions." From that perspective, it might appear that the multiplied

---

[14]Ibid., p. 41.

[15]Ware, *The Orthodox Way*, p. 123; see also his explanation elsewhere: "It becomes something not merely said by the lips, not merely thought by the mind, but offered spontaneously by the whole of one's being—lips, intellect, emotions, will, and body. The prayer fills the entire consciousness, and no longer has to be forced out but says itself" (*The Orthodox Church*, p. 65).

thousandfold repetitions of the Jesus Prayer, as encouraged within Orthodoxy, would violate that directive.

Two responses can be made. In the first place, *repetition* is not forbidden. What is proscribed is *vain* repetitions—that is, repetitions *to no purpose.* In the passage cited, the Lord himself clarified that such "vain repetitions" or "empty phrases" are offered in the hope of thereby attracting God's attention and being heard. This is not the goal of Orthodoxy's encouraged repetition of the Jesus Prayer. For Eastern Christianity, the reason for such repetitions is a particular purpose, one enjoined by Scripture itself—namely, to "pray without ceasing."

That leads to a second response. While it might seem strange to many Western Christians to repeat a prayer in this fashion, such repetition is something they accept in other areas of their lives where they hope to develop good patterns. Anyone who wants to develop as a basketball player spends many hours shooting a basketball, often from the same spot. Similarly, those who want to develop in soccer will practice dribbling a soccer ball for hours on end. The purpose of such repetition in sport lies beyond the repetition itself. Through repetition, one hopes to develop the abilities to engage in the respective activities with skill, so that the actions "become part of you," are instinctive, come "by second nature." Without such practice, one will never develop the requisite abilities in virtually any sport. Should prayer receive less deliberative attention by those who are called to be "spiritual athletes" for Christ?

Actually, Orthodoxy's repetition of the Jesus Prayer is hardly different from the memorization of Scripture passages or catechism answers so readily encouraged within Western Christendom. In attempting such memorization, one repeats the passage or answer numerous times, trying so to drive it into the depths of one's memory by these purposeful repetitions that one thereafter will remember the passage or the answer. From an Orthodox perspective, readying oneself by repetition of the Jesus Prayer to offer prayer unceasingly is a worthy goal for a Christian—indeed, a goal commanded by St. Paul.

CONCLUDING OBSERVATIONS

The Jesus Prayer is not normative for Orthodox Christians. It should not be supposed that all the Orthodox faithful have followed the practices above and sought to attain unceasing prayer. Even so, we should not adjudge that the only ones who have done so would be the monks who have the untrammeled time to engage in such repetition. Eastern Christianity has stressed throughout the centuries that unceasing prayer is not the private preserve of monasticism; rather, it is within the grasp of all Christians who will attempt it. To be sure, the repetition encouraged in *The Way of a Pilgrim* requires blocks of uninterrupted time. Difficult as that may be to obtain, some semblance of it is not unattainable for the determined; many Christians set aside time for reflection and contemplation in spiritual retreats, and many attend conferences or take classes to receive further instruction in Christian faith and practice. With planning, one could arrange time for uninterrupted repetition of the Jesus Prayer, such that one could begin so to get acclimatized to it that it becomes second nature to us. We could spend our time far less positively.

We in Western Christendom should recognize that our common approaches to St. Paul's command to "pray without ceasing" really do not get at what the apostle actually enjoins upon Christians. Prayer is hardly unknown among us, but unceasing prayer is a stranger to us. What Eastern Orthodoxy has developed as a way to attain unceasing prayer offers us a viable option. The repetition necessary to make the Jesus Prayer second nature to us is not itself foreign, if we consider what we do in other areas of our lives where we prize the development of good abilities. Surely, a life of unceasing prayer is at least as desirable as a good golf swing or tennis forehand. And the reward of such effort, under divine blessing, should make it eminently desirable to us—a life of unceasing prayer, to God's glory and our spiritual enrichment. If we in Western Christianity can learn how to engage in unceasing prayer from our brothers and sisters in Orthodoxy, we will have learned a great deal from them.

Quite apart from the question of "praying without ceasing," the Jesus Prayer is an extraordinary gem of spirituality. It offers a concise expression of the Christian message in the form of a simple prayer that covers everything conceivable we might need for body and soul. It offers a sparkling condensation of the Christian hope and richly rewards meditation. Without a doubt, Western Christians can benefit richly from reflecting on and using it.

EPILOGUE

AS WE HAVE SEEN, THE ORTHODOX TRADITION offers stimulating insights into the faith "once for all entrusted to the saints" (Jude 3). Building on the ancient heritage of the Greek church fathers, Orthodoxy has sought to remain faithful to the apostolic witness passed on through the subsequent centuries. Eastern Orthodoxy has asked different questions of Scripture than Western Christianity has—and different questions lead to different answers. Eastern Christianity has heard these answers from the Lord in the apostolic witness and has articulated from them a distinctive presentation of the Christian faith.

An Eastern Christian who reads this volume might be surprised to note some elements dear to his tradition and, probably, to his own piety and thought that are missing in this book. However, it has not been the intention for this volume to offer a compendium of the whole of Orthodox teaching, piety or practice. Rather, I have endeavored to set forth significant key elements of the Eastern Christian tradition and make them accessible to Western Christians. Still, I hope that Orthodox who read this book will find in it a helpful reminder of much of their faith and practice, and that they will find benefit in the comparisons with Western Christian patterns.

The main purpose of this book, though, has been so to consider some distinctive emphases and approaches of Eastern Orthodoxy that Western Christians may receive benefit and stimulation. Some of these can be more readily assimilated into Western Christian teaching and practice than others; some will unquestionably remain more challenging. In either case, I hope that this book will enable Western Christians to taste and see how the Lord has been gracious (Ps 34:8) to our brothers and sisters in Orthodoxy.

As I indicated in the prologue, I do not view Eastern Orthodoxy as perfect or without its own tensions or flaws. Certainly, the teaching of Scripture and the history of the church warn us against any such triumphalism, whether for one's own or any other tradition. Even so, it has been my experience that Christians can learn and benefit from the insights of those who stand in other traditions within the church—and especially so from the Orthodox. I pray that this volume will enable some Western Christians to open themselves anew to the Christian faith through the insights of their Orthodox brothers and sisters. May some of the light that God has enabled them to see fall upon both the sacred page and the paths that we in the West, as well as in the East, should be walking to his glory. We are all called to walk "in right paths for his name's sake" (Ps 23:3), in "the ancient paths, where the good way lies" (Jer 6:16): may light from the Christian East enable us better to see and walk in those paths.

For Further Reading

In what appears below, I have listed and briefly commented on books helpful for understanding Eastern Orthodoxy. Almost all of them are by leading Orthodox scholars; the few written by Western Christians show insightful understanding of Orthodoxy. I have organized the list in categories, so that readers interested in pursuing study on one or another topic may find relevant works more easily.

Reference Works

Gillquist, Peter E., and Alan Wallerstedt et al. *The Orthodox Study Bible: New Testament and Psalms.* Nashville: Thomas Nelson, 1993. A valuable resource: annotations, introduction and various appendices offer insights into Orthodox understandings of Scripture.

Nassif, Bradley. *The Westminster Handbook to Eastern Orthodox Theology.* Philadelphia: Westminster John Knox, 2007. A concise, accessible presentation of Orthodox doctrine.

Perry, Ken, David J. Melling, Dimitri Brady, Sidney H. Griffith and John F. Healey, eds. *The Blackwell Dictionary of Eastern Christianity.* Oxford: Blackwell, 2001. A rich resource for information on the Orthodox (and Oriental Orthodox) churches, with more than 700 articles.

Prokurat, Michael, Alexander Golitzin and Michael D. Peterson. *Historical Dictionary of the Orthodox Church.* Lanham, Md.: Scarecrow Press, 1996. An excellent resource offering concise introductions to significant events, controversies, developments, leaders, etc., in the lengthy history of Orthodoxy.

Roberson, Ronald. *The Eastern Christian Churches: A Brief Survey.* 6th ed. Rome: Pontifical Oriental Institute, 1991. A concise, well-informed survey of the present situation in all branches of Eastern Christianity by a sympathetic Roman Catholic specialist in Orthodoxy.

General Introductions

Binns, John. *An Introduction to the Christian Orthodox Churches.* Cambridge: Cambridge University Press, 2002. A solid historical overview of Eastern Christianity from the time of Constantine to the post-Communist period, offering insights into Orthodox teaching and practice.

Coniaris, A. M. *Introducing the Orthodox Church: Its Faith and Life.* Minneapolis: Light & Life Publishing, 1982. An excellent, accessible introduction by a respected Orthodox theologian.

Ware, Bishop Kallistos (Timothy). *The Orthodox Church.* 2nd rev. ed. New York: Penguin, 1993. Unquestionably one of the best introductions to Orthodoxy, written by one of contemporary Orthodoxy's most respected figures.

Historical Treatments

Adeney, Walter F. *The Greek and Eastern Churches.* Clifton, N.J.: Reference Book Publishers, 1965 [reprint of 1908 edition]. A lengthy treatment (628 pages), now dated in its interpretations, but with a great amount of information.

Hussey, Joan. *The Orthodox Church in the Byzantine Empire.* Oxford: Clarendon, 1986. An outstanding historical presentation by a leading expert on the Byzantine Empire.

Meyendorff, John. *Byzantine Theology: Historical Trends and Doctrinal Themes.* 2nd ed. New York: Fordham University Press, 1979. The best treatment available of the doctrinal perspectives laid out during the formative Byzantine period of Orthodox history. The first section follows the controversies in historical sequence; the second considers the doctrines dealt with during the period.

Pelikan, Jaroslav. *The Spirit of Eastern Christendom (600-1700).* Chicago: University of Chicago Press, 1974. The best available treatment in English on the history of doctrine in Eastern Orthodoxy, written by an outstanding historian of Christian thought.

Schmemann, Alexander. *Historical Road of Eastern Orthodoxy.* Crestwood, N.Y.: St. Vladimir's Seminary Press, 1977. A popularly written treatment which capably sets forth the history of Orthodoxy.

Zernov, Nicholas. *The Russians and Their Church.* 3rd ed. Crestwood, N.Y.: St. Vladimir's Seminary Press, 1978. A good overview of the influence of Orthodoxy on Russia and its people.

Eastern Orthodox Doctrine and Thought

Bouteneff, Peter. *Sweeter Than Honey: Orthodox Thinking on Dogma and Truth.*

Crestwood, N.Y.: St. Vladimir's Seminary Press, 2006. A fine treatment of Orthodoxy's approach to and expectations about doctrine, responding insightfully to common assumptions about truth at the beginning of the third millennium.

Bulgakov, Sergius. *The Orthodox Church.* Revised translation by Lydia Kesich. Crestwood, N.Y.: St. Vladimir's Seminary Press, 1988. Stimulating treatment of several topics in Orthodox thought and practice by a leading Russian Orthodox thinker of the early twentieth century.

Giannaras, Chrestos, and Christos Yannaras. *Elements of Faith: An Introduction to Orthodox Theology,* translated by Keith Schram. Edinburgh: T & T Clark, 1991. A clear presentation of Orthodox doctrine by Greek Orthodox theologians.

Guroian, Vigen. *Incarnate Love: Essays in Orthodox Ethics.* 2nd ed. Notre Dame, Ind.: University of Notre Dame Press, 2002. A careful exploration of ethics from a distinctively Orthodox perspective.

John of Damascus, St. *The Orthodox Faith.* In *Saint John of Damascus: Writings,* translated by Frederic H. Chase Jr., pp. 165-406. Washington, D.C.: The Catholic University of America Press, 1958. The classic treatment of Orthodox doctrine, relied on for centuries as the best presentation of the faith.

Lossky, Vladimir. *The Mystical Theology of the Eastern Church.* Crestwood, N.Y.: St. Vladimir's Seminary Press, 1976. A treatment that incorporates the mystical style and approach which has shaped Orthodox doctrine.

———. *Orthodox Theology: An Introduction.* Crestwood, N.Y.: St. Vladimir's Seminary Press, 1978. Brief treatment, organized according to topics of dogmatics. A challenging read.

———. *The Vision of God,* translated by Asheleigh Moorhouse. Crestwood, N.Y.: St. Vladimir's Seminary Press, 1983. Nine chapters, moving from the Greek church fathers through the views of St. Gregory Palamas, dealing with how the Orthodox tradition has understood the promise of "seeing God"—a topic on which Western and Eastern Christian views are in significant disagreement.

Meyendorff, John. *Christ in Eastern Christian Thought.* Crestwood, N.Y.: St. Vladimir's Seminary Press, 1975. Careful scholarly treatment of Christology as it was articulated during the Byzantine era.

Schmemann, Alexander. *For the Life of the World: Sacraments and Orthodoxy.* Crestwood, N.Y.: St. Vladimir's Seminary Press, 1973. A reflection, originally written for young peoples' studies societies, offering an Orthodox worldview as it arises from Orthodox perspectives on the sacraments.

Staniloae, Dumitru. *The Experience of God—Orthodox Dogmatic Theology.* Vol. 1:

Revelation and Knowledge of the Triune God. Vol. 2: *The World: Creation and Deification.* Edited and translated by Ioan Ionita and Robert Barringer. Brookline, Mass.: Holy Cross Orthodox Press, 1994. The first two volumes of a projected six-volume English translation of the outstanding Romanian Orthodox theologian's treatment of Orthodox dogmatics.

Ware, Bishop Kallistos (Timothy). *How Are We Saved? The Understanding of Salvation in the Orthodox Tradition.* Minneapolis: Light & Life Publishing, 1996. A simple presentation of Orthodoxy's understanding of salvation.

Eastern Orthodox Spirituality

Arseniev, Nicholas. *Mysticism and the Eastern Church.* Crestwood, N.Y.: St. Vladimir's Seminary Press, 1979. Popularly written presentation of the mystical approach to joy and life in Orthodoxy.

Chryssavgis, John. *In the Heart of the Desert: The Spirituality of the Fathers and Mothers.* Bloomington, Ind.: World Wisdom, 2003. A survey of ancient texts by men and women in Christian antiquity who lived in monastic seclusion or communities in the desert, and a presentation of their exhortations, counsel, prayers and struggles.

[Gillet, Lev, under the designation, "A Monk of the Eastern Church."] *The Jesus Prayer.* Rev. ed. Crestwood, N.Y.: St. Vladimir's Seminary Press, 1987. An introduction to the history and practice of the Jesus Prayer.

Maloney, George A., ed. *Pilgrimage of the Heart: A Treasury of Eastern Christian Spirituality.* San Francisco: Harper & Row, 1983. Excellent introduction by the editor, followed by numerous excerpts from Orthodox leaders from antiquity to the present. Excerpts are organized into twelve chapters dealing with significant themes in Orthodox teaching and practice.

McGuckin, John Anthony. *Standing in God's Holy Fire: The Byzantine Tradition.* Maryknoll, N.Y.: Orbis, 2001. An introduction to the emphases and leading authorities of Orthodox spirituality during the Byzantine period.

Meyendorff, John. *St. Gregory Palamas and Orthodox Spirituality.* Crestwood, N.Y.: St. Vladimir's Seminary Press, 1974. Overview of the teaching of Palamas and his influence on subsequent Orthodoxy.

[Scrima, Andrei, under the designation "A Monk of the Eastern Church."] *Orthodox Spirituality: An Outline of the Orthodox Ascetical and Mystical Tradition.* Crestwood, N.Y.: St. Vladimir's Seminary Press, 1978. A concise introduction to Orthodox spirituality.

Sigrist, Bishop Seraphim. *Theology of Wonder.* Torrance, Calif.: Oakwood Publications, 1999. A concise, contemporary presentation of the mystical approach of Orthodoxy.

Speake, Graham. *Mount Athos: Renewal in Paradise.* New Haven, Conn.: Yale University Press, 2002. A beautifully illustrated treatment of the history of monasticism on the "holy mountain," the main center of Orthodox monasticism for the past millennium.

Ware, Bishop Kallistos (Timothy). *The Orthodox Way.* Rev. ed. Crestwood, N.Y.: St. Vladimir's Seminary Press, 1995. A devotional, profound consideration of Orthodox teaching as it shapes human life. Considered a masterpiece by Eastern Christians.

The Way of a Pilgrim and The Pilgrim Continues His Way. [Author unknown.] Translated by Helen Bacovcin. New York: Image Books, 1992. A classic of Russian spirituality: a nineteenth-century novel focused on the use of the Jesus Prayer by simple believers.

Icons

Evdokimov, Paul. *The Art of the Icon: A Theology of Beauty,* translated by Steven Bigham. Redondo Beach, Calif.: Oakwood Publications, 1990. Profound reflections by a leading Russian Orthodox theologian on the significance and meaning of icons.

Giakalis, Ambrosios. *Images of the Divine: The Theology of Icons at the Seventh Ecumenical Council.* Leiden: E. J. Brill, 1994. A scholarly examination of various facets of the teaching on icons as endorsed at Nicea II in 787.

Ouspensky, Leonid, and Vladimir Lossky. *The Meaning of Icons.* Crestwood, N.Y.: St. Vladimir's Seminary Press, 1983. Careful introductions to the meaning of icons and the techniques of iconography, followed by beautiful reproductions of numerous icons (arranged according to types) and reflections on each icon.

Parry, Kenneth. *Depicting the Word: Byzantine Iconophile Thought of the Eighth and Ninth Centuries.* Leiden: E. J. Brill, 1996. A scholarly examination of the philosophical and theological themes in the views of the defenders of icons.

Pelikan, Jaroslav. *Imago Dei: The Byzantine Apologia for Icons.* Princeton, N.J.: Princeton University Press, 1990. The best presentation of the Orthodox argument in favor of icons.

Sahas, Daniel J. *Icon and Logos: Sources in Eighth-Century Iconoclasm.* Toronto: University of Toronto Press, 1986. Introduction to and annotated translation of the sixth session of the Seventh Ecumenical Council, which declared the legitimacy of icons.

Ugolnik, Anthony. *The Illuminating Icon.* Grand Rapids: Eerdmans, 1989. A standard presentation of the Orthodox teaching about icons.

Eastern Orthodox-Western Christian Interaction

Calian, Carnegie Samuel. *Theology Without Boundaries: Encounters of Eastern Orthodoxy and Western Tradition.* Louisville, Ky.: Westminster John Knox, 1992. Wide-ranging discussion of contacts and problems between Eastern Orthodoxy and Western Christianity.

Clendenin, Daniel B. *Eastern Orthodox Christianity: A Western Perspective.* 2nd rev. ed. Grand Rapids: Baker, 2003. An introduction to Orthodoxy by an evangelical who taught in Russia during the early 1990s.

Doulis, Thomas, ed. *Toward the Authentic Church—Orthodox Christians Discuss Their Conversion: A Collection of Essays.* Minneapolis: Light & Life Publishing, 1996. Stories recounting why some Western Christians have gravitated to Orthodoxy.

Fairbairn, Donald. *Eastern Orthodoxy Through Western Eyes.* Louisville, Ky.: Westminster John Knox, 2003. A sympathetic but critical presentation by a Reformed theologian who taught for several years in Ukraine.

Gillquist, Peter E. *Becoming Orthodox: A Journey to the Ancient Christian Faith.* Brentwood, Tenn.: Wolgemuth & Hyatt, 1989. The intriguing story of how some evangelical leaders were drawn toward ancient Christianity, established an Evangelical Orthodox Church and eventually were accepted within the structures of Eastern Orthodoxy.

Gillquist, Peter E., ed. *Coming Home: Why Protestant Clergy Are Becoming Orthodox.* Ben Lomond, Calif.: Conciliar Press, 1992. Interesting stories about what brought ordained clergy from various segments of Western Christianity to embrace Eastern Orthodoxy.

Mathewes-Green, Frederica. *At the Corner of East and Now: A Modern Life in Ancient Christian Orthodoxy.* New York: Jeremy P. Tarcher/Putnam, 1999. An engagingly written account of how the author was drawn, reluctantly but ultimately gladly, into Orthodoxy.

———. *Facing East: A Pilgrim's Journey into the Mysteries of Orthodoxy.* New York: HarperSanFrancisco, 1997. A winsomely written account of life in an Orthodox parish over the course of a year by a convert from mainline Protestantism.

Schaeffer, Frank. *Dancing Alone: The Quest for Orthodox Faith in the Age of False Religion.* Brookline, Mass.: Holy Cross Orthodox Press, 1994. A stridently written account of the conversion of this son of an influential evangelical to Greek Orthodoxy.

———. *Letters to Father Aristotle: A Journey Through Contemporary American Orthodoxy.* Salisbury, Mass.: Regina Orthodox Press, 1995. A straightforward, sharply written criticism of what this evangelical convert to Greek Orthodoxy sees as deficient in contemporary Orthodox practice.

Stamoolis, James, ed. *Three Views on Eastern Orthodoxy and Evangelicalism.* Grand Rapids: Zondervan, 2004. Five Orthodox and evangelical scholars dialogue on similarities and differences.

Stylianopoulos, Theodore G., ed. *God's Living Word: Orthodox and Evangelical Essays on Preaching.* Brookline, Mass.: Holy Cross Orthodox Press, 1983. Collection of essays and responses by Greek Orthodox and by evangelical spokesmen.

Name Index

Subject Index

Scripture Index